ANIMAL CRUELTY AND FREEDOM OF SPEECH:

WHEN WORLDS COLLIDE

New Directions in the Human-Animal Bond

Alan M. Beck, Series Editor

ANIMAL CRUELTY AND FREEDOM OF SPEECH:

WHEN WORLDS COLLIDE

**Abigail Perdue and
Randall Lockwood**

Purdue University Press,
West Lafayette, Indiana

Library of Congress Cataloging-in-Publication Data

Perdue, Abigail, author.
  Animal cruelty and freedom of speech : when worlds collide / Abigail Perdue,
Randall Lockwood.
    pages cm. -- (New directions in the human-animal bond)
  Includes bibliographical references and index.
  ISBN 978-1-55753-633-4 (hardback) -- ISBN 978-1-61249-321-3 (epdf) -- ISBN
978-1-61249-322-0 (epub)
  1. Animal welfare--Law and legislation--United States. 2. Animal welfare--
Law and legislation--United States--Cases. 3. Animal rights--United States. 4.
Animals--Law and legislation--United States. 5. Freedom of speech--United
States. 6. Human-animal relationships--United States. I. Lockwood, Randall,
1948- author. II. Title.
  KF3841.P47 2014
  344.7304ʾ9--dc23

2013039397

Notice to Readers

This publication was cite-checked in summer 2012. While all references to cases,
statutes, and other legal materials were current at that time, the authors, editor,
and publisher are not responsible for errors or omissions due to legal matters or
events taking place after that date.

TABLE OF CONTENTS

Foreword

Companion animals are very much part of our American self-image and personality; more than sixty percent of all households in the United States have a pet—more than forty percent have more than one. It is common to hear people refer sincerely to their pets as "members of the family." We name our companion animals, like we name our children, in appreciation of their individuality, and have a well-developed veterinary infrastructure to address their health needs. This dedication to our animals very much informs a concern for their welfare and abhorrence of animal cruelty. Evidence that we have little acceptance of cruelty is that dogfighting, which is considered a particularly egregious form of cruelty, is outlawed in all fifty states, as well as the District of Columbia, Puerto Rico, and the Virgin Islands.

But Americans also have a great dedication to their freedom of speech and of self-expression; indeed, the protection that guarantees those freedoms is part of the *First* Amendment of the Constitution of the United States. But what happens when our concern for animals and their welfare and our freedom of self-expression are in conflict?

Animal Cruelty and Freedom of Speech uses *United States v. Stevens*, a case argued before the Supreme Court of the United States in 2009, to illustrate an issue that documented these two competing and compelling interests. Studying this case in detail allows us to understand the issues of animal cruelty while appreciating our constitutional freedoms. The case in point is one of only two animal rights cases ever handled by the Supreme Court of the United States and the only case discussing the competing interests of animal cruelty and free speech. It brought into question a federal law, 18 U.S.C. 48 (Section 48), criminalizing the creation, sale, or possession of the depiction of acts of animal cruelty. While many had hailed the law as something that would benefit both people and animals, others argued the law would threaten free expression. The Supreme Court found that the law did not address an exception to First Amendment rights and it was declared unconstitutional in April 2010. In response, President Barack Obama signed the Animal Crush Video Prohibition Act of 2010 (Crush Act), the constitutionality of which is still under review.

This book details the history, scope, and purpose of the Section 48 and then explores the facts and legal precedent underlying *United States v. Stevens*. It analyzes the Supreme Court's decision to invalidate the law and explains how an alternative outcome could have been reached. Finally, the authors examine the newly enacted Crush Act. As they observe, "Depictions of animal cruelty have been and will remain part of the media landscape whether they are used to advocate for animal protection or to satisfy the base motives of those who would exploit animals for utilitarian, prurient, or pathological purposes."

This issue has social and educational importance. It will be taught and discussed both in constitutional and animal law courses around the country, as well in other social studies classes. Moreover, human-animal relationships and our natural concern for animal welfare is a topic of interest not only to animal law attorneys and law students, but also to professionals in many fields including law enforcement, animal control, and animal protection—indeed, to all that are concerned about animals and legal freedoms.

Animal Cruelty and Freedom of Speech, which uses an exemplar court case to explore a broader issue, is somewhat like Purdue University Press' very popular book, *Inside Animal Hoarding*. This new book fits nicely in Purdue University Press books that address social policy issues related to animals.

As Americans, we love our pets as much as we love our freedom of expression. We must find ways to balance these values so people and animals can continue to share and benefit from each other.

Alan M. Beck
Center for the Human-Animal Bond
College of Veterinary Medicine
Purdue University
West Lafayette, Indiana

Acknowledgments

I first met Dr. Lockwood in the spring of 2009 when I was asked to work on a unique *pro bono* project—helping to draft an amicus brief in *United States v. Stevens* in support of the Government on behalf of the American Society for the Prevention of Cruelty to Animals. It was during my work on that project that I first learned about the existence of crush videos and the tortuous lives of fighting dogs. A long-time animal lover, I was shocked to learn of these disturbing enterprises. Dr. Lockwood was incredibly helpful in drafting the brief. Eventually, after I entered academia, I published a law review article on the case. But there was still more to be said about the law, the decision, and the culture of cruelty giving rise to each. And so this book was born.

The creative birthing process was more strenuous and difficult than I could have imagined, but it was also incredibly rewarding. There are no words that can adequately express my sincere gratitude to all of the amazing individuals who supported me during the process.

My thanks go to Dr. Alan Beck, Charles Watkinson, and Jennifer Lynch at Purdue University Press, whose patience, guidance, and flexibility made this project possible. I also owe a major debt of gratitude to my colleagues at my former law firm, at my alma mater, Washington and Lee University, where I drafted the law review article that preceded the book, and at Wake Forest University School of Law for their invaluable insight and peer editing. I am particularly grateful to Professor Harold Lloyd whose thoughtful feedback and own insightful research on *Stevens* truly enriched the piece. I am also extremely appreciative of my wonderful research assistants through the years, including Lea Koh, Tee Hassold, Stephen White, Stephen Frost, Kelsey Meuret, Breonna Hammond, and Evan Leadem, who worked tirelessly to make sure that I crossed every *t*.

Most of all, I extend heartfelt thanks to my amazing family and friends, especially my parents, Janet and David Perdue, my mamaw and papaw, Mary and

Hoover Asbury, my sister and brother-in-law, Rachel and Alexander Turner, my beloved nephews, Heath and Wyatt, my grandfather and grandmother, Herbert and Maxine Perdue, my aunt and uncle, Christine and Turner Smith, and our fur-covered "family" members—Mandy, Megan, Dozy, Hank, Harriet, Lambie, and Violet. They instilled in me a love and respect for all of God's creatures.

Last but certainly not least, I would like to acknowledge the strength and support of my Heavenly Father without whom I would not have had the heart and stamina for this undertaking. As Jesus observed in Luke 12:6, "What is the price of five sparrows? A couple of pennies? Yet God does not forget a single one of them." Because His eye is on the sparrow, so is mine. And like Him, I strive to show mercy, compassion, and love to all living creatures, humans and animals alike.

Dr. Lockwood wishes to thank Dr. Alan Beck for his support and persistence in advocating for the publication of this work as well as the ASPCA staff, particularly President Ed Sayres, Chief of Staff, General Counsel Melissa Norden, and Chief Counsel Stacy Wolf, for their commitment to responding to the challenges to the "Crush Act" and other legal protections for animals. He also wishes to thank his wife, Julie Stern, and daughter, Susan Lockwood, for their patience in listening to endless discussions of animal cruelty cases in general and particularly disturbing cases of sexual mistreatment of animals. His household had to invoke a rule where the phrase "unicorns and rainbows" was the signal to change the topic to something uplifting to preserve family unity and sanity.

We hope our book will illuminate the issues inherent in animal cruelty and be a voice for positive change.

Introduction

The movie begins. Hypnotic music plays eerily in the background. A woman saunters out of the shadows carrying a puppy by the scruff of its neck. Her face and upper body are obscured, so the viewer's eyes are drawn down her body to her spiked heels. The puppy begins to whimper and squirm as the actress tapes it to the floor. The music fades, and the woman's voice breaks the silence. She screams at the animal as it twists and kicks, trying desperately to escape. But fighting is futile because the puppy is pinned to the floor. The actress kicks the animal again and again, each time with increasing force. Blood spurts from its eyes and nose. Its piercing shrieks compete with the woman's increasingly abusive epithets, which never subside. Fighting through the pain, the dying puppy struggles to escape as the woman's stiletto heels grind its bones into dust. After a slow and tortuous death, the animal lies in pieces on the floor. The movie ends.[1]

Regrettably, the existence of "crush videos" like the one described above is rooted in fact, not fiction. Indeed, the discovery in the 1990s of a market in crush videos caught many professionals involved in animal cruelty investigation and prosecution off guard. The reality of this strange fetish even surprised investigators well-acquainted with the large market for materials related to animal sexual assault, who often felt that they had seen it all. The unusually swift public policy reaction to crush videos was perhaps poorly planned and potentially harmful to efforts to protect animals from harm.

Concerns over the crush video industry were growing at the same time that law enforcement was taking a closer look at the continuing proliferation of illicit material and seeking new tools for preventing and responding to it. Law enforcement was also increasingly concerned about the use of newer channels of marketing and distribution of potentially illicit material via the Internet and underground publications.

1

Recognizing the tremendous societal harms caused by the creation and sale of depictions of animal cruelty, Congress enacted 18 U.S.C. §48 (Section 48) —a federal law criminalizing their creation, sale, or possession.[2] Proponents of Section 48 predicted that countless benefits to humans and animals would flow from its enforcement. Opponents argued that Section 48 imperiled free expression. Thus, the stage was set for a unique collision of two traditionally "liberal" concerns—the prevention of animal cruelty and the First Amendment guarantee of free speech.

On April 20, 2010, the Supreme Court of the United States in *United States v. Stevens*[3] affirmed the decision of the United States Court of Appeals for the Third Circuit (Third Circuit), declaring Section 48 to be unconstitutional. In response, President Barack Obama signed the Animal Crush Video Prohibition Act of 2010 (Crush Act) into law on December 9, 2010. It remains to be seen whether the Crush Act will stamp out the practices driving this clandestine industry or whether it, too, will ultimately succumb to legal challenges.

Stevens has far-reaching implications for humane law enforcement, animal advocates, animal law students and practitioners, the media, and anyone concerned about changing public policies regarding animal protection. The history of the case and its aftermath provide important lessons about the challenges of using the legal system to protect animals.

Stevens mirrors a Hollywood epic with elements of sex, violence, greed, animals, criminal investigations, political infighting and an uncertain outcome. The story unfolds in four parts, each posing unique public policy implications. First there is the "discovery" of crush videos and the public and political response, culminating in the enactment of Section 48. This discovery came at a time of growing recognition of the connections between animal cruelty and interpersonal violence as well as a heated debate regarding the clinical significance of sexual interactions with animals and the role of government in regulating such behavior, particularly given earlier Supreme Court decisions involving religious animal sacrifice rituals.

Second are the growing concerns about organized dogfighting and whether Section 48 encompassed dogfighting depictions. Third is the escalation of this case to America's highest court, provoking a national debate on regulation of media depictions of animals and animal cruelty and the government's role in preventing animal cruelty. Finally, there is the aftermath of the Supreme Court's decision, including attempts to correct any shortcomings of the original law and a movement to restrict efforts to create depictions of animal cruelty that can serve to raise awareness of animal cruelty in large-scale agriculture.

Our book details the history, scope, and purpose of Section 48 and then explores the facts and law underlying *Stevens*. It analyzes the Supreme Court's decision to invalidate the law and explains how an alternative outcome could have been reached. Finally, the book examines the newly enacted Crush Act. We hope our detailed analysis of *Stevens* will provide insight and guidance to animal advocates, legal scholars, and law enforcement professionals in drafting, implementing, and enforcing laws that protect humans and animals alike.

Notes

1. Portions of this book are excerpted from Abigail Lauren Perdue, *When Bad Things Happen to Good Laws: The Rise, Fall, and Future of Section 48*, 18 VA. J. SOC. POL'Y & L. 469 (2011), and have been reprinted herein with the permission of the Journal and Author.
2. As used herein, the phrases "cruelty to animals" and "animal cruelty" refer only to *criminal* animal cruelty. Unless otherwise specified, the phrase "depictions of animal cruelty" refers to portrayals of criminal acts of cruelty against live animals.
3. U.S. v. Stevens, 559 U.S. 460 (2010).

CHAPTER 1

Cruelty Unspoken: Law and Policy Regarding Animals and Sexual Deviance

Stevens grew out of efforts to restrict a form of human-animal sexual interaction that the public found particularly disturbing—namely the production of "crush videos" catering to a previously little known fetish. This concern did not arise in a vacuum. Effects to enact and enforce legislation related to interspecies sexual practices have had a lengthy and uneven history.

Bestiality, or animal sexual assault, is one of the rarest forms of animal cruelty and, over the last few decades, has rarely been prosecuted as a primary offense in the absence of other charges of animal cruelty or other crimes. Ironically, such crimes have the longest history of investigation and prosecution in Western society.

The proscription of sexual contact with animals dates from Old Testament times. Deuteronomy states, "cursed be he that lieth with any manner of beast,"[1] while Exodus warns "whosoever lieth with a beast shall surely be put to death."[2] The severity of the penalties for such acts had little or nothing to do with concern about the harm to animals, but rather was based on the notion that such actions upset the natural order of the universe and could lead to the production of monstrous offspring that were the work of the Devil.[3]

The penalty for such activities in many Western cultures was often death for both the human and non-human participants. Such a trial was depicted as the starting point for the 1993 film *The Advocate* (released in the United Kingdom as *The Hour of the Pig*), which was based upon the career and case files of Bartholomew Chassenée, a lawyer in fifteenth-century France who served as an advocate for animals that were accused of crimes.[4] Many well-documented cases of such prosecutions exist.[5] However, the societal response to bestiality was often inconsistent. There were few prosecutions for bestiality in Colonial America despite the strong Puritan presence.[6] In contrast, there were approximately 700 executions for bestiality in Sweden from 1635 to 1778.[7]

5

The response of the modern American legal system to sexual activity involving animals has also been inconsistent. Sodomy laws once existed in every state and criminalized various sexual behaviors, including oral and anal sex, even between consenting adults, as well as homosexual behavior, gross lewdness, gross indecency, pedophilia, necrophilia and bestiality. Often all of these were included within the catch-all categories of sodomy or crimes against nature. Since the 1970s, the American Civil Liberties Union (ACLU) and other groups have successfully challenged state sodomy laws, usually on the grounds of persecution of individuals based on their sexual orientation and the criminalization of behaviors transpiring between consenting adults. More than 30 states have subsequently repealed their sodomy laws through legislative or court action.[8]

The repeal of sodomy laws often had the effect of essentially decriminalizing animal sexual assault, unless the act involved some other crime such as animal cruelty, indecent exposure, trespass or breaking and entering. In response to this unintended change, many state legislatures re-enacted provisions specifically targeting bestiality as distinct from other traditional "crimes against nature." Approximately 37 states have enacted laws that prohibit sexual contact between humans and animals. Most of these laws were enacted in the last decade: Pennsylvania in 1999, Iowa in 2001, Illinois and Maryland in 2002, Washington (state) and Arizona in 2006, Indiana, Tennessee, and Colorado in 2007, Alaska in 2010, and Florida in 2011. About half of these states provide for felony penalties in cases of animal sexual assault, with provisions for imprisonment for up to twenty years and fines of up to $50,000.[9]

This climate of increasing concern about sexual offenses involving animals helped set the stage for public reaction to revelations about the existence of crush videos. However, public and professional opinion did not unilaterally favor greater investigation and prosecution of such offenses. Efforts to restore criminal penalties for bestiality have been met with opposition from a contingent of self-described *zoophiles* who maintain a large Internet presence. Detailed how-to guides for the sexual abuse of animals involving various species can be found, along with information on laws, zoonotic diseases, personal advertisements, pro-zoophile resources, and even advice about how animal abusers can come out to their family and friends. Although such proponents maintain that their behavior constitutes a lifestyle choice analogous to other non-traditional sexual orientations, this view is countered by the prevailing legal, legislative, and societal view that such contact constitutes interspecies sexual assault.

The debate over the dangers of human-animal sexual interaction was further complicated by a number of scholarly reactions. In a 2001 review of Midas Dekkers' (2000) *Dearest Pet: On Bestiality*, animal rights philosopher Peter Singer argued that sexual activities between humans and animals that result in harm to the animal should be illegal, but that "sex with animals does not always involve cruelty" and that "mutually satisfying activities" of a sexual nature may sometimes occur between humans and animals. Singer claims that our discomfort with zoophilia originates in our view of humans as separate and morally superior from the rest of the animal world rather than the direct harm to the animal.[10]

This apparent defense of animal sexual assault attracted voluminous criticism from animal protection groups and fellow philosophers. Regan criticized Singer's position as a consequence of his adapting a utilitarian approach to animal rights, rather than a strictly rights-based one, and noted that the rights-based position distances itself from non-consensual sex.[11] In an essay entitled "Pets or Meat," Case raises the issue of how to differentiate the act of bestiality from other "tricks" pets are forced to perform, sometimes through coercion.[12]

More relevant to later arguments presented in support of strong legislation related to human-animal sexual interactions in general and Section 48 in particular was the growing body of literature from psychologists, clinical social workers and criminologists connecting aberrant sexual conduct with animals to the potential risks posed by the perpetrators to human beings. Beirne was the major voice for reinterpreting bestiality or zoophilia as "animal sexual assault." He makes the connection to violence against humans clear, noting that sexual abuse of animals parallels sexual abuse of women and children. It is also problematic because (1) human-animal sexual contact is almost always coercive; (2) often causes pain or death for the animal; and (3) animals are unable to consent or to communicate about their abuse.[13] Likewise, Ascione notes that bestiality may be considered cruel even in cases when physical harm to an animal does not occur, drawing a parallel to cases of adult sexual activity with a child where consent is presumed to be impossible.[14]

Other research indicated that the sexual abuse of animals is often anecdotally linked to the sexual abuse of women and children. This form of domestic violence involves the use of animals for degradation and sexual exploitation of the battered partner. Bestiality may be a part of further tormenting and humiliating the victim.[15] Child sexual abusers may also sexually abuse animals to enhance, expand, or extend the abuse of the genuinely powerless and unsuspecting victim.[16] Some case studies of sexual abuse of children include reports of forcing children to interact sexually with animals.[17]

Animal sexual contact is higher in some clinical and adjudicated populations. In one study, psychiatric patients exhibited a significantly higher prevalence rate (55%) of bestiality than control groups of medical inpatients (10%) and psychiatric staff members (15%).[18] Research also indicates a connection between animal sexual abuse and other types of violent crimes. Forty percent of the perpetrators of sexually motivated homicides who had been sexually abused as children report that they had sexually abused animals.[19] Duffield et al. report on seven young in-carcerated psychiatric patients identified as having committed a sexual act with an animal.[20] They characterize this sample as "severely disturbed young persons who may suffer with other psychiatric disorders, such as severe conduct disor-der, personality disorder, substance abuse, or psychosis."[21] Other clinical findings supported greater concern about animal sexual assault. Frazier looked at thirty sexually violent juveniles. Of these, 90% reported having abused animals with 37% reporting *sexual* abuse of animals.[22]

The specific concern about the public health and safety issues raised by sexu-ally-oriented animal cruelty grew, in part, out of a much broader growth of public policy concern about the large and growing body of literature showing the con-nection between many forms of animal cruelty and the potential for acts of vio-lence against people.[23] Although much of this literature existed well before 1980, it attracted little attention until popularized by animal advocacy groups, social service workers and growing public fascination with the life histories of violent offenders. Arguments based on this expanding body of literature were often at the core of proposed legislation, as well as the legal arguments raised in support of preserving the principles of Section 48.

It was in the context of growing concern about bestiality and zoophilia that the crush video market was discovered. In the mid-1990s, investigators for sev-eral animal protection groups began systematically monitoring Internet traffic promoting bestiality. At the same time, law enforcement agencies began more systematic surveillance of pornographic sights, primarily over concern about the market in child pornography. The discovery of crush videos took the debates about animals and human sexuality to a new level. Although many people argued that the human-animal interactions in the context of bestiality or zoophilia were often benign or even "romantic," no such whitewash of the animal assault in the con-text of these videos was possible. By definition, the animals were always injured or killed, usually in slow and painful ways that already violated most existing animal cruelty codes. However, discovering and prosecuting such cruelty based on the acts themselves would prove difficult.

The path from revelations of the reality of crush videos to legislative action was, as we will see, uncharacteristically short for any federal legislation. The first awareness came in mid-1997 when British Customs seized several Squish Productions videos entering the country from California. These and related productions became known to various humane investigators and in May 1998 such evidence was brought to the attention of Tom Connors, Deputy District Attorney for Ventura County (California) District by the Humane Society of the United States.[24] Over the next several months, through participation in chat rooms and other conversations, Ventura County investigators determined that Gary Lynn Thomason, running a business called *Steponit*, had produced a crush video depicting rats, mice and baby mice ("pinkies") being crushed and killed by a female under the heel of her shoe.[25]

Officers eventually conducted a search of Thomason's apartment for any evidence of his production and distribution of videos and found thirty or forty videos in a closet. Other items seized were a computer containing chat room conversations relating to crush videos as well as clips taken from crush videos and still images. In August 1999, Thomason and Diane Aileen Chaffin, the "star" of several of the videos, were arrested in California for and subsequently convicted of felony animal cruelty under state law. Their appeal was denied in 2000.[26]

Although Thomason and Chaffin were successfully prosecuted for animal cruelty, California prosecutors expressed concern at the obstacles they faced in pursuing such actions. They noted that buying and selling depictions of animal cruelty was not illegal under any state or federal law. Furthermore, although law enforcement officials could prosecute the acts of torturing and killing the animals, it was often difficult to determine where and when those acts had taken place in order to establish jurisdiction and timeliness.[27]

Notes

1. Deut. 27:21 AV.
2. Exod. 22:19 AV.
3. Piers Bierne, "Rethinking Bestiality: Towards a Concept of Interspecies Sexual Assault," *Theoretical Criminology* 1, no. 3 (1997): 321.
4. Sadakat Kadri, *The Trial: A History, from Socrates to O.J. Simpson* (New York: Random House, 2005), 155.
5. E. P. Evans, *The Criminal Prosecution and Capital Punishment of Animals* (London: Faber and Faber Limited, 1906), 18.
6. Bierne, "Rethinking Bestiality," 323.
7. Jonas Liliequist, "Peasants against Nature: Crossing the Boundaries between Man and Animal in Seventeenth-and Eighteenth-Century Sweden," *Journal of the History of Sexuality* 1, no. 3 (1991): 394.
8. "History of Sodomy Laws and the Strategy that Led Up to Today's Decision," American Civil Liberties Union, last modified June 16, 2003, http://www.aclu.org/lgbt-rights_hiv-aids/history-sodomy-laws-and-strategy-led-todays-decision.

9.   Rebecca F. Wisch, "Overview of State Bestiality Laws," *Animal Legal and Historical Center*, last modified 2010, http://www.animallaw.info/articles/ovuszoophilia.htm.

10. Peter Singer, "Heavy Petting," *Utilitarianism*, last modified 2001, http://www. utilitarian.net/singer/by/2001----.htm.

11. Tom Regan, *Animal Rights, Human Wrongs* (Lanham: Rowan and Littlefield, 2003), 64, 86.

12. Mary Anne Case, "Pets or Meat," *Chicago-Kent Law Review* 80, no. 3 (2005): 1149.

13. Bierne, "Rethinking Bestiality," 323.

14. Frank R. Ascione, "Children Who Are Cruel to Animals: A Review of Research and Implications for Developmental Psychopathology," *Anthrozoös* 6, no. 4 (1993): 229.

15. Lenore E. A. Walker, *The Battered Woman Syndrome*, 3rd ed. (New York: Springer, 2009), 394.

16. Carol J. Adams, "Bringing Peace Home: A Feminist Philosophical Perspective on the Abuse of Women, Children, and Pet Animals," *Hypatia* 9, no. 2 (Spring 1994): 69.

17. Ascione, "Children Who Are Cruel to Animals," 229.

18. William A. Alvarez and Jack P. Freinhar, "A Prevalence Study of Bestiality (Zoophilia) in Psychiatric In-Patients, Medical In-Patients, and Psychiatric Staff," *International Journal of Psychosomatics* 38, no. 1–4 (1991): 45.

19. Robert K. Ressler et al., "Murderers Who Rape and Mutilate," *Journal of Interpersonal Violence* 1, no. 3 (1986): 277–80.

20. Gary Duffield, Angela Hassiotis, and Eileen Vizard, "Zoophilia in Young Sexual Abusers," *Journal of Forensic Psychiatry* 9, no. 2 (1998): 294–304.

21. Ibid., 303.

22. Monique R. Frazier, "Physically and Sexually Violent Juvenile Offenders: A Comparative Study of Victimization History Variables," Unpublished doctoral dissertation, Department of Psychology, Utah State University, Logan, UT (1998).

23. See, e.g., Frank R. Ascione, and Randall Lockwood, "Animal Cruelty: Changing Psychological, Social and Legislative Perspectives," In *State of the Animals 2000*, 39–53. Washington, D.C.: Humane Society Press, 2001.

24. Punishing Depictions of Animal Cruelty and the Federal Prisoner Health Care Co-Payment Act of 1999: Hearing Before the Subcomm. on Crime, 116th Cong. 41 (1999) (statement of Tom Connors, Deputy District Attorney for Ventura County, CA).

25. Ibid., 42.

26. *People v. Thomason*, 84 Cal. App. 4th 1064, 1066 (2000).

27. Punishing Depictions of Animal Cruelty and the Federal Prisoner Health Care Co-Payment Act of 1999: Hearing Before the Subcomm. on Crime, 116th Cong. 41 (1999) (statement of Tom Connors, Deputy District Attorney for Ventura County, CA).

CHAPTER 2

Dogfighting in America:
A Historical and Sociolegal Perspective

Throughout the decade preceding the enactment of Section 48, while many humane investigators were focused on animal sexual assault and the connections between animal cruelty and interpersonal violence, others turned their attention to the "blood sports" of dogfighting and cockfighting. Dogfighting has presented a challenge to American law enforcement for nearly 150 years and was one of the main reasons for the formation in 1866 of the American Society for the Prevention of Cruelty to Animals (ASPCA), which conducted the first law enforcement action against dogfighters in America.[1] One of the most notorious dogfighting operations was Kit Burns' Sportsman's Hall in New York City—the scene of dogfights, cockfights, ratting, and other events.[2] In 1868, ASPCA officers raided the establishment.[3] Burns was fined $800, but criminal charges were dismissed.[4] Ultimately Burns leased his property for prayer meetings and dogfighting was driven into secret locations outside the city.[5] Dogfighting proliferated in several major cities, including Philadelphia, Boston, and Chicago.[6]

Throughout most of the twentieth century, despite the continuing efforts of animal protection organizations and a handful of law enforcement agencies that actively addressed the crime of dogfighting, the activities remained underground, and the participants were rarely held accountable. Laws addressing animal cruelty and dogfighting in particular were usually weak and/or poorly enforced.

In the last twenty years, tolerance of dogfighting dwindled. Legislators, law enforcement agencies, and the public awakened to the reality that crimes against animals do not occur in a vacuum. Increasingly, they recognized that animal cruelty and dogfighting often involve participants who have been or will be involved in many other serious crimes, including interpersonal violence.

In the last decade, agencies have been given better tools to address these crimes. Once a misdemeanor in many states, dogfighting now carries felony penalties

11

in all states and at the federal level.[7] Attending a dogfight is now a serious crime in most states.[8] Animal cruelty, which is always a component of dogfight enterprises, can also result in felony penalties in nearly every state.[9]

A major factor in raising awareness of dogfighting was the arrest and conviction of NFL quarterback Michael Vick on federal and state charges related to dogfighting in 2007.[10] The publicity surrounding Vick's prosecution, as well as other dogfighting cases involving high profile individuals, created growing public pressure on law enforcement to respond. In 2009, the largest dogfight raid in U.S. history highlighted the importance of coordinating the skills and resources of many agencies in responding to dogfighting.[11] Nearly 400 dogs were seized during simultaneous operations at more than 20 locations in eight states, resulting in 27 arrests.[12] The raids combined the resources of federal and state law enforcement agencies and local and national animal protection groups.

One factor that caused authorities to take a closer look at dogfighting is the recognition that dogfighting and dogfighters had changed in the last two decades. Dogfighters increasingly made use of underground publications and, eventually, the Internet, to share and sell information and products to promote dogfighting, including materials to promote the sale of particular lineages of fighting dogs, instruct others in the tools and methods of dogfighting and recruit new participants. Since most dogfighting aficionados could only attend a few fights each year, there was a market for depictions of fights to feed their interest and provide tips for raising and training fighting dogs.

At a time when the resources of law enforcement agencies were spread thin, some jurisdictions questioned the importance of using these resources to respond to dogfighting and other crimes against animals.

As mentioned above, dogfighting is illegal in all fifty states and the District of Columbia, Puerto Rico, and the Virgin Islands. As of 2009, dogfighting is a felony in all states. In most states, the possession of dogs for the purpose of fighting is also a felony offense.[13] Being a spectator at a dogfight is currently a felony in a growing number of states.[14] The Federal Animal Fighting Prohibition Enforcement Act of 2007 provides for felony penalties for interstate commerce, import and export relating to commerce in fighting dogs, fighting cocks, and cockfighting paraphernalia.[15] Each violation can result in up to three years in jail and a $250,000 fine.[16] Furthermore, several states make it a crime to encourage, entice, assist, or cause another person do any illegal activities related to dogfighting.[17] These "aiding and abetting" provisions substantially broaden the reach of state dogfighting laws, making it a crime to knowingly or intentionally engage in any behavior that furthers or supports dogfighting activities.[18]

Perhaps this is because dogfighting is a gateway crime. Many communities report growing involvement of juvenile offenders in dogfighting, often as a part of gang involvement. The sense of power and control gained from having an aggressive dog, as well as the potential financial gain, can lure juveniles into an underground scene that often includes other criminal activities.

In addition to the animal cruelty and illegal gambling that are at the core of dogfighting activity, virtually all dogfight raids involve the discovery and seizure of illegal drugs, and about two-thirds result in the seizure of illegal weapons.[19] Such raids also frequently lead to the arrest of many offenders with outstanding warrants.[20] Disputes over dogfights have also been associated with serious assaults and several homicides.[21]

Dogfighting is a classic example of a *broken-window* crime. The evidence of its presence in an area may be very visible, particularly in the case of street fighting, but the difficulty of mounting an effective law enforcement response may create the perception that no one cares about the threats this crime presents to the community.

Although state and local law enforcement agencies were increasingly aware of all of these reasons for pursuing dogfighting operations, prior to 2008 federal laws were typically much weaker than state animal cruelty or dogfighting laws, producing a general lack of interest in federal action against crimes that often involved extensive interstate traffic, communication and exchange of information. The federal government has authority to investigate animal fighting ventures and to enter cooperative agreements with the Federal Bureau of Investigation (FBI), the Bureau of Alcohol, Tobacco, Firearms and Explosives, the Treasury Department, and any other federal, state, or local government agency to assist in those investigations. The Secretary of Agriculture and his or her agents from the USDA Office of the Inspector General may also secure and execute warrants to search for and seize dogs involved in fighting ventures in the district where those dogs are located.

Federal felony level penalties for animal fighting were finally instituted in May 2007 under the Animal Fighting Venture Prohibition Act.[22] Violation is punishable by fines and up to five years in prison or both.[23] In addition, as of November 1, 2008, the federal sentencing guidelines have been amended to designate a heightened base offender level for individuals convicted of felonies under the animal fighting venture law.[24] The guidelines also contemplate upward departure from the sentencing guidelines for offenses that involve extraordinary cruelty to animals which cause results such as maiming or death.[25]

In April 2003, James Fricchione, the publisher of *Sporting Dog Journal* since 2001, was arrested at his home in Orange County, New York.[26] Police seized eighteen pit bulls, many of them injured, along with assorted dogfighting paraphernalia.[27] In March 2004, he was found guilty of one count of dogfighting and four counts of cruelty to animals.[28] He was sentenced to two to seven years in state prison, fined $5,000, and prohibited from owning any animals for ten years.[29] His conviction was upheld on appeal.[30] It is important to note that no charges were filed related to the publication and distribution of *Sporting Dog Journal*.

Notes

1. Randall Lockwood, *Dogfighting: A Guide for Community Action* (Washington, D.C.: U.S. Department of Justice, 2012), 6.
2. Ibid.
3. Ibid.
4. Ibid.
5. Ibid.
6. Ibid.
7. Ibid., 4.
8. Ibid.
9. Ibid.
10. Ibid.
11. Ibid., 5.
12. Ibid.
13. Ibid., 7.
14. Ibid.
15. Ibid.
16. Ibid.
17. *Combating Dogfighting: Prosecutors' Guide to Dogfighting Cases* (New York: ASPCA, 2010), 6.
18. Ibid.
19. Lockwood, *Dogfighting*, 7.
20. Ibid.
21. Ibid.
22. Animal Fighting Venture Prohibition Act, 7 U.S.C. §2156 (2008).
23. Ibid.
24. Ibid.
25. Ibid.
26. "Fricchione," Inhumane.org, accessed April 18, 2013, http://www.inhumane.org/data/JFricchione.htm.
27. Ibid.

28. Ibid.
29. Ibid.
30. Ibid.

CHAPTER 3

Showcasing Animal Abuse: Regulating Media Depictions of Animal Cruelty

A central theme in the public policy issues surrounding *Stevens* is the regulation of depictions of animal abuse and neglect. What is the dividing line between bad taste, exploitation, entertainment, education, advocacy, and potentially criminal behavior? How can we prove that a depiction has serious value warranting First Amendment protection? Different media providers seek to attract public attention (and associated financial gain) in many different ways. They may entertain, enlighten, educate, enrage, or advocate. They may choose to stand out from the mass of mass media by shocking and offending viewers. Most advocacy groups, whether for people or animals, seek support and funding through appeals that often depict the pain and suffering of the populations they serve, whether they be starving children, battered women, endangered wildlife, or abused animals.

Depictions of killing or harming animals are as old as visual artistic expression. Many early cave paintings are depictions of hunting and killing prey.[1] Perhaps the earliest cinematic depiction of animal cruelty is Thomas Edison's 1903 film "Electrocuting an Elephant."[2] The brief film documents Edison's use of alternating current to execute Topsy, a 28-year-old elephant kept at Coney Island who had killed three men, including a severely abusive trainer who had attempted to feed her a lit cigarette.[3]

The ASPCA opposed plans to kill Topsy as inhumane. Edison offered to execute her using alternating current, which was done before an audience of 1,500 people. The movie was then shown to audiences across the country.[4] Edison had a commercial purpose for placing this disturbing film into wide circulation; he and his colleagues routinely demonstrated and documented the electrocution of dogs, cats, and other animals to illustrate the hazards of alternating current being promoted by his arch rival, George Westinghouse.[5] This was a primary tactic in the competition between Westinghouse's technology of using alternating current as a means of producing and distributing electric power and Edison's direct current generating plants that eventually lost out.[6] Topsy's electrocution and the widespread showing of the film aimed to show that this new form of power could even kill an elephant. Had Section 48 been in place at the time, perhaps Edison could have successfully claimed exemption based on the scientific and historical value of the event.

Cinematic history is full of depictions of animal cruelty, both real and simulated. As Stevens pointed out, "[i]mages of the intentional wounding or killing of animals covered by Section 48 pervade our society, media, and literature because animals pervade our lives."[7] Stevens listed many films in wide release rated as "unacceptable" by the American Humane Association (AHA) due to depictions of actual animal cruelty.[8]

It took almost a generation after the first showing of movies that depicted animal cruelty for the public to begin to express concern over such treatment. The prevailing utilitarian view of horses and other animals as expendable commodities essentially inhibited any real expressions of outrage. Animals were merely stock or props. The fact that nearly 150 horses were killed in filming the chariot race scene in the 1925 version of *Ben Hur* went unchallenged and, in fact, the success of the film helped establish MGM as a major movie studio.[9]

This attitude began to change with reaction to a scene in the 1939 movie *Jesse James* in which a horse was ridden off a 70-foot cliff to its real death. A more urbanized population than even a decade before was less inclined to dismiss such needless cruelty. That led to the contract between AHA and the Hays Office (and later the Screen Actors Guild) giving AHA the right to review scripts and have representatives on site to supervise animal action in films.[10] A parallel process occurred in Great Britain, as animal welfare advocates pushed for national legislation to address the problem—resulting in the Cinematograph Films (Animals) Act enacted in 1937.[11] The wording of the Act resembles that of Section 48. It specifies:

> No person shall exhibit to the public, or supply to any person for public exhibition . . . any cinematograph film (whether produced in Great Britain or elsewhere) if in connection with the film any scene represented in the film was organized or directed in such a way as to involve the cruel infliction of pain or terror on any animal or the cruel goading of any animal to fury.[12]

Despite such monitoring, animal cruelty continued to be a part of many films in the U.S., including some that were highly successful. Disney's *True-Life Adventures* series frequently attracted criticism for its claims that the often anthropomorphic depictions of animals in the wild were real.[13] This assertion was later proven to be true of one of the series' most successful films. In 1982, the Canadian Broadcasting Company (CBC) television news magazine program, *The Fifth Estate*, produced a documentary about animal cruelty in film. The documentary focused much of its coverage on "White Wilderness" (1958), one of the most successful *True-Life Adventures*.[14] The film contains a now legendary scene of lemmings leaping off a cliff to their death. This dramatic scene became etched in the public consciousness, giving rise to the popular view that such behavior is natural and common. The segment drew very little criticism until recent times and, in fact, the film won the 1958 Academy Award for Best Documentary. The CBC investigators discovered that the lemming scene was filmed near downtown Calgary and not at the Arctic Ocean as implied. The lemmings did not voluntarily jump into the river but were reportedly pushed in by a rotating platform installed by the film crew. A lemming expert interviewed for the exposé claimed that the particular species of lemming shown in the film is not known to migrate or commit mass suicide.[15]

Since then, "White Wilderness" has come to symbolize the "nature fakers" that put animals at risk or even to death for education and entertainment. The treatment of the animals in the film could have perhaps been prosecuted under today's laws in some states that extend protection to all animals, including rodents, but the filmmaker's actions did not violate any Canadian or American laws at the time. Although dozens of animals died slowly in the production of the scene, it perhaps could have avoided sanction on the basis of its alleged educational value had Section 48 been in place at the time.

The increased attention to animal maltreatment in the media reflected both a cultural shift in public concern about animal welfare, but also the commercial recognition that depictions of animal cruelty were potentially damaging to films seeking wider distribution. However, such concerns have not eliminated traffic in films that clearly depict actual animal cruelty. In fact, a number of films have exploited the shock value of such maltreatment to attract publicity as well as a niche audience of people seeking to view such material. These films featured actual on-camera deaths of a variety of animals, including seals being clubbed to death and animals being killed on the slaughterhouse line.[16]

Scenes of dogfighting have been depicted in several advocacy pieces described below, but few commercial films have provided scenes comparable to what appeared in Stevens' videos. The most noteworthy is *Amores Perros*, a 2000 Mexican film that grossed over $5 million and was nominated for an Academy Award as Best

Foreign Language Film.[17] The film included controversial scenes of dogfighting. According to UK news outlet *The Guardian*, director Alejandro Ganzalez Iñárritu explained that no dogs were harmed during the making of the film.[18] In the scenes where dogs are apparently attacking each other, they were reportedly actually playing. Their muzzles were covered with fine fishing line, so that they were unable to bite each other. In the shots where dogs are apparently dead or dying, they were sedated (under the supervision of the Mexican SPCA). The realism of the scenes was reportedly enhanced through sound editing.

It is important to separate the treatment of animals in media from the depiction of such treatment. The early attempts to regulate media depictions of animals by the AHA in America and the British Board of Film Censors/Classification in the United Kingdom were necessary due to the lack of strong animal welfare legislation that could protect the animals being used.[19] Even today, some of the animals whose treatment is regulated by AHA guidelines would not be covered under animal cruelty statutes in some states where filming might take place (for example, fish, invertebrates, and some wildlife).[20] However, the egregious forms of abuse that gave rise to contemporary monitoring, such as horse tripping, are now specifically prohibited, and any treatment resulting in unnecessary suffering or death of most vertebrates would fall under existing animal cruelty laws in nearly every state.[21]

The regulation of depictions of animal cruelty has become even more confounded by the development of technologies that essentially separate such depictions from any actual treatment of live animals. Virtually all modern cinematic representations of animals at risk involve puppetry, robotics or computerized graphic imagery (CGI). One of the most popular movies in recent years, *Men in Black* (1997), features a key scene in which the protagonist, Will Smith, repeatedly stomps on scattering cockroaches to goad a giant roach-like alien into attacking him. Although the scene clearly involved model and CGI insects (and AHA was on scene), the depiction itself is reminiscent of many actual crush videos involving the crushing of insects.

The result of the technological changes is that films that might depict serious animal abuse have been produced without harm to any actual animals (such as *Rise of the Planet of the Apes*, 2011).[22] Conversely, films that carry a powerful animal liberation theme but make use of live animal actors have been criticized for alleged animal maltreatment in the production of the film. One such case involved the film *Project X* (1987), which told the story of the rescue of chimpanzees from lethal experiments at a military laboratory. TV personality Bob Barker accused the film's producers of animal cruelty. The AHA, which was responsible for monitoring animal action during the movie's production, filed a $10 million defamation lawsuit against Barker, arguing that the animal cruelty claims were based on hearsay. In 1994, over Barker's objections, his insurance company settled the lawsuit for $300,000.[23]

Some advocates recognized the potential power of film and video as a tool for exposing cruel practices even before animal protection movements became skilled in the use of mass media to tell their stories. Even if film was not specifically being used to advocate for animals, potential targets of such advocacy expressed concern about this power. As early as 1942, the hunting lobby labeled the Walt Disney film *Bambi* as anti-hunting propaganda.[24] In England in 1949 the producers of *Gone to Earth* (1950) complained that they were being prevented from completing their film about a woman and her pet fox because the British Field Sports Society feared the film would fuel anti-foxhunt sentiment.[25]

One of the most powerful non-fiction depictions of real-life killing of animals was the French slaughterhouse documentary *Le Sang des Bêtes (The Blood of Beasts)* (1949). The film contrasts peaceful life in the outskirts of Paris with the gory conditions inside the nearby slaughterhouses. It documents the fate of the animals and that of the workers in graphic detail. The film continues to influence documentary filmmakers today and has received over 200,000 Youtube views.[26]

One of the first videos produced by a major media source that created great controversy was CBS's *Guns of Autumn* (1975) documentary on hunting. The video, narrated by Dan Rather, depicted many scenes of hunting bear, deer, and other animals in unfavorable light. Although widely praised by animal protection groups, such as the Humane Society of the United States (HSUS) and the Fund for Animals, it drew vehement criticism from gun and hunting groups.[27] An attempt to produce a more balanced piece, *Echoes of the Guns of Autumn*, did not placate critics. The Michigan United Conservation Club filed a libel lawsuit against CBS, claiming that CBS had defamed "all Michigan hunters," which was estimated to be a constituency of one million people.[28] A federal appellate court ruled in CBS's favor, noting that many of those claiming harm were not shown, named, or in any way mentioned in either video.[29] The court noted that "vague, general references to a comparatively large group do not constitute actionable defamation."[30]

As animal protection groups grew in both resources and sophistication throughout the 1980s and 90s, they saw the enormous potential for effective use of media to document and expose many forms of animal cruelty and inhumane killing. Numerous groups prepared video material depicting the alleged cruelties of many activities including rodeo, laboratory experimentation, factory farming, hunting, trapping, fur production, dogfighting, cockfighting, slaughter, puppy mills, whaling, and many more. After the passage of Section 48 and its broadened application to dogfighting in *Stevens*, many legal experts warned of the intrinsic problem of trying to regulate potentially identical content that allegedly tried to serve two different purposes—instructing others in the conduct of dogfighting and hog hunting versus exposing the cruelties inherent in dogfighting or hog hunting. Stevens highlighted this potential discrepancy, stating:

> While the Humane Society tells this Court that "gruesome depictions" of dogfighting "do not merit the dignity of full First Amendment protection" and do not "convey any ideas or information" (HSUS Br. 20), the Humane Society's own website employs such images as part of its advocacy effort to convey ideas and information. . . . Furthermore, outside of Court, the Society lauds as a "must see" Hollywood producer David Roma's documentary about Pit Bulls that contains horrific images from modern-day dogfights of dogs with portions of their eyes, ears, and noses torn away and a dog disemboweled after a fight in the pit. See Bobby Brown & David Roma, *Off the Chain* (24/7 Food Inc. and Illucid Productions 2005) (Humane Society review on cover: "This film is a must see—exposing the ultimate betrayal of man's best friend."). Stevens' dogfighting images, by contrast, lack any such images of blood or serious injury to the dogs.[31]

Notes

1. Linda Kalof, *Looking at Animals in Human History* (London: Reaktion Books, 2007), 2.
2. Mark Essig, *Edison and the Electric Chair* (New York: Walker & Company, 2003), 279.
3. "Bad Elephant Killed," *The Commercial Advertiser*, New York, 5 January 1903.
4. Essig, *Edison and the Electric Chair*, 279.
5. Ibid., 143–45.
6. Ibid., 276.
7. Brief for the Respondent at 22, *United States v. Stevens*, 559 U.S. 460 (2010) (No. 08-769).
8. Ibid., 2n-10b.
9. Jonathan Burt, *Animals in Film* (London: Reaktion Books, 2002), 153.
10. Ibid.
11. Ibid., 137.
12. Ibid. (citing Cinematograph Films (Animals) Act 1937, Act, I,(I)).
13. Bosley Crowther, "Disney's Nature: 'The Vanishing Prairie' Has Animals Like Those in Familiar Cartoons," New York Times, 22 August 1954, X1.
14. *See* Bob McKeown, "Cruel Camera," *Fifth Estate* video, May 5, 1982, http://www.cbc.ca/fifth/cruelcamera/video2.html.

15. Riley Woodford, "Lemming Suicide Myth: Disney Film Faked Bogus Behavior," Alaska Department of Fish and Game, last modified 2003, http://www.adfg.alaska.gov/index. cfm?adfg=wildlifenews.view_article&articles_id=56.

16. John Alan Schwartz, *Faces of Death*, directed by John Alan Schwartz (1978), video; Paulo Cavera and Franco Prosperi, *Mondo Cane*, directed by Paulo Cavera (1962), video.

17. *Amores Perros*, directed by Alajandro Gonzalez (Mexico: Altavista Films, 2000), DVD.

18. "Going to the Dogs," *Guardian.co.uk*, last modified August 22, 2000, http://film.guardian. co.uk/interview/interviewpages/0,6737,357271,00.html.

19. Burt, *Animals in Film*, 139.

20. "State Animal Cruelty Laws," *aspca.org*, last modified 2013, http://www.aspca.org/ Fight-Animal-Cruelty/Advocacy-Center/state-animal-cruelty-laws.aspx.

21. Burt, *Animals in Film*, 153.

22. *Rise of the Planet of the Apes*, directed by Rupert Wyatt (Hollywood, CA: Twentieth Century Fox, 2011), DVD.

23. Lucinda Smith, Leah Feldon, and Eleanor Hoover, "Speaking Up for 'Abused' Animals, Bob Barker is Hit with a Lawsuit," *People Magazine*, September 1989, http://www. people.com/people/archive/article/0,,20121207,00.html.

24. Ralph H. Lutts, "The Trouble with Bambi: Walt Disney's Bambi and the American Vision of Nature," *Forest & Conservation History* 36, no. 4 (1992): 161–69.

25. Burt, Animals in Film, 7.

26. "Le Sang des Bêtes (Blood of the Beasts) part 1/3," YouTube video, posted by "thior-paiwk," December 9, 2007, https://www.youtube.com/watch?v=QFAUA8_mfXs.

27. Marilyn Greenwald, *Cleveland Amory* (Lebanon, NH: University Press of New England, 2009), 135.

28. Ibid.

29. Mich. United Conservation Clubs v. CBS News, A Div. of CBS, Inc., 665 F.2d 110, 112 (6th Cir. 1981).

30. Ibid.

31. Brief for the Respondent, 21.

CHAPTER 4

Freedom of Religion and Animal Sacrifice: *Church of the Lukumi Babalu Aye, Inc. v. City of Hialeah*

The Church of the Lukumi Babalu Aye, Inc., (Church) is a not-for-profit corporation that was organized under the laws of the State of Florida as a place of religious worship in the seventies. In 1987, the Church acquired property in Hialeah, Florida, for the purpose of securing a place to practice a religion known as "Santeria" (Way of the Saints) and to establish a theological school, an Afro-Cuban museum, counseling services, and similar programs.[1] The Church's goal was to raise awareness of Santeria, including its sacrificial rites.

Hialeah has been described as "a working-class community of Cubans and Hispanics living in small houses and old apartments in an industrial city known largely for its famous racetrack with 400 pink flamingos."[2] Hialeah residents were less than thrilled about the Church's plans. According to David O'Brien, an attorney representing several of the Church's neighbors remarked: "Santeria is not a religion. It is a throwback to the dark ages. It is a cannibalistic, Voodoo-like sect which attracts the worst elements of society, people who mutilate animals in a crude and most inhumane manner."[3] A local pastor labeled Santeria "black magic [and] a cult."[4] Soon after the plans were announced, Church leaders began receiving death threats, and protesters appeared at pre-opening events carrying signs with messages like "Jesus Up, Satan Down."[5] The public outcry against the Church was too loud to ignore.

On June 9, 1987, the Hialeah City Council held an emergency public session. Approximately three hundred people attended, and the scene was described as a "mob atmosphere."[6] According to O'Brien, audience members described Santeria as "barbaric," "medieval," and "satanic" and purportedly booed Church leaders.[7]

During the emergency session, the council adopted Resolution 87-66, which emphasized residents' concerns "'that certain religions may propose to engage in practices which are inconsistent with public morals, peace or safety,' and declared that '[t]he City reiterates its commitment to a prohibition against any and all acts of any and all religious groups which are inconsistent with public morals, peace or safety.'"[8] The council also passed Ordinance No. 87-40, which largely adopted the language of Florida's anti-cruelty act and aimed to prevent the Church, or any other person or group, from practicing animal sacrifice within city limits.[9] Later on, the council enacted Resolution 87-90, which emphasized the council's "'great concern regarding the possibility of public ritualistic animal sacrifices'" and "declared the city policy 'to oppose the ritual sacrifices of animals' within Hialeah."[10] It announced that any person or organization practicing animal sacrifice within city limits would be prosecuted.[11]

These measures proved insufficient. In September 1987, the council enacted additional ordinances, including No. 87-52, which prohibited ritual animal sacrifice, regardless of whether the sacrificial animal would be consumed, and No. 87-72, which prohibited the slaughter of any animals on premises not properly zoned for slaughterhouse use.[12] Violations were punishable by fines not exceeding $500 or imprisonment not exceeding sixty days, or both.[13]

The Church and its president, Ernesto Pichardo, challenged the ordinances pursuant to 42 U.S.C. § 1983 in the United States District Court for the Southern District of Florida. Named defendants were the City of Hialeah, its mayor, and city council members in their individual capacities. The complaint alleged violations of the Free Exercise Clause and sought a declaratory judgment as well as injunctive and monetary relief. In granting summary judgment for the defendants, the District Court concluded that the defendants possessed absolute immunity and "that the ordinances and resolutions adopted by the Council did not constitute an official policy of harassment, as alleged by petitioners."[14] After a bench trial on the remaining claims, the District Court held that Hialeah had not violated the Free Exercise Clause.

The Church appealed the case all the way to the Supreme Court of the United States, which struck the ordinances for violating the Free Exercise Clause. Because *Lukumi* was the first Supreme Court case pitting concerns regarding animal cruelty against the First Amendment, it naturally took center stage during the subsequent proceedings in *Stevens*.

The Church

Ernesto Pichardo became a Santeria initiate in Cuba when he was sixteen.[15] Only four years after entering the priesthood in the order of *Shango*, he and his brother, Fernando—a *babalawo*—their mother, *iyalosha* Carman Pla Oni Yemaya, their stepfather, *babalosha* Raul Rodriguez, and attorney Gino Negretti founded the Church.[16] Fernando became the administrative director and corporate secretary. By the time of the litigation, Ernesto had become president of the Church and risen to the rank of *italero*—the highest rank within the Santerian church aside from *babalawo*.[17]

By 1986, the Church was offering accredited courses on Santeria to law enforcement and actively recruiting new members. Furthermore, the Church created a sixteen-member committee to organize the opening of a new church facility.[18]

The Church served as a place of worship for the Lukumi religion, sometimes referred to as *Yoba*, *Yoruba*, or *Santeria*. The Lukumi-Yoruba people once consisted of more than 250 different ethnic groups. As O'Brien explains, *Lukumi* is derived from the Yoruba *"Omo Ife,"* (Children of Ife); Ife is akin to the Eden of Judeo-Christian tradition.[19]

In the sixteenth, seventeenth, and eighteenth centuries, many of the *Yoruba* people were captured as slaves and transported to Cuba. At the time, some justified slavery by framing it as missionary work. Slaves were sometimes baptized before being loaded onto slave ships, which often bore Catholic-inspired names. The practice of Lukumi was prohibited because slaves were expected to convert to Christianity.[20]

"Santeria" is a Spanish word meaning the worship or way of the saints that describes a subset of traditional religions originating in western Africa. In Cuba, the Lukumi religion of Africa became known as Santeria because followers worshipped spirits, or manifestations of God, called *orishas,* alongside Catholic saints, or *santos*.[21] Yoruban slaves incorporated Catholicism to evade detection and consequent punishment. For example, Santerian practitioners viewed Saint Peter, who was traditionally associated with iron, as *Shango*, the god of lightning and thunder.[22] Indeed, O'Brien observes that orishas were publicly celebrated in accordance with Catholic rites and celebrations on various saints' days.[23] Santeria devotees also observe the Catholic sacraments.[24]

According to Professor Joseph Murphy:

> Catholicism offered a world of symbolism that could be translated into African meanings. The saints provided symbols behind which the orisha could live on. The more symbolically austere traditions of Protestantism did not have this panoply of sacred objects for Africans to identify and reinterpret. Catholic symbolism provided a haven for the orishas, symbolic building blocks to recreate the way of the orishas in the New World.[25]

This blending of cultures, known as *syncretism*, allowed Yoruban slaves to safely and secretly practice Santeria while masking their religion in a heavy veil of

Catholicism. For four hundred years, Santeria endured as a clandestine religion secretly practiced by slaves and their descendants. It remained underground largely due to fears of persecution, discrimination, and stigma.[26] The veil of secrecy under which Santeria is usually practiced also means that no one knows how many Santerian practitioners currently exist.[27]

The Santerian community is comprised of units individually known as a *casa* or *ile* (house). A priest typically heads the house but is also godfather or godmother to an extended family *en santo* (in the spirit).[28] Unlike many other religions, Santeria has no scriptures and is transmitted by word-of-mouth. Santeria is based on interpretation of an oral tradition; no organized worship or centralized authority and no written code or tradition exists. Santeria involves an interrelationship of beliefs and conduct as well as special ceremonies for life cycle events, including birth, marriage, and death.[29] Herbal medicine, prayer, protective charms, chants, magic, marriage and death rites, and food and animal offerings are important parts of this religion.

Santeria teaches that God gives every individual a destiny that is fulfilled with the aid and energy of orishas, which are considered powerful but not immortal. Their survival depends on animal sacrifice, and the blood of sacrificial animals is poured on sacred stones thought to embody the orishas to nourish the orishas. Accordingly, sacrifices are performed as part of birth, marriage, initiation, healing, and death rites as well as during annual celebrations and as a means of therapy or crisis prevention. Sacrificial animals include chickens, pigeons, doves, ducks, guinea hens, goats, sheep, and turtles. The typical killing method is cutting the carotid arteries in the neck. The sacrificed animal is then consumed, except where it is used as part of healing and death rituals.[30]

Because Santerians were persecuted in Cuba, "the religion and its rituals were practiced in secret."[31] Cuban exiles fleeing Fidel Castro transmitted Santeria to America, primarily to south Florida where Hialeah is located. By some estimates, as of 1993, approximately fifty to sixty thousand Santeria practitioners lived and worshipped in south Florida.[32] Pichardo testified that in the late 1980s, ten *italeros* existed in Dade County alone and a conference of Santerian priests was held annually in New York.[33] Yet even today the open practice of Santeria is rare.

Animal Sacrifice

The use of animal sacrifice made Santeria the subject of litigation pitting the public interest in freedom of religion against the public concern over preventing animal cruelty. Animals are sacrificed during Santerian rituals to "feed" *orishas*. As O'Brien explains, divination is based on the *ifa* divination cycle, which is comprised of 256 *odu*s, which are further subdivided into groups of sixteen. *Ifa* divination is most often performed through the casting of shells or stones. Divination tells the priest what type of animal to sacrifice and the purpose of the sacrifice.[34]

Sacrificial animals, except those used in certain rituals, are often consumed. Only certain specially trained priests perform animal sacrifice, and those priests do not obtain, maintain, butcher, cook, or dispose of the sacrificial animals.[35]

Each priest plays a distinct role in the sacrificial process. No single priest or follower knows exactly how each separate function is performed. One priest may handle post-sacrificial cleanup, while another maintains the animal before the sacrifice. One priest transports the animal to the killing spot, a second performs the sacrifice, and a third priest discards the carcass, typically in the garbage of followers' or priests' homes.[36] During the *Lukumi* proceedings, testimony regarding the method of disposal of sacrificial animals primarily related to carcasses allegedly found in public places, which in large part triggered enactment of the challenged ordinances.

Although sacrificial animals are supposed to be clean and disease-free, Santerian priests do not appear to receive training in how to verify this; according to court documentation, they rely upon personal observation to make such determinations.[37] The frequency and volume of Santerian animal sacrifice remain a mystery. The number of animals sacrificed and the number of pots of blood collected to feed the orishas hinge upon the number of deities involved, which in turn, depends upon the type of ritual.[38]

Pichardo testified that 600 initiations occur annually in private homes in Dade County; 20 to 30 animals are usually sacrificed during a single initiation rite, which suggests that in Dade County alone, 12,000 to 18,000 animals are sacrificed annually in initiation rites.[39]

Although the carcasses of sacrificed animals are typically discarded in the garbage, there appears to be no religious prohibition against animal burial, incineration, or disposal in sanitary waste containers. During the *Lukumi* proceedings, Pichardo testified that the Church would comply with legal requirements regarding carcass disposal. He appears to have conceded, however, that there was no effective way to control or monitor practitioners outside the Church.[40] The carcasses of sacrificed animals had reportedly been found near rivers or canals, road signs, and sometimes on non-practitioners' lawns or doorsteps, fueling the public outcry against the Church.[41]

Furthermore, although some practitioners believed that a priest must obey the law in order to comply with Santerian principles, Pichardo admitted that a priest could interpret *ifa* "to require that an animal carcass be left in the open, or even neglect to consult the *ifa* at all regarding the disposal."[42] He conceded that although he would consider such behavior to be deviant, some Santerian priests might order the disposal of animal carcasses in public places if they interpreted *ifa* to require it.[43]

As to the killing method, it is taught by an oral apprenticeship. The apprentice observes where and how the teaching priest inserts the knife. The teaching priest and the apprentice hold the knife while the teaching priest guides the apprentice through the killing stroke several times. Once the teaching priest becomes satisfied that the apprentice can perform the sacrifice, the apprentice is permitted to kill the animal without assistance.[44]

The sacrificial animal is placed on a table on its left side. Usually, an apprentice holds the animal's legs, and the priest stands on the other side of the animal. The priest holds the animal's head such that it faces away from the priest and extends beyond the edge of the table. The priest typically uses his left hand to hold the animal's head high on the nose area. Whether the priest is left- or right-handed, he always wields the knife, which is usually four inches long, with his right hand. The priest inserts the knife into the right-hand side of the animal's neck and pushes it through, severing the main arteries although not slitting the throat.[45]

Expert testimony heard during the *Lukumi* proceedings revealed that there is no guarantee that the priest can simultaneously sever both carotid arteries. Arterial lining can recoil and close the artery to prevent hemorrhaging. Based on this testimony, the District Court found that the killing method was not "reliable or painless."[46] Rather, some young animals have deeper arteries within the vertebrae so that they are unlikely to instantaneously be rendered unconscious.[47] A chicken, for example, possesses a total of four carotid arteries, which are rubbery and slide, increasing the risk that one will be missed.[48]

Expert testimony also indicated that the sacrificial animal is highly likely to experience pain and fear. While awaiting sacrifice, the animal is typically maintained in close confinement with animals of other species, causing intense stress and anxiety. The animal is led to the killing spot and will perceive the body secretions of the other sacrificial animals that have just been killed. Animals in fear often secrete chemical metabolites known as *pheromones*, and the odor of these pheromones can trigger an intense fear reaction in the sacrificial animal approaching the killing spot.[49] Animals may not appear afraid even though they are because of "tonic immobility"; in other words, an intensely fearful animal freezes.[50] Fearful animals often defecate or urinate unless they have been deprived of food or water.[51]

After the sacrifice, the animal is decapitated, and its blood is drained into clay pots placed under its head.[52] Furthermore, "[t]he pots of blood are placed before the deities until the animal's carcass is removed" and then discarded.[53] By some accounts, this blood might occasionally be drunk, placed on followers, or left in pots for long periods of time, although Pichardo described such practices as deviant.[54]

Sacrificial animals are typically purchased from *botanicas*, stores that specialize in selling articles related to Santeria, or local farms that breed animals for sacrifice. Such animals are allegedly often kept in dirty, overcrowded conditions and are not always adequately fed and watered.[55]

As mentioned earlier, the remains of sacrificial animals being discarded in public places purportedly prompted enactment of the challenged ordinances. At the time of the proceedings, there were no documented instances of any infectious disease originating from the discarded remains. However, it is undisputed that carcasses attract flies, rats, and other animals that carry diseases.[56] For instance, flies transmit dysentery, cholera, and hepatitis.[57]

District Court Decision

As explained above, the Church sued the city, its mayor, and the city council members in the United States District Court for the Southern District of Florida. The complaint alleged violations of the Free Exercise Clause and sought a declaratory judgment and injunctive and monetary relief. The District Court granted summary judgment because the defendants possessed absolute immunity and "the ordinances and resolutions . . . did not constitute an official policy of harassment."[58]

The Church argued that the ordinances were invalid because they conflicted with Florida law permitting ritual animal slaughter in limited circumstances, but the District Court found no conflict because the ordinances only banned slaughter that fell outside that exemption.[59] Nor was the District Court convinced that the ordinances were invalid because they provided for a criminal penalty whereas state law only imposed a civil penalty because the statute at issue expressly authorized municipalities to enact an ordinance that did not mirror the state law penalty.[60]

The Church's primary challenge to the ordinances involved the First Amendment. The District Court began its analysis by noting that Santeria came to this country through immigrants:

> Migration has been the lifeblood of this country. As each of the tens
> of thousands came, they brought with them their unique heritages
> which were ultimately integrated and woven into the fabric which is
> America. The strength of that fabric has grown over two centuries.

Those who fled poverty found opportunity; those who were deprived
of the opportunity of expression found freedom of speech; and those
who were deprived of the opportunity to worship God found freedom of religion. These newfound freedoms, however, were not un-
abridged and absolute.[61]

After a nine-day bench trial on the claims not already resolved by summary
judgment, the District Court ruled for Hialeah and found no violation of the Free
Exercise Clause. Seven weeks later on October 5, 1989, the District Court issued
a comprehensive opinion upholding the ordinances.[62] Specifically, the District
Court observed:

Although the ordinances are not religiously neutral but were intended to stop the practice of animal sacrifice in the City of Hialeah,
the ordinances were not passed to interfere with religious beliefs, but
rather to regulate conduct. The ordinances have three compelling
secular purposes: 1) to prevent cruelty to animals; 2) to safeguard the
health, welfare and safety of the community; and 3) to prevent the
adverse psychological effect on children exposed to such sacrifices.[63]

However, these public interests would ultimately prove insufficient to warrant
abridging the First Amendment freedoms of Santeria practitioners.

First Amendment Concerns

The Church argued that the ordinances violated the free exercise of its members'
First Amendment rights. The Church claimed that the city council had discrimi-
nated against it with regard to licensing and zoning applications and also complained of alleged harassment by law enforcement officials. The District Court was
not persuaded and found that the allegation of increased police scrutiny related to
a perimeter created for the Church's protection due to "intense and often hostile
media coverage" surrounding the case.[64]

The Church's primary allegation was that the council passed the ordinances to
discriminate against the Church and to prevent it from establishing a physical presence in violation of the First Amendment.[65] The District Court observed that the
Free Exercise Clause of the First Amendment, which applies to the states through
the Fourteenth Amendment, provides that "Congress shall make no law respecting an establishment of religion, or prohibiting the free exercise thereof."[66] The
Supreme Court would later confirm that Santeria is a religion within the meaning
of the First Amendment and that although animal sacrifice may be repugnant to
some, "religious beliefs need not be acceptable, logical, consistent, or comprehen-

sible to others in order to merit First Amendment protection."[67] The District Court had determined that no record evidence supported this contention; rather, it established that the city council aimed to stop animal sacrifice practiced by any person or group regardless of religious affiliation.[68] The District Court observed that First Amendment protection is not absolute.[69] The District Court emphasized that before it balanced competing religious and governmental interests, it must first decide two threshold issues: whether the law regulates conduct rather than belief and whether the law has both a secular purpose and effect. It decided that the government had met both tests because the law proscribed the conduct of animal sacrifice, not any religious belief regarding the practice.[70] Second, the District Court concluded that the ordinances were facially neutral because some do not mention religious conduct at all; another provided notice that the state exemption for ritual slaughter applied exclusively to commercial ritual slaughter performed in slaughterhouses, not Santerian slaughter occurring in private homes.[71]

However, the District Court recognized that the ordinances were not religiously neutral in application and were prompted by concern over the Church. The District Court concluded that the true purpose of the ordinances was to prevent animal sacrifice, not to exclude the Church from Hialeah. The District Court also determined that the ordinances did not facially target religious conduct; further, "specifically regulating [religious] conduct" does not violate the First Amendment "when [the conduct] is deemed inconsistent with public health and welfare." Thus, the District Court concluded that the ordinances' effect on the Church's religious conduct was "incidental to the ordinances' secular purpose and effect."[72]

The District Court emphasized that the Supreme Court has upheld laws with secular purposes even if they implicate religious practices.[73] Indeed, the District Court rejected a facial challenge to the ordinances because "[a] statute is overbroad on its face only if it is unconstitutional 'in every conceivable application' or seeks to prohibit a broad range of protected conduct."[74]

Next, the District Court balanced the governmental interests in prohibiting the conduct against freedom of religion.[75] In so doing, the District Court observed several compelling governmental interests underlying the ordinances: (i) animal sacrifices pose a substantial health risk to animals, participants, and the public; (ii) emotional injury to child observers of animal sacrifice; (iii) protecting animals from the method of killing used in Santeria sacrifice, which it found to be unreliable and inhumane; and (iv) restricting animal sacrifice of animals to areas zoned for slaughterhouse use. The District Court concluded that these compelling interests justified the ordinances.[76]

Safeguarding Public Health

With regard to safeguarding public health, the District Court found cases banning ritual snake-handling and marijuana use as part of religious services persuasive because the evidence revealed a risk of physical harm to Church members and the public arising from sacrifice-related disease and infestation.[77] Specifically, the District Court observed that "animal carcasses are often left in public places, leading to an increased risk of disease."[78] Sacrificial animals are often obtained from sources that have not maintained the animals in sanitary conditions, and the animals are sometimes not inspected, which increases the risk of disease and salmonella.[79] Priests who select animals may lack training in recognizing disease.[80] Therefore, the District Court found that Hialeah had proven that Santerian animal sacrifices imperiled public health.[81]

Protecting Children's Welfare

Animal sacrifice also raised concerns regarding the welfare of children exposed to the practice. Research psychologist Dr. Raul Huesmann, whose research focused on the effects of the observation of violence on the development of aggressive and violent behavior, opined that the observation of animal sacrifice, even as part of an initiation rite, would likely produce psychological processes, namely desensitization, tolerance, and imitation, in observers that not only encourage tolerance of aggression and violence but might also increase the possibility of the child-viewer exhibiting such behavior toward animals or humans.[82] Although the District Court pointed out that other factors could also promote aggressive, violent behavior, it accepted Dr. Huesmann's assertion that a correlation exists between a child's observation of violence, especially when perpetrated by individuals perceived as having high status, and the risk of developing violent and aggressive behavior.[83] As the District Court explained, "the younger the child, the stronger the effect. . . . The observation of animal sacrifice can have a detrimental effect on a child's mental health and on that child's future behavior."[84]

The District Court reached this conclusion in the face of contradictory testimony from a clinical psychologist, Dr. Angel Velez-Diaz, who felt that because child-viewers of animal sacrifice have been prepared for what they see, no negative effects ensue from viewing; his views were found to be less credible because he had not conducted studies regarding the impact of observation of violence by children.[85]

The District Court was also not persuaded by the testimony of an educator at Miami Dade Community College who testified that, based on her study of children's attitudes toward death, children exposed to death viewed it as a more natural process. She did not consider animal sacrifice to be a violent act. The District Court found her statements less persuasive because she was unfamiliar with Dr. Huesmann's studies, her studies focused on death not violence, and she lacked personal knowledge about animal sacrifice or child observers of it.[86]

In sum, the District Court found that exposure to animal sacrifice could harm the psychological well-being of children and increase the likelihood that such children will exhibit aggression.[87] Therefore, based on the expert testimony discussed above, Hialeah demonstrated that preventing harm to children was a strong governmental interest that further justified enactment of the ordinances.

Preventing Animal Cruelty

According to the District Court, "equally compelling [was] the City's interest in the protection of animals from cruelty and unnecessary killing."[88] The District Court found that 12,000 to 18,000 animals were annually sacrificed in Santerian initiation rites alone.[89] The District Court emphasized the well-established and long-recognized public policy in preventing animal cruelty. Expert testimony established that the killing method is unreliable and inhumane and that sacrificial animals are often kept in dirty and overcrowded conditions that engender fear and stress. Sometimes they are not given adequate food or water, and it is undisputed that they endure great pain during the sacrifice.[90]

The District Court further observed that Hialeah had a compelling interest in prohibiting the slaughter or sacrifice within city areas not zoned for slaughterhouse use and that the mere fact that slaughter is religiously motivated does not diminish that interest.[91] Pichardo was unable to guarantee that Santerians would comply with such zoning regulations, leading the District Court to conclude that a less restrictive ordinance would be difficult, if not impossible, to enforce.[92]

The District Court also concluded that an exception to the sacrifice prohibition for religious conduct would "'unduly interfere with fulfillment of the governmental interest'" because any narrower restrictions—that is, regulation of disposal of animal carcasses—would be unenforceable as a result of the secret nature of Santeria.[93]

Therefore, in upholding the ordinances, the District Court concluded:
> A balance of the compelling government interest served by the ordinances against the burden of Plaintiffs of not being allowed to ritually sacrifice animals, with all of the attendant risks to public health and animal welfare, must be resolved in favor of the City. Even absolute

proscriptions of religious conduct are constitutional when the law serves a compelling state interest. Compelling governmental interests, including public health and safety and animal welfare, fully justify the absolute prohibition on ritual sacrifice at issue here, and any effort to exempt purportedly religious conduct from the strictures of the City's laws would significantly hinder the attainment of those compelling interests. Therefore, this Court holds that the challenged ordinances do pass constitutional muster.[94]

The ordinances passed by the City of Hialeah regulating the ritual sacrifice of animals are consistent with both state statutes and the United States Constitution. The ordinances target the indiscriminate slaughter of animals in areas of the City not zoned for such activities because of the many attendant risks to both public health and animal welfare. The ordinances are not targeted at the Church of the Lukumi Babalu Aye and practitioners of Santeria, but are meant to prohibit all animal sacrifice, whether practiced by an individual, a religion, or a cult. Additionally, there was no proof of any discriminatory action by the City against the Plaintiff Church or any of its practitioners.[95]

In discussing the Church's legal defeat, counsel for the Church opined: "It is a dark day for religious freedom. We've made criminals out of 70,000 people in South Florida."[96] An appeal was inevitable. The American Civil Liberties Union (ACLU) selected Douglas Laycock, then professor at the University of Texas School of Law, to take the lead on the appeal due to his expertise in constitutional law and appellate advocacy.[97] However, the appeal was no more successful than the initial challenge.

On June 11, 1991, a three-judge panel of the United States Court of Appeals for the Eleventh Circuit affirmed the District Court's decision in a one-paragraph *per curiam* opinion.[98] In response, the Church petitioned the Supreme Court of the United States to review the case. On March 23, 1993, the Supreme Court granted the Church's petition for certiorari.[99] In addition to the parties' briefing, ten amicus briefs were filed: four in support of the Church and one filed by the U.S. Catholic Conference, which supported neither side. The five opposition briefs filed in support of Hialeah came from an assortment of animal protection and animal rights groups. The brief from the Humane Society of the United States (HSUS) was joined by the American Society for the Prevention of Cruelty to Animals (ASPCA), the Massachusetts SPCA and the Animal Legal Defense Fund. An additional brief was submitted by the Washington Humane Society. A brief from the People for the Ethical Treatment of Animals (PETA) was joined by the New Jersey Animal Rights Alliance and the Foundation for Animal Rights Advocacy. A fourth brief was filed by the International Society for Animal Rights along with Citizens for Animals and Farm Animal Reform Movement. An additional brief was filed by the Institute for Animal Rights Law along with the American Fund for Alternatives to Animal Research, Farm Sanctuary, United Animal Nations, and United Poultry Concerns.[100]

At the Supreme Court

On June 11, 1993, the Supreme Court issued a lengthy decision, striking the ordinances as unconstitutional. The Supreme Court has held that "a law that is neutral and of general applicability need not be justified by a compelling governmental interest even if the law has the incidental effect of burdening a particular religious practice."[101] Thus, the Supreme Court addressed whether the ordinances were facially neutral but observed that such facial neutrality is not determinative. Rather, "official action that targets religious conduct for distinctive treatment cannot be shielded by mere compliance with the requirement of facial neutrality. The Free Exercise Clause protects against governmental hostility which is masked as well as overt."[102] The Supreme Court determined that "a law lacks facial neutrality if it refers to a religious practice without a secular meaning discernable from the language or context."[103]

According to the Supreme Court, the record indicated that the ordinances' goal was to suppress animal sacrifice during Santerian worship. Use of the words "sacrifice" and "ritual" bolstered that conclusion.[104] Furthermore, Resolution 87-66 stated that "'residents and citizens of the City of Hialeah have expressed their concern that certain religions may propose to engage in practices which are inconsistent with public morals, peace or safety,'" and "'reiterate[d]'" Hialeah's commitment to prohibit "'any and all [such] acts of any and all religious groups.'"[105]

The Supreme Court determined that the ordinances operated to target Santeria even though they implicated many secular concerns like the prevention of animal cruelty. For instance, Ordinance 87-71 prohibited animal sacrifice, which it defined as the "'unnecessar[y] kill[ing of] . . . an animal in a public or private ritual or ceremony not for the primary purpose of food consumption.'"[106] According to the Court, this language singled out Santeria because the definition excluded animal killings except for religious sacrifice and exempted kosher slaughter.[107]

Elsewhere the Court observed that a different ordinance exempted licensed food establishments, again narrowing the impact of the law to Santeria.[108]

The ordinances' careful and narrow language troubled the Supreme Court because, while killings for religious reasons were deemed unnecessary, hunting, fishing, animal slaughter for food, eradication of insects and pests, and veterinary euthanasia were considered necessary and permissible.[109] The Supreme Court reasoned that because the ordinances require an evaluation of the underlying justification for the killing, they represent a system of "'individualized governmental assessment of the reasons for the relevant conduct.'"[110] The Supreme Court emphasized that in such circumstances the government "'may not refuse to extend that system to cases of 'religious hardship' without compelling reason.'"[111] The Supreme Court noted that because the application of the ordinances judged religious animal killings to be less deserving of protection than non-religious killing, it singled out religious practice for discriminatory treatment.[112]

The Supreme Court also determined that most of the ordinances were overbroad because they prohibited more religious conduct than necessary to achieve their goals.[113] For example, the Court pointed out that if improper disposal is the harm of animal sacrifice, Hialeah "could have imposed a general regulation on the disposal of organic garbage."[114] With regard to Hialeah's interest in mandating proper care of sacrificial animals, the Supreme Court reasoned that the appropriate response is regulation of conditions and treatment of animals regardless of why an animal is kept.[115] Put differently, more narrowly tailored ordinances would still be effective in preventing animal cruelty.

The Supreme Court also found the timing of the enactment of the ordinances suspicious. The minutes and taped excerpts of the June 9 city council session reflected significant hostility toward Santeria and animal sacrifice by residents, city council members, and other city officials.[116] For all of these reasons, the Supreme Court concluded that the ordinances aimed to suppress Santeria.

Turning to an examination of whether the ordinances were of general applicability, the Supreme Court noted that the Free Exercise Clause "'protect[s] religious observers against unequal treatment.'"[117] The Supreme Court determined that the ordinances were substantially underinclusive to protect public health or prevent animal cruelty because they failed to prohibit nonreligious conduct that similarly imperiled those interests.[118] The Supreme Court concluded that the ordinances targeted religiously motivated conduct.[119]

The next step in the First Amendment analysis was whether the ordinance could survive strict scrutiny. As explained above, a law that is not neutral or generally applicable but which burdens a religious practice must survive strict scrutiny; in other words, it must be narrowly tailored to achieve a compelling government interest.[120]

The Supreme Court concluded that the ordinances did not survive strict scrutiny because even if the governmental interests underlying the statute were compelling, the ordinances were not sufficiently narrow to advance those interests; rather they were overbroad in some respects and underinclusive in others.[121] As the Supreme Court explained, Hialeah had failed to show that the governmental interests were compelling because "where [the] government restricts only conduct protected by the First Amendment and fails to enact feasible measures to restrict other conduct producing substantial harm or alleged harm of the same sort, the interest given in justification of the restriction is not compelling."[122] For the foregoing reasons, the Supreme Court reversed. However, the decision was anything but unanimous. Rather, nearly all of the justices wrote separately.

Justice Scalia concurred in part and Chief Justice Rehnquist joined. According to Justice Scalia, the Court should not have considered the subjective motivation of the Hialeah city council members because it is "virtually impossible to determine" a legislative body's motive.[123] He observed that pure motives, such as the prevention of animal cruelty, do not matter if a law "singles out a religious practice for special burdens."[124]

Justice Souter concurred, urging the Court to reexamine precedent stating that there is no First Amendment violation where the prohibition of a religious practice flows from the enforcement of a facially neutral and generally applicable law.[125]

Justice Blackmun's concurrence, which Justice O'Connor joined, emphasized that the First Amendment's protection of religion extends beyond those singular occasions in which the government targets a religion for burdensome treatment; a statute that burdens the free exercise of religion "'may stand only if the law in general, and the State's refusal to allow a religious exemption in particular, are justified by a compelling interest that cannot be served by less restrictive means.'"[126] Justice Blackmun argued that when a state enacts legislation that intentionally or unintentionally burdens a religious practice, it must justify that burden by "'showing that it is the least restrictive means of achieving some compelling state interest.'"[127] He considered the ordinances overinclusive and underinclusive in relation to the interests they purportedly advanced. He also implied that a law that singles out a religious practice for disfavored treatment is not narrowly tailored to a compelling governmental interest; put differently, "regulation that targets religion in this way, ipso facto, fails strict scrutiny."[128] Justice Blackmun also clarified the narrow scope of the decision, stating:

A harder case would be presented if petitioners were requesting an exemption from a generally applicable anticruelty law. The result in the case before the Court today, and the fact that every Member of the Court concurs in that result, does not necessarily reflect this Court's views of the strength of a State's interest in prohibiting cruelty to animals. This case does not present, and I therefore decline to reach, the question whether the Free Exercise Clause would require a religious exemption from a law that sincerely pursued the goal of protecting animals from cruel treatment. The number of organizations that have filed amicus briefs on behalf of this interest, however, demonstrates that it is not a concern to be treated lightly.[129]

In a settlement agreement resulting from the case, Hialeah paid $500,000 for the Church's legal expenses incurred in the six years of litigation. Hialeah also paid one dollar to the Church as a symbol of reconciliation. In the aftermath of *Lukumi*, Pichardo observed that the community appeared less hostile toward Santeria.[130] No one knew that *Lukumi* would soon play a key role in yet another case pitting First Amendment freedoms against the interest in preventing animal cruelty.

Appendix

City of Hialeah, Florida, Resolution No. 87-66

City of Hialeah, Florida, Resolution No. 87-66, adopted June 9, 1987, provides:

"WHEREAS, residents and citizens of the City of Hialeah have expressed their concern that certain religions may propose to engage in practices which are inconsistent with public morals, peace or safety, and

"WHEREAS, the Florida Constitution, Article I, Declaration of Rights, Section 3, Religious Freedom, specifically states that religious freedom shall not justify practices inconsistent with public morals, peace or safety.

"NOW, THEREFORE, BE IT RESOLVED BY THE MAYOR AND CITY COUNCIL OF THE CITY OF HIALEAH, FLORIDA, that:

"1. The City reiterates its commitment to a prohibition against any and all acts of any and all religious groups which are inconsistent with public morals, peace or safety."

City of Hialeah, Florida, Ordinance No. 87-40

City of Hialeah, Florida, Ordinance No. 87-40, adopted June 9, 1987, provides:

"WHEREAS, the citizens of the City of Hialeah, Florida, have expressed great concern over the potential for animal sacrifices being conducted in the City of Hialeah; and

"WHEREAS, Section 828.27, Florida Statutes, provides that 'nothing contained in this section shall prevent any county or municipality from enacting any ordinance relating to animal control or cruelty to animals which is identical to the provisions of this Chapter . . . except as to penalty.'

"NOW, THEREFORE, BE IT ORDAINED BY THE MAYOR AND CITY COUNCIL OF THE CITY OF HIALEAH, FLORIDA, that:

"Section 1. The Mayor and City Council of the City of Hialeah, Florida, hereby adopt Florida Statute, Chapter 828—'Cruelty to Animals' (copy attached hereto and made a part hereof), in its entirety (relating to animal control or cruelty to animals), except as to penalty.

"Section 2. Repeal of Ordinances in Conflict. "All ordinances or parts of ordinances in conflict herewith are hereby repealed to the extent of such conflict.

"Section 3. Penalties. "Any person, firm or corporation convicted of violating the provisions of this ordinance shall be punished by a fine, not exceeding $500.00, or by a jail sentence, not exceeding sixty (60) days, or both, in the discretion of the Court.

"Section 4. Inclusion in Code. "The provisions of this Ordinance shall be included and incorporated in the Code of the City of Hialeah, as an addition or amendment thereto, and the sections of this Ordinance shall be renumbered to conform to the uniform numbering system of the Code.

"Section 5. Severability Clause. "If any phrase, clause, sentence, paragraph or section of this Ordinance shall be declared invalid or unconstitutional by the judge or decree of a court of competent jurisdiction, such invalidity or unconstitutionality shall not affect any of the remaining phrases, clauses, sentences, paragraphs or sections of this ordinance.

"Section 6. Effective Date. "This Ordinance shall become effective when passed by the City Council of the City of Hialeah and signed by the Mayor of the City of Hialeah."

City of Hialeah, Florida, Resolution No. 87-90

City of Hialeah Resolution No. 87-90, adopted August 11, 1987, provides:

"WHEREAS, the residents and citizens of the City of Hialeah, Florida, have expressed great concern regarding the possibility of public ritualistic animal sacrifices in the City of Hialeah, Florida; and

"WHEREAS, the City of Hialeah, Florida, has received an opinion from the Attorney General of the State of Florida concluding that public ritualistic animal sacrifices is a violation of the Florida State Statute on Cruelty to Animals; and

"WHEREAS, the Attorney General further held that the sacrificial killing of animals other than for the primary purpose of food consumption is prohibited under state law; and

"WHEREAS, the City of Hialeah, Florida, has enacted an ordinance mirroring state law prohibiting cruelty to animals.

"NOW, THEREFORE, BE IT RESOLVED BY THE MAYOR AND CITY COUNCIL OF THE CITY OF HIALEAH, FLORIDA, that:

"Section 1. It is the policy of the Mayor and City Council of the City of Hialeah, Florida, to oppose the ritual sacrifices of animals within the City of Hialeah, Florida. Any individual or organization that seeks to practice animal sacrifice in violation of state and local law will be prosecuted."

City of Hialeah, Florida, Ordinance No. 87-52

City of Hialeah, Ordinance No. 87-52, adopted September 8, 1987, provides:

"WHEREAS, the residents and citizens of the City of Hialeah, Florida, have expressed great concern regarding the possibility of public ritualistic animal sacrifices within the City of Hialeah, Florida; and

"WHEREAS, the City of Hialeah, Florida, has received an opinion from the Attorney General of the State of Florida, concluding that public ritualistic animal sacrifice, other than for the primary purpose of food consumption, is a violation of state law; and

"WHEREAS, the City of Hialeah, Florida, has enacted an ordinance (Ordinance No. 87-40), mirroring the state law prohibiting cruelty to animals.

"WHEREAS, the City of Hialeah, Florida, now wishes to specifically prohibit the possession of animals for slaughter or sacrifice within the City of Hialeah, Florida.

"NOW, THEREFORE, BE IT ORDAINED BY THE MAYOR AND CITY COUNCIL OF THE CITY OF HIALEAH, FLORIDA, that:

"Section 1. Chapter 6 of the Code of Ordinances of the City of Hialeah, Florida, is hereby amended by adding thereto two (2) new Sections 6-8 "Definitions" and 6-9 "Prohibition Against Possession Of Animals For Slaughter Or Sacrifice," which is to read as follows:

"Section 6-8. Definitions

"1. Animal—any living dumb creature.

"2. Sacrifice—to unnecessarily kill, torment, torture, or mutilate an animal in a public or private ritual or ceremony not for the primary purpose of food consumption.

"3. Slaughter—the killing of animals for food.

"Section 6-9. Prohibition Against Possession of Animals for Slaughter Or Sacrifice.

"1. No person shall own, keep or otherwise possess, sacrifice, or slaughter any sheep, goat, pig, cow or the young of such species, poultry, rabbit, dog, cat, or any other animal, intending to use such animal for food purposes.

"2. This section is applicable to any group or individual that kills, slaughters or sacrifices animals for any type of ritual, regardless of whether or not the flesh or blood of the animal is to be consumed.

"3. Nothing in this ordinance is to be interpreted as prohibiting any licensed establishment from slaughtering for food purposes any animals which are specifically raised for food purposes where such activity is properly zoned and/or permitted under state and local law and under rules promulgated by the Florida Department of Agriculture.

"Section 2. Repeal of Ordinance in Conflict. All ordinances or parts of ordinances in conflict herewith are hereby repealed to the extent of such conflict.

"Section 3. Penalties. Any person, firm or corporation convicted of violating the provisions of this ordinance shall be punished by a fine, not exceeding $500.00, or by a jail sentence, not exceeding sixty (60) days, or both, in the discretion of the Court.

"Section 4. Inclusion in Code. The provisions of this Ordinance shall be included and incorporated in the Code of the City of Hialeah, as an addition or amendment thereto, and the sections of this Ordinance shall be renumbered to conform to the uniform numbering system of the Code.

"Section 5. Severability Clause. If any phrase, clause, sentence, paragraph or section of this Ordinance shall be declared invalid or unconstitutional by the judge or decree of a court of competent jurisdiction, such invalidity or unconstitutionality shall not affect any of the remaining phrases, clauses, sentences, paragraphs or sections of this ordinance.

"Section 6. Effective Date. This Ordinance shall become effective when passed by the City Council of the City of Hialeah and signed by the Mayor of the City of Hialeah."

City of Hialeah, Florida, Ordinance No. 87-71

City of Hialeah, Ordinance No. 87-71, adopted September 22, 1987, provides:

"WHEREAS, the City Council of the City of Hialeah, Florida, has determined that the sacrificing of animals within the city limits is contrary to the public health, safety, welfare and morals of the community; and

"WHEREAS, the City Council of the City of Hialeah, Florida, desires to have qualified societies or corporations organized under the laws of the State of Florida, to be authorized to investigate and prosecute any violation(s) of the ordinance herein after set forth, and for the registration of the agents of said societies.

"NOW, THEREFORE, BE IT ORDAINED BY THE MAYOR AND CITY COUNCIL OF THE CITY OF HIALEAH, FLORIDA, that:

"Section 1. For the purpose of this ordinance, the word sacrifice shall mean: to unnecessarily kill, torment, torture, or mutilate an animal in a public or private ritual or ceremony not for the primary purpose of food consumption.

"Section 2. For the purpose of this ordinance, the word animal shall mean: any living dumb creature.

"Section 3. It shall be unlawful for any person, persons, corporations or associations to sacrifice any animal within the corporate limits of the City of Hialeah, Florida.

"Section 4. All societies or associations for the prevention of cruelty to animals organized under the laws of the State of Florida, seeking to register with the City of Hialeah for purposes of investigating and assisting in the prosecution of violations and provisions of this Ordinance, shall apply to the City Council for authorization to so register and shall be registered with the Office of the Mayor of the City of Hialeah, Florida, following approval by the City Council at a public hearing in accordance with rules and regulations (i.e., criteria) established by the City Council by resolution, and shall thereafter, be empowered to assist in the prosecution of any violation of this Ordinance.

"Section 5. Any society or association for the prevention of cruelty to animals registered with the Mayor of the City of Hialeah, Florida, in accordance with the provisions of Section 4 hereinabove, may appoint agents for the purposes of investigating and assisting in the prosecution of violations and provisions of this Ordinance, or any other laws of the City of Hialeah, Florida, for the purpose of protecting animals and preventing any act prohibited hereunder.

"Section 6. Repeal of Ordinances in Conflict. All ordinances or parts of ordinances in conflict herewith are hereby repealed to the extent of such conflict.

"Section 7. Penalties. Any person, firm or corporation convicted of violating the provisions of this ordinance shall be punished by a fine, not exceeding $500.00, or by a jail sentence, not exceeding sixty (60) days, or both, in the discretion of the Court.

"Section 8. Inclusion in Code. The provisions of this Ordinance shall be included and incorporated in the Code of the City of Hialeah, as an addition or amendment thereto, and the sections of this Ordinance shall be renumbered to conform to the uniform numbering system of the Code.

"Section 9. Severability Clause. If any phrase, clause, sentence, paragraph or section of this Ordinance shall be declared invalid or unconstitutional by the judgment or decree of a court of competent jurisdiction, such invalidity or unconstitutionality shall not affect any of the remaining phrases, clauses, sentences, paragraphs or sections of this Ordinance.

"Section 10. Effective Date. This Ordinance shall become effective when passed by the City Council of the City of Hialeah and signed by the Mayor of the City of Hialeah."

City of Hialeah, Florida, Ordinance No. 87-72

City of Hialeah, Ordinance No. 87-72, adopted September 22, 1987, provides:

"WHEREAS, the City Council of the City of Hialeah, Florida, has determined that the slaughtering of animals on the premises other than those properly zoned as a slaughter house, is contrary to the public health, safety and welfare of the citizens of Hialeah, Florida.

"NOW, THEREFORE, BE IT ORDAINED BY THE MAYOR AND CITY COUNCIL OF THE CITY OF HIALEAH, FLORIDA, that:

"Section 1. For the purpose of this Ordinance, the word slaughter shall mean: the killing of animals for food.

"Section 2. For the purpose of this Ordinance, the word animal shall mean: any living dumb creature.

"Section 3. It shall be unlawful for any person, persons, corporations or associations to slaughter any animal on any premises in the City of Hialeah, Florida, except those properly zoned as a slaughter house, and meeting all the health, safety and sanitation codes prescribed by the City for the operation of a slaughter house.

"Section 4. All societies or associations for the prevention of cruelty to animals organized under the laws of the State of Florida, seeking to register with the City of Hialeah for purposes of investigating and assisting in the prosecution of violations and provisions of this Ordinance, shall apply to the City Council for authorization to so register and shall be registered with the Office of the Mayor of the City of Hialeah, Florida, following approval by the City Council at a public hearing in accordance with rules and regulations (i.e., criteria) established by the City Council by resolution, and shall thereafter, be empowered to assist in the prosecution of any violations of this Ordinance.

"Section 5. Any society or association for the prevention of cruelty to animals registered with the Mayor of the City of Hialeah, Florida, in accordance with the provisions of Section 4 hereinabove, may appoint agents for the purposes of investigating and assisting in the prosecution of violations and provisions of this Ordinance, or any other laws of the City of Hialeah, Florida, for the purpose of protecting animals and preventing any act prohibited hereunder.

"Section 6. This Ordinance shall not apply to any person, group, or organization that slaughters, or processes for sale, small numbers of hogs and/ or cattle per week in accordance with an exemption provided by state law.

"Section 7. Repeal of Ordinances in Conflict. All ordinances or parts of ordinances in conflict herewith are hereby repealed to the extent of such conflict.

"Section 8. Penalties. Any person, firm or corporation convicted of violating the provisions of this ordinance shall be punished by a fine, not exceeding $500.00, or by a jail sentence, not exceeding sixty (60) days, or both, in the discretion of the Court.

"Section 9. Inclusion in Code. The provisions of this Ordinance shall be included and incorporated in the Code of the City of Hialeah, as an addition or amendment thereto, and the sections of this Ordinance shall be renumbered to conform to the uniform numbering system of the Code.

"Section 10. Severability Clause. If any phrase, clause, sentence, paragraph or section of this Ordinance shall be declared invalid or unconstitutional by the judgment or decree of a court of competent jurisdiction, such invalidity or unconstitutionality shall not affect any of the remaining phrases, clauses, sentences, paragraphs or sections of this ordinance."

"Section 11. Effective Date. This Ordinance shall become effective when passed by the City Council of the City of Hialeah and signed by the Mayor of the City of Hialeah."[131]

Notes

1. David M. O'Brien, *Animal Sacrifice and Religious Freedom: Church of the Lukumi Babalu Aye v. City of Hialeah* (Lawrence, Kansas: University of Kansas Press, 2004), 33.
2. Ibid., 33.
3. Ibid., 35.
4. Ibid.
5. Ibid., 38.
6. Ibid., 42.
7. Ibid., 42–43.
8. *Church of the Lukumi Babalu Aye, Inc. v. City of Hialeah*, 508 U.S. 520, 526 (1993).

9.   Ibid.
10. Ibid., 527.
11. Ibid.
12. *Church of the Lukumi Babalu Aye, Inc. v. City of Hialeah*, 723 F.Supp. 1467, 1476 (S.D. Fla. 1989), rev'd, 508 U.S. 520 (1993).
13. O'Brien, *Animal Sacrifice*, 47.
14. *Lukumi*, 508 U.S. at 528.
15. *Lukumi*, 723 F.Supp. at 1474 n.24.
16. O'Brien, *Animal Sacrifice*, 23.
17. *Lukumi*, 723 F.Supp. at 1469.
18. O'Brien, *Animal Sacrifice*, 26.
19. Ibid., 3
20. *Lukumi*, 723 F.Supp. at 1469.
21. *Lukumi*, 508 U.S. at 524.
22. *Lukumi*, 723 F.Supp. at 1470 n.4.
23. O'Brien, *Animal Sacrifice*, 7.
24. *Lukumi*, 508 U.S. at 524.
25. O'Brien, *Animal Sacrifice*, 8.
26. *Lukumi*, 723 F.Supp. at 1470.
27. Ibid.
28. O'Brien, *Animal Sacrifice*, at 14.
29. *Lukumi*, 723 F.Supp. at 1470.
30. *Lukumi*, 508 U.S. at 525.
31. Ibid.
32. Ibid.
33. *Lukumi*, 723 F.Supp. at 1470.
34. Ibid., 1471 n.14.
35. Ibid., 1471.
36. Ibid., 1471 n.12.
37. Ibid., 1471.
38. Ibid., 1473 n.21.
39. Ibid., 1473 n.22.
40. Ibid., 1471.
41. Ibid., 1474 n.29.
42. Ibid., 1471 n.14.
43. Ibid.
44. Ibid., 1472.
45. Ibid.
46. Ibid.
47. Ibid.
48. Ibid., 1473.
49. Ibid.
50. Ibid., 1473 n.19.

51. Ibid.
52. Ibid., 1473.
53. Ibid.
54. Ibid., 1473 n.21.
55. Ibid.
56. Ibid.
57. Ibid., 1475 n.33.
58. *Lukumi*, 508 U.S. at 528; see also *Church of the Lukumi Babalu Aye, Inc. v. City of Hialeah*, 688 F.Supp. 1522 (S.D. Fla. 1988).
59. *Lukumi*, 723 F.Supp. at 1480.
60. Ibid., 1481–82.
61. Ibid., 1482.
62. O'Brien, *Animal Sacrifice*, 90.
63. *Lukumi*, 723 F.Supp. at 1476-77.
64. Ibid., 1479.
65. Ibid.
66. Ibid., 1482.
67. *Lukumi*, 508 U.S. at 531 (quoting *Thomas v. Review Bd. of Ind. Emp't Sec. Div.*, 450 U.S. 707, 714 (1981)).
68. *Lukumi*, 723 F.Supp. at 1479.
69. Ibid., 1482.
70. Ibid.
71. Ibid., 1483–84.
72. Ibid.
73. Ibid.
74. Ibid., 1484 n.53.
75. Ibid., 1484.
76. Ibid., 1487.
77. Ibid., 1485.
78. Ibid.
79. Ibid.
80. Ibid.
81. Ibid.
82. Ibid., 1475.
83. Ibid.
84. Ibid.
85. Ibid., 1476.
86. Ibid.
87. Ibid., 1486.
88. Ibid.
89. Ibid., 1473 n.22.
90. Ibid., 1486.
91. Ibid.

92. Ibid., 1487 n.59.
93. Ibid., 1486 (quoting *United States v. Lee*, 455 U.S. 252, 259 (1982)).
94. Ibid., 1487.
95. Ibid., 1488.
96. O'Brien, *Animal Sacrifice,* 93.
97. Ibid., 94
98. Ibid., 96; see also *Church of Lukumi v. City of Hialeah*, 936 F.2d 586 (11th Cir. 1991).
99. Ibid., 100.
100. Ibid., 102.
101. *Lukumi*, 508 U.S. at 531.
102. Ibid., 534.
103. Ibid., 533.
104. Ibid., 534.
105. Ibid., 535.
106. Ibid., 535–36.
107. Ibid., 536.
108. Ibid.
109. Ibid., 537.
110. Ibid. (quoting *Emp't Div. of Human Res. of Ore v. Smith*, 494 U.S. 872, 884 (1990)).
111. Ibid.
112. Ibid., 537–38.
113. Ibid., 546.
114. Ibid., 538.
115. Ibid., 539.
116. Ibid., 541.
117. Ibid., 542 (quoting *Hobbie v. Unemployment Appeals Comm'n of Fla.*, 480 U.S. 138, 148 (1987) (Stevens, J. concurring in judgment)).
118. Ibid., 543.
119. Ibid., 545.
120. Ibid., 546.
121. Ibid.
122. Ibid., 546–47.
123. Ibid., 558.
124. Ibid., 559.
125. Ibid., 559–60.
126. Ibid., 577–78 (quoting *Emp't Div. of Human Res. of Ore v. Smith*, 494 U.S. 872, 907 (1990)).
127. Ibid., 578 (quoting *Thomas v. Review Bd. of Ind. Emp't Sec. Div.*, 450 U.S. 707, 718 (1981)).
128. Ibid., 579.
129. Ibid., 580.
130. O'Brien, *Animal Sacrifice,* 160.
131. *Lukumi*, 508 U.S. at 548–57.

CHAPTER 5

Freedom of Speech and Animal Protection: *United States v. Stevens*

In response to growing concerns regarding the crush video industry, Representative Elton Gallegly (R-CA) introduced the "Crush Video Bill"—H.R. 1887—on May 20, 1999, with broad bipartisan support from 52 co-sponsors. On September 30, 1999, the House of Representatives Subcommittee on Crime heard testimony about crush videos from law enforcement, Actors and Others for Animals, the Doris Day Animal League, and the American Humane Association.[1] Some testifying analogized the crush video industry to the production of child pornography.[2] Several members of the Subcommittee expressed concern about the bill's stipulation that the depictions would be illegal if the act depicted was unlawful in the state where the video was sold—a concern later echoed by the Supreme Court.[3]

Less than two weeks later, on October 13, 1999, an exceptions clause was added to the bill to address free speech concerns raised in the Subcommittee hearings, and the bill was favorably reported by the House Judiciary Committee, paving the way for a full House of Representatives vote just six days later.[4] After rigorous legislative debate, Representative Gallegly's bill overwhelmingly passed on October 19, 1999, receiving 372 ayes and only 42 nays.[5] Proponents of Section 48 alluded to the link between human and animal violence, the impact of depictions of animal cruelty on viewers, especially children, and the need to make a moral statement that wanton acts of extreme animal cruelty are intolerable in America.[6] Opponents of Section 48 argued, *inter alia*, that Section 48 was not sufficiently narrowly tailored and that preventing animal cruelty is not a compelling interest.[7] One month later, the Senate version of the bill was approved unanimously—a rarity for any legislation, particularly an animal-related law.[8]

In December 1999, then-President Bill Clinton signed 18 U.S.C. §48 (Section 48) into law. President Clinton expressed the need to limit Section 48's focus and intent on aberrant sexual practices. As he explained, "so construed, the Act would prohibit types of depictions described in the statute's legislative history, of wanton cruelty to animals designed to appeal to a prurient interest in sex."[9]

Section 48 criminalized the creation, sale, or possession of certain depictions of animal cruelty.[10] It stated in pertinent part:

> Whoever knowingly creates, sells, or possesses a depiction of animal cruelty with the intention of placing that depiction in interstate or foreign commerce for commercial gain, shall be fined under this title or imprisoned not more than 5 years, or both.... Subsection (a) does not apply to any depiction that has serious religious, political, scientific, educational, journalistic, historical, or artistic value.[11]

Subsection (c)(1) defined the term "depiction of animal cruelty" as:

> Any visual or auditory depiction, including any photograph, motion-picture film, video recording, electronic image, or sound recording of conduct in which a living animal is intentionally maimed, mutilated, tortured, wounded, or killed, if such conduct is illegal under Federal law or the law of the State in which the creation, sale, or possession takes place, regardless of whether the maiming, mutilation, torture, wounding, or killing took place in the State.[12]

Subsection (c)(2) defined *state* as "each of the several States, the District of Columbia, the Commonwealth of Puerto Rico, the Virgin Islands, Guam, American Samoa, the Commonwealth of the Northern Mariana Islands, and any other commonwealth, territory, or possession of the United States."[13]

Section 48 appeared to have its desired effect. The market in crush videos reportedly declined, even absent arrests under Section 48 for distribution of such videos. It seemed that the mere threat of prosecution had decreased the market for crush videos—or had at least driven it deep underground.[14] The law provided a potentially effective tool for stopping the distribution of materials that allowed people to profit from depictions of animal cruelty.

Ironically, the first prosecution under Section 48 that proceeded to trial ultimately resulted in the law's invalidation. The alleged perpetrator was filmmaker Robert J. Stevens. Through his business—"Dogs of Velvet and Steel"—and website—Pitbulllife.com—Stevens purportedly sold dogfighting videos and paraphernalia out of his home in Pittsville, Virginia.[15] He advertised via *Sporting Dog*

Journal—an underground periodical that purportedly promotes the criminal dogfighting industry, allegedly by publishing the results of illegal dogfights.[16]

Although Stevens did not participate in actual dogfighting, he was prominent in the dogfighting world, particularly known for writing and distributing *Dogs of Velvet and Steel*, a self-published instructional book clearly aimed at dogfighters.[17] Like many contributors to dogfighting literature, Stevens claimed to have no interest in promoting illegal dogfighting. However, his book describes his attendance at many fights and provides extensive information on the training and conditioning of dogs for fighting.[18]

Law enforcement agents mail-ordered three videos from Stevens. Two of the tapes—"Pick-A-Winna" and "Japan Pit Fights"—portrayed organized dogfights. The third video—"Catch Dogs and Country Living"—depicted a pit bull tearing off the lower jaw of a domestic pig.[19]

"Japan Pit Fights" features fights involving three dogs Stevens had sent to Japan.[20] The time and location of the fights is not specified.[21] "Pick-a-Winna" claims to recreate the ambiance of old-time dogfights. Narration encourages viewers to pay attention to the dogs' behavior and fight styles to see if they can predict the outcome. In doing so, one could argue that Stevens instructs viewers in the proper training, conditioning, and handling of fighting dogs.[22] "Catch Dogs" is the most brutal of the three videos. Although the video is supposedly about the use of pit bulls in legal pig hunting, it begins with a depiction of a Japanese dogfight, allegedly to demonstrate the "core of the breed."[23] The video goes on to show a pit bull grabbing a captive pig. Within three minutes the dog has torn away the pig's lower jaw and much of its nose and throat. The video does not demonstrate actual field hunting of pigs with dogs.[24]

The agents obtained a warrant and searched Stevens' residence where they found dogfighting videos, merchandise, and records indicating sales in excess of $50,000.[25] While not insignificant, this is a relatively small amount compared to the income dogfights, stud fees, and sales of pups generate. Indeed, a single fight may involve bets in excess of $10,000, and total purses for an evening of organized dogfighting activity commonly exceed $50,000 to $100,000 at a single venue.[26] Also, unlike crush videos, dogfighting videos sometimes show the faces of participants and, in fact, are often an important part of the evidence used to build a successful dogfight prosecution. In addition, sometimes video evidence seized in present-day investigations of dogfighting involve smartphone video recordings, which may contain metadata about the time and location where the video was made unless those capabilities have been specifically disabled.[27]

Stevens' arrest was unique in the world of dogfighting. Some viewed it as an overreaction because no one alleged that Stevens was actively involved in dog-fighting at his property. No dogs, dogfight training or conditioning equipment, or other paraphernalia were seized.[28] The only charges against Stevens related to the application of Section 48 to his video distribution enterprise.[29] Stevens was well-known in the dogfighting world and to humane agencies that investi-gated fighting, but he was not considered a major breeder, trainer or promoter.[30] However, the blatant marketing of materials that seemed to violate Section 48 made him a target.

By contrast, law enforcement viewed Stevens' arrest as spotlighting Section 48 as a new tool that could be used against dogfighters. The case was included in the American Prosecutors Research Institute guide *Animal Cruelty Prosecution: Op-portunities for Early Response to Crime and Interpersonal Violence* as a demonstra-tion of how the law could be applied to dogfighting enterprises.[31]

Despite the controversy, Stevens' conduct came within the embrace of Section 48 as written. The first two videos, depicting actual fights in Japan and the U.S., clearly involved the maiming of animals in the context of dogfighting, which was illegal in the state to which the videos were sent (Pennsylvania) and every other state. The third video, featuring the torture and mutilation of a domestic pig as well as an illegal dogfight, also depicted activities that violated laws in virtually every state in which the videos might have been sold.[32]

In 2004, Stevens was indicted on three counts of knowingly selling depictions of animal cruelty with the intent to place the depictions in interstate commerce for profit in violation of Section 48.[33] Stevens moved to dismiss his indictment by arguing that Section 48 was void for vagueness under the Due Process Clause of the Fifth Amendment and facially invalid under the Free Speech Clause of the First Amendment.[34] In denying his motion, the District Court held that the depictions of animal cruelty that Section 48 targeted do not constitute protected speech.[35] Perhaps it was inevitable that Section 48 would be challenged on First Amendment grounds. It was problematic from the start that the case chosen to test the law did not indisputably comport with the original legislative intent underpinning Sec-tion 48 and potentially contravened President Clinton's remarks that Section 48's enforcement should be limited to "wanton cruelty to animals designed to appeal to a prurient interest in sex."[36]

In reaching its decision, the District Court analogized to pornography and explained that "if the government has a sufficiently compelling interest in pro-hibiting the sale of depictions of sexual activity between consenting adults, it has an equal, if not greater, interest in preventing the torture, maiming, mutilation and wanton killing of animals that are unable to consent to such treatment."[37] It compared Section 48 to a law prohibiting child pornography that the United States Supreme Court had upheld in *New York v. Ferber*[38] and determined that Section 48 was not substantially overbroad because it applied only to depictions of intentional and illegal acts of animal cruelty involving live animals, which lack redeeming social value and are intended for interstate commercial sale.[39]

The case proceeded to trial, and on January 13, 2005, a jury convicted Stevens on each of the three counts. He was sentenced to concurrent prison sentences of 37 months apiece, followed by three years of supervised release.[40]

Displeased with the trial verdict, Stevens appealed his conviction to the Third Circuit.[41] On July 18, 2008, the Third Circuit, over a three-judge dissent, vacated Stevens' conviction and declared Section 48 to be facially unconstitutional.[42] In reaching its decision, the Third Circuit majority was reluctant to hold that the animal cruelty depictions at issue constituted unprotected speech absent guidance from the Supreme Court.[43] The Third Circuit rejected the District Court's analogy to *Ferber* and relied instead on the Supreme Court's holding in *Church of the Lukumi Babalu Aye, Inc. v. City of Hialeah (Lukumi)*,[44] which the Third Circuit interpreted to mean that preventing animal cruelty is not a compelling interest.[45] Although the Third Circuit opined in a footnote that Section 48 may be overbroad, it rested its holding on strict scrutiny grounds since "voiding a statute on overbreadth grounds is 'strong medicine.'"[46]

Writing for the majority, Judge Smith emphasized that the Supreme Court had "not recognized a new category of speech that is unprotected by the First Amendment in over twenty-five years."[47] The majority recounted the legislative history of Section 48, concluding that its purpose was to prohibit crush videos, not the dogfighting videos that resulted in Stevens' conviction.[48] The majority first explained why depictions of animal fighting constitute protected speech and then why Section 48 did not survive strict scrutiny.

The majority reasoned that Section 48 regulated speech, not conduct, because it targeted depictions of animal cruelty rather than the acts of cruelty themselves, most or all of which were already prohibited by existing anti-cruelty laws. According to the District Court, the government conceded that the depictions at issue did not fall into existing categories of protected speech. In a footnote, the majority acknowledged the government's reliance upon *Chaplinsky* to argue that the government interest in restricting the speech should be weighed against the value of the speech.[49] However, without much additional elaboration, the majority concluded that "the only possible way to conclude that Section 48 regulates un-protected speech is through an analogy to the *Ferber* rationale."[50]

Evidencing its reluctance to designate a new category of unprotected speech, the majority cautioned that:

> Without guidance from the Supreme Court, a lower federal court should hesitate before extending the logic of *Ferber* to other types of speech. The reasoning that supports *Ferber* has never been used to create whole categories of unprotected speech outside of the child pornography context. Furthermore, *Ferber* appears to be on the margin of the Supreme Court's unprotected speech jurisprudence.[51]

In applying the *Ferber* factors to the facts of *Stevens*, the Third Circuit con-cluded that preventing animal cruelty does not trump free speech rights for the following reasons: (i) *Lukumi* suggests that preventing animal cruelty is not a compelling interest; (ii) Congress rarely finds a compelling interest for content-based restrictions and when it does, those interests relate to human, not animal, welfare; (iii) Section 48 did not regulate the underlying acts of animal cruelty; and (iv) the Third Circuit found an insufficient link between the statute and the interest in preventing animal cruelty.[52]

Citing *Ashcroft v. Free Speech Coalition*, the majority iterated that the "mere tendency of speech to encourage unlawful acts is not a sufficient reason for ban-ning it. . . . The prospect of crime . . . by itself does not justify laws suppressing protected speech."[53] Similarly, general references to speech repugnant to public mores cannot serve as a compelling government interest sufficient to override constitutional protections of speech.[54]

Turning to the second *Ferber* factor, that child pornography is "intrinsically related to the sexual abuse of children,"[55] the Third Circuit opined that:

> while animals are sentient creatures worthy of human kindness and human care, one cannot seriously contend that the animals them-selves suffer continuing harm by having their images out in the mar-ketplace. . . . when an animal suffers an act of cruelty that is captured on film . . . the fact that the act of cruelty was captured on film in no way exacerbates or prolongs the harm suffered by that animal.[56]

With regard to the third *Ferber* factor—the drying-up-the-market theory—the Third Circuit conceded that the theory was potentially apt in the animal cruelty context but stated that no empirical evidence in the record confirmed the theory's validity.[57]

The fourth *Ferber* factor examines the value of the speech.[58] The government argued that Section 48's broad exemptions clause meant that only speech with little or no redeeming social value would be prohibited, but the Third Circuit stated that "the exceptions clause cannot on its own constitutionalize §48."[59]

Finally, the Third Circuit explained that the attempted analogy to *Ferber* failed "because of the inherent differences between children and animals. Those profound differences require no further explication here."[60]

Having decided that Section 48 regulates protected speech, the majority next considered whether the statute survived strict scrutiny and held that it did not. The majority determined that the law was underinclusive because it only regulated depictions of animal cruelty sold within interstate commerce for commercial gain; it did not prohibit a video of animal cruelty sold within a single state or made for personal gain. Yet the majority simultaneously deemed the statute to be overinclusive because a party could be prosecuted for selling a depiction of animal cruelty in Pennsylvania that had been created in Virginia even if the conduct depicted was legal in Virginia, so long as it was illegal in Pennsylvania.[61] According to the majority, "if the government interest is to prevent acts of animal cruelty, the statute's criminalization of depictions that were legal in the geographic region where they were produced makes *§48* overinclusive."[62] Third, the Supreme Court permitted prohibition of child pornography in *Ferber* because regulation of the speech decreased the likelihood of the illegal conduct and ensuing harm. The majority stated that with respect to crush videos, the government's claims that films are made deliberately obscuring the date, location, and face of the participant, making arrest nearly impossible were unpersuasive because crush videos constitute only a portion of the speech that Section 48 banned.[63]

The government argued that handlers in dogfighting videos are deliberately shown from the waist or elbows down, making it virtually impossible to determine when and where such fights occur for purposes of the statute of limitations and other enforcement matters.[64] However, with respect to the videos at issue in *Stevens*, the majority concluded that this argument was "empirically inaccurate" because handlers' faces are sometimes clear and in the film, whereas in "Japan Pit Fights" the individuals depicted could not be prosecuted because dogfighting is legal in Japan.[65] There is no effort to conceal any of the faces of the people in the third video, and Stevens mentioned their names and the hunt locations.[66] Therefore, the majority concluded that Section 48 was not narrowly tailored using the least restrictive means and thus, failed to survive strict scrutiny.[67]

Notably, in footnote 16, the majority opined that Section 48 might also be unconstitutionally overbroad.[68] As the majority explained:

The Government is too quick to conclude that a reading of the statute that covers a wide variety of ostensibly technical violations like hunting and fishing will not lead to prosecutions. This Court is required to examine the plain language of the statute to determine whether "a substantial amount of protected speech is prohibited or chilled in the process" of regulating depictions of animal cruelty. Even if we incorrectly assume that §48 constitutionally reaches the type of depictions sold by Stevens, we must pose reasonable but challenging hypotheticals to determine the statute's sweep.[69]

The statute potentially covers a great deal of constitutionally protected speech, and prosecutions that stray far from crush videos may chill this type of speech. Section 48 broadly proclaims that "the term 'depiction of animal cruelty' means any visual or auditory depiction, including any photograph, motion-picture film, video recording, electronic image, or sound recording of conduct in which a living animal is intentionally maimed, mutilated, tortured, wounded, or killed, if such conduct is illegal under Federal law or the law of the State in which the creation, sale, or possession takes place, regardless of whether the maiming, mutilation, torture, wounding, or killing took place in the State." If a person hunts or fishes out of season, films the activity, and sells it to an out-of-state party, it appears that the statute has been violated. Similarly, the same person could be prosecuted for selling a film which contains a depiction of a bullfight in Spain if bullfighting is illegal in the state in which this person sells the film. The only possible protections for this violator are prosecutorial discretion and the exceptions clause in section (b). If this depiction has "religious, political, scientific, educational, journalistic, historical, or artistic value" but the value is not "serious," then this violator only has prosecutorial discretion to fall back on. The penalty for these hypothetical violations includes a fine and up to five years in prison. We do not believe that the constitutionality of §48 should depend on prosecutorial discretion for a statute that sweeps this widely. There is no reason to believe that prosecutors will limit themselves to targeting crush videos through §48.[70]

However, because voiding a statute on overbreadth grounds is "strong medicine" and should be used "sparingly and only as a last resort," we are satisfied to rest our analyst on strict scrutiny grounds alone.[71]

Ironically, the language that the majority confined to a single footnote would ultimately become the linchpin in the Supreme Court's decision invalidating Section 48.

Judges Cowen, Fuentes, and Fisher dissented[72] on the ground that the videos at issue were not entitled to First Amendment protection in part because they lack redeeming social value and because the history and breadth of America's anticruelty laws evince that the prevention of animal cruelty is an important government interest.[73] Writing on behalf of the dissenting judges, Judge Cowen opined that animal cruelty erodes public mores and has "a deleterious effect on the individual inflicting the harm."[74] Analogizing to *Ferber*, the dissenters averred that prohibiting depictions of animal cruelty would dry up the lucrative dogfighting industry. The dissenters further concluded that Section 48 was neither overbroad nor impermissibly vague and that constitutional concerns regarding the statute should be addressed on a case-by-case basis.[75]

According to the dissent, the Supreme Court has consistently held that certain speech may be prohibited when its social value is plainly outweighed by the government's compelling interest regulating it. *Ferber* articulated critical considerations in determining which speech is unprotected. The dissent agreed with the government that the prevention of animal cruelty constitutes a compelling government interest.[76] In support of this assertion, the dissenting opinion cited the numerous and longstanding state and federal anti-cruelty and animal protection laws across the nation[77] as well as Supreme Court precedent deeming a vast array of interests as compelling.[78]

Finally, the dissent explained that *Lukumi* was distinguishable and did not support the assertion that the prevention of animal cruelty does not constitute a compelling government interest because the ordinances at issue there failed because their true rationale was the unconstitutional suppression of the Santeria religion.[79] Justice Blackmun made clear that "the result in [*Lukumi*], does not necessarily reflect this Court's views of the strength of a State's interest in prohibiting cruelty to animals."[80]

The dissent rejected any suggestion that "Congress cannot have a compelling interest to advance a goal when the subject of the regulation is not directly within its constitutional sphere of legislative authority."[81] Nor did the dissenters find Section 48 to be sufficiently underinclusive or overinclusive so as to warrant invalidation.[82] According to the dissent, "Congress could have reasonably decided to focus its attention on purely interstate conduct, lest enforcement efforts be hampered by costly constitutional litigation. This is especially so in light of the indication that the materials Congress sought to prohibit 'were almost exclusively distributed for sale through interstate or foreign commerce.'"[83]

The dissent interpreted the reach of Section 48 quite differently than the majority. Under the dissent's reading of the statute, a party may be prosecuted for possessing a depiction of animal cruelty in Virginia originally made in the Northern Mariana Islands even where the underlying activity depicted is legal in the Northern Mariana Islands, but only if the act is otherwise illegal in Virginia or in the state or territory to which the party knowingly directs the sale of the depiction.[84] "Were the acts legal in both Virginia and the Northern Mariana Islands, Party Z could not be prosecuted for selling the depiction in Virginia to someone back in the Northern Mariana Islands."[85]

Next, the dissent determined that the speech prohibited had little or no redeeming social value because the statute's broad exemptions clause excluded speech having "serious religious, political, scientific, educational, journalistic, historical, or artistic value."[86] If a serious work, not so exempted, required a depiction of animal cruelty, the cruelty or the animal could be simulated without running afoul of Section 48.[87] Therefore, the dissent concluded that Section 48 was constitutional because it merely "outlaws depictions that 'are no essential part of any exposition of ideas, and are of such slight social value as a step to truth that any benefit that may be derived from them is clearly outweighed by the social interest in order and morality.'"[88]

However, the dissent went further, explaining how application of *Ferber* supported its conclusion. The dissent read *Ferber* to signify that a "category of speech may be constitutionally restricted where it depicts—and thus necessarily requires—the intentional infliction of physical harm on a class of especially vulnerable victims in violation of law, where the distribution of such depictions spurs their production but laws prohibiting the underlying acts are woefully underenforced, and where the speech's social value is so *de minimis* as to be outweighed by the important governmental goal of protecting the victims."[89] It clarified that human abuse was much more reprehensible than animal abuse, but that alone was insufficient to claim that animal abuse could not constitute a compelling interest.[90]

After reiterating that the prevention of animal cruelty is a compelling interest, which satisfies the first *Ferber* factor, the dissent observed that the speech at issue is intrinsically related to the underlying crime of animal cruelty because creation of the depiction necessitates an act of illegal animal cruelty.[91] Thus, the harm "arises directly and necessarily from the *creation* of the depictions itself."[92] As for the consequent psychological harm to victims, the dissent noted that during training, fighting dogs are deliberately abused and tortured to predispose them to violence. Losing dogs may be left to die untreated from their injuries or cruelly executed. Animals depicted in crush videos are stomped to death during the filmmaking process.[93]

Unlike the majority, which arguably gave Stevens' overbreadth and vagueness arguments short shrift, the dissent encountered these issues head on and stated that the statute was neither unconstitutionally overbroad nor vague.[94] As the dissent explained, overbreadth is "strong medicine that is not to be casually employed."[95]

As to Stevens' argument that Section 48 is overbroad because it criminalizes depictions of conduct that was not illegal when or where it occurred, the dissent pointed out that a state may prohibit the distribution of unprotected materials produced outside the state because "'the maintenance of the market itself 'leaves open the financial conduit by which the production of such material is funded and materially increases the risk that [local] children will be injured.'"[96] The Supreme Court has also ruled that it was permissible for the government to annihilate the child pornography market at all levels, which included penalizing distributors not actually involved in the conduct.[97] Therefore, Section 48 is not overbroad merely because it attacks the commercial distribution network of the depictions, rather than the acts of cruelty they depict.[98] Turning to Stevens' final argument that the statute could extend to technical violations of hunting and fishing statutes, the dissent noted that the Supreme Court had recently rejected similar arguments in *United States v. Williams* where it upheld a federal statute criminalizing the promotion and possession of child pornography over an overbreadth challenge.[99] According to the dissent, Section 48 posed no realistic danger to such depictions.[100]

Turning to Stevens' allegation that Section 48 is impermissibly vague because its definition of depiction of animal cruelty is predicated on state law and states define "animal" differently, the dissent explained that a statute is void for vagueness if it "fails to provide people of ordinary intelligence a reasonable opportunity to understand what conduct it prohibits" or "authorizes or even encourages arbitrary and discriminatory enforcement."[101] In rejecting this argument, the dissent observed that a federal law is not unconstitutionally vague just because it incorporates state law; indeed, such incorporation is common. Therefore, the dissent concluded that the statute was not void for vagueness.[102]

On December 15, 2008, the United States filed a petition for writ of certiorari, which the Supreme Court granted on April 20, 2009.[103] The Supreme Court heard oral argument on October 6, 2009.[104] On April 20, 2010, the Supreme Court declared Section 48 to be unconstitutionally overbroad.[105]

Notes

1. Kerry Adams, Note, *Punishing Depictions of Animal Cruelty: Unconstitutional or a Valid Restriction on Speech?*, 12 Barry L. Rev. 203, 206 (2009).
2. Ibid., 206–07: see Randall Lockwood, *Animal Cruelty Prosecution: Opportunities for Early Response to Crime and Interpersonal Violence* (Alexandria, VA: American Prosecutors Research Institute, 2006), 32–33; Michael Reynolds, Note, *Depictions of the Pig Roast: Restricting Violent Speech Without Burning the House*, 82 S. Cal. L. Rev. 341, 344 (2009).
3. Adams, 206.
4. H.R. Rep. No. 106-397 (1999).
5. Adams, 207.
6. Ibid., 206.
7. Ibid., 206–07; Emma Ricaurte, Comment, *Son of Sam and Dog of Sam: Regulating Depictions of Animal Cruelty Through the Use of Criminal Anti-Profit Statutes*, 16 ANIMAL L. 171, 183 (2009) ("In Congress, opponents of the bill argued that although people may find depictions of the intentional maiming, mutilating, wounding, or killing of animals 'disturbing,' the fact that society finds particular speech offensive is not a sufficient reason to suppress it. Opponents also raised constitutional concerns. They argued that the depictions could not be categorized as obscene under the obscenity exception to the First Amendment. They also asserted that there was no compelling interest and, even if there were, the bill was not narrowly tailored.") (internal citations omitted).
8. Adams, 204.
9. Ibid., 221.
10. As used herein, the phrases "cruelty to animals" and "animal cruelty" refer only to *criminal* animal cruelty. Unless otherwise specified, the phrase "depictions of animal cruelty" refers to portrayals of criminal acts of cruelty against live animals.
11. 18 U.S.C. §48 (2009).
12. Ibid.
13. Ibid.
14. Reynolds, 345-46.
15. Ibid., Robert Barnes, "Supreme Court overturns anti-animal cruelty law in First Amendment case," *Washington Post*, April 21, 2012.
16. Joe Mandak, "Men Charged in Publication of Dogfighting Magazine," *Associated Press*, July 26, 2004 (Owner of *Sporting Dog Journal* James Jay Fricchione and John Kelly were charged with animal cruelty and conspiracy to commit animal cruelty—felonies warranting fines up to $15,000 and seven years in prison. The magazine purportedly serves a sizeable international audience of subscribers. According to Pennsylvania Attorney General, Jerry Pappert, the bimonthly circular published information on dogfights, stud services, and dogfighting paraphernalia. The magazine also conferred champion and grand champion status on winning dogs.).

17. Brief for Appellant at 6, *United States v. Stevens*, 533 F.3d 218 (3d Cir. 2008) (No. 05-2497) [hereinafter Brief for Appellant].
18. Brief for the United States at 4, *United States v. Stevens*, 559 U.S. 460 (2010) (No. 08-769) [hereinafter Gov't Brief].
19. *United States v. Stevens*, 533 F.3d 218, 221 (3d Cir. 2008); see Elizabeth L. Kinsella, Note, *A Crushing Blow: United States v. Stevens and the Freedom to Profit from Animal Cruelty*, 43 U.C. DAVIS L. REV. 347, 369 (2009) (While creators of depictions of animal cruelty typically edit out identifying information in animal cruelty videos so as to prevent prosecution arising from the underlying acts of animal cruelty caught on tape, "Catch Dogs" "contained names and addresses of dog suppliers, locations of hunts, and clear images of participants' faces. The State could prosecute offenders for the underlying acts of animal cruelty without banning the depictions of that crime.").
20. Brief Amicus Curiae of International Society for Animal Rights in Support of Petitioner at 9, *United States v. Stevens*, 559 U.S. 460 (2010) (No. 08-769) [hereinafter ISAR Brief]; Gov't Brief, 4.
21. Brief for Appellant, 5; Gov't Brief, 4; Kinsella, 366.
22. Kinsella, 366.
23. The Humane Society of the United States. "Who is Bob Stevens?," *The Humane Society of the United States*. November 9, 2009, http://www.humanesociety.org/news/news/2009/11/bob_stevens_110909.html.
24. Ibid.
25. ISAR Brief, 9; Gov't Brief, 4.
26. ISAR Brief, 9.
27. *Stevens*, 533 F.3d at 234.
28. Brief for Appellant, 6.
29. Ibid., 5.
30. The Humane Society of the United States. "Frequently Asked Questions about Bob Stevens," *The Humane Society of the United States*. November 9, 2009, http://www.humanesociety.org/news/news/2009/11/faq_bob_stevens_110909.html.
31. Lockwood, *Animal Cruelty Prosecution*, 33.
32. Kinsella, 366.
33. Brief for Appellant, 5; Gov't Brief, 4; Kinsella, 366.
34. Brief for the Respondent at 5, *United States v. Stevens*, 559 U.S. 460 (2009) (No. 08-769) [hereinafter Brief for the Respondent].
35. *United States v. Stevens*, 130 S.Ct. 1577, 1583 (2009).
36. Adams, 206.
37. Gov't Brief, 5.
38. Ibid.; *New York v. Ferber*, 458 U.S. 747, 774 (1982).
39. Gov't Brief, 5.
40. Kinsella, 366.
41. *Stevens*, 553 F.3d at 218.
42. *United States v. Stevens*, 559 U.S. 460, 1583 (2010); Gov't Brief, 5–6.

43. *Stevens*, 130 S. Ct. at 1583–84; Gov't Brief, 5–6; Kinsella, 366.

44. *Stevens*, 130 S. Ct. at 1583–84; Gov't Brief, 6 (discussing *Church of the Lukumi Babalu Aye, Inc., v. City of Hialeah*, 508 U.S. 520, 547 (1993)); Kinsella, 366–67 ("In facially invalidating the statute, the Third Circuit declined to recognize a new category of unprotected speech without express direction from the Supreme Court. Out of the traditionally unprotected categories, the court found the speech regulated by §48 somewhat similar only to Ferber. Addressing the five Ferber factors favoring creation of a new category of unprotected speech, the Stevens court rejected a government argument that depictions of animal cruelty were analogous to depictions of child pornography. Having determined that §48 was a content-based regulation of protected speech, the Stevens court applied strict scrutiny review. It held the statute failed this heightened standard of review for two reasons. First, the regulation served no compelling interest. The court found preventing animal cruelty was not a sufficiently compelling interest in the context of free speech to justify a content-based regulation. Second, even assuming the asserted interest was compelling, the statute failed to satisfy the narrow tailoring requirement. In sum, because §48 was unconstitutional, Stevens' conviction could not stand.").

45. See Gov't Brief, 6; Kinsella, 372 (The *en banc* Third Circuit "erroneously suggested [that] there is no compelling government interest in preventing animal cruelty in the First Amendment context.").

46. Gov't Brief, 6 (quoting *Broadrick v. Oklahoma*, 413 U.S. 601, 613 (1973)).

47. *Stevens*, 553 F. 3d at 220.

48. Ibid., 222.

49. Ibid.

50. Ibid., 224 n.6.

51. Ibid., 225.

52. Ibid., 226–32.

53. Ibid., 229–30 (quoting *Ashcroft v. Free Speech Coalition*, 535 U.S. 234, 245–53 (2002)).

54. Ibid., 230.

55. Ibid. (quoting *Ferber*, 458 U.S. at 759).

56. Ibid., 230.

57. Ibid.

58. Ibid., 231.

59. Ibid.

60. Ibid., 232.

61. Ibid., 232–34.

62. Ibid., 234.

63. Ibid.

64. Ibid.

65. Ibid., 234, 248.

66. Ibid., 234.

67. Ibid., 235.

68. Ibid., 235, n.16.

69. Ibid.
70. Ibid.
71. Ibid. (internal citations omitted).
72. Ibid., 236.
73. See Gov't Brief, 6–7; Kinsella, 367 ("Detailing the long-standing history of animal cruelty laws in the United States, these judges agreed with the government that its interest in protecting animals was compelling. The dissenting circuit judges further argued that the depictions prohibited under §48 were of such minimal social value as to fall outside of First Amendment protection. Applying the Ferber factors, these judges would have recognized depictions of animal cruelty as a narrow category of unprotected speech, and thus would have upheld both the constitutionality of §48 and Stevens' conviction.").
74. Gov't Brief, 7.
75. Ibid.
76. *Stevens*, 533 F. 3d at 236–37.
77. Ibid., 238–39 (citing proscribe animal fighting, 7 U.S.C. § 2156 (require that livestock be slaughtered humanely), 7 U.S.C. § 1901 (help establish humane guidelines governing the purchase, sale, and handling of animals), 7 U.S.C. § 2142 (create standards to protect pets in pounds and shelters), 7 U.S.C. § 2158 (prevent the "cruel and inhumane" soring of horses), 15 U.S.C. §§ 1821–1831 (protect free-roaming horses and burros from capture, branding, harassment, and death), 16 U.S.C. §§ 1331–1340 (help conserve endangered species), 16 U.S.C. §§ 1531–43 (and protect marine mammals), 16 U.S.C. §§ 1361–1421h).
78. Ibid., 237 n.19 (*see, e.g., Grutter v. Bollinger*, 539 U.S. 306, 328 (2003) ("attaining a diverse student body"); *Simon & Schuster, Inc. v. Members of N.Y. State Crime Victims Bd.*, 502 U.S. 105, 118 (1991) ("ensuring that victims of crime are compensated by those who harm them" and "that criminals do not profit from their crimes"); *Eu v. San Francisco County Democratic Cent. Comm.*, 489 U.S. 214, 226 (1989) ("[m]aintaining a stable political system"); *Federal Election Comm'n v. Nat'l Conservative Political Action Comm.*, 470 U.S. 480, 496-97 (1985) (preventing governmental corruption)).
79. Ibid., 240.
80. Ibid. (citing *Lukumi*, 508 U.S. at 580).
81. Ibid., 241.
82. Ibid., 241–42 n.23.
83. Ibid., 242 (quoting H.R. Rep. No. 106-397, at 3 (summarizing witness testimony on nature of commercial market for depictions of animal cruelty)).
84. Ibid., 242 n.23.
85. Ibid.
86. Ibid., 242 (quoting 18 U.S.C. §48[b]).
87. Ibid. at 242 (citing H.R. Rep. No. 106-397, at 5 ("The committee believes that no reasonable person would find any redeeming value in the material proscribed by [18 U.S.C. §48]")).

88. Ibid., 243 (citing *Chaplinsky v. New Hampshire*, 315 U.S. 568, 572 (1942)).

89. Ibid., 243

90. Ibid., 243 n.24.

91. Ibid., 244.

92. Ibid.

93. Ibid., 244–45 (citing H.R. Rep. No. 106-397, at 2 (describing crush videos as "videotapes
     . . . depicting [] small animals being slowly crushed to death")).

94. Ibid., 247–49.

95. Ibid. (quoting *Los Angeles Police Dep't. v. United Reporting Publishing Corp.*, 528 U.S.
     32, 39 (1999)).

96. Ibid., 248 (citing *People v. Ferber*, 52 N.Y.2d 674, 422 N.E.2d 523, 531, 439 N.Y.S.2d
     863 (N.Y. 1981) (Jasen, J., dissenting)); see also 18 U.S.C. § 2252A (federal child por-
     nography statute explicitly reaches works produced overseas).

97. Ibid. (citing *Ferber*, 458 U.S. at 759–60).

98. Ibid., 248.

99. Ibid. (citing *United States v. Williams*, 128 S. Ct. 1830, 1843–45 (2008)).

100. Ibid., 249.

101. Ibid. (citing *Hill v. Colorado*, 530 U.S. 703, 732 (2000)).

102. Ibid., 249.

103. *United States v. Stevens*, 556 U.S. 1181 (2009).

104. Kinsella, n.40.

105. *Stevens*, 556 U.S. at 1592.

CHAPTER 6

Clash of the Titans: Friends of the Court Battle over Section 48

When the Supreme Court entertains an issue as controversial and significant as animal cruelty or freedom of speech, let alone a unique case involving both, everyone wants to weigh in. It is no surprise then that numerous amicus briefs were filed in *United States v. Stevens.*[1] Amici included a vast array of entities and organizations from the American Society for the Prevention of Cruelty to Animals (ASPCA) and the Humane Society of the United States (HSUS) to the National Rifle Association of America, Inc. (NRA) and the American Civil Liberties Union (ACLU). A group of American Animal Law professors filed a brief that was purportedly in support of neither party but instead asked the Supreme Court to address the Third Circuit's conclusion that preventing animal cruelty fails to constitute a compelling government interest.[2] However, on balance most amici predictably chose a side in this mammoth legal battle. Animal rights organizations filed in favor of the United States, while hunting/fishing organizations and First Amendment proponents advocated for Stevens.

The Endangered Dog Breeders Association (EBA) and the American Dog Breeders Association (ADBA) were one exception. They combined forces to file a joint amicus brief asking the Court to invalidate Section 48 because it exceeded the scope of congressional intent.[3] EBA and ADBA self-described as "several organizations representing dog and animal owners dedicated to fighting breed specific or other anti-pet legislation and promoting wholesome animal welfare activities."[4] EBA is an Oklahoma-based non-profit corporation formed in the 1980s purportedly "to combat breed specific legislation and the preservation of the bull breeds."[5] The ADBA was founded as a registry for the American Pit Bull Terrier in 1909 and later expanded to become an all-breed registry, which, by its own account, holds sanctioned dog shows and weight pulls throughout the United States.[6]

Law Professors—First Amendment Scholars

Academics weighed in on both sides. Law professors who teach and publish on freedom of speech and constitutional law, including but not limited to Erwin Chemerinsky, prominent constitutional law scholar, Rodney Smolla, renowned First Amendment scholar and former dean of Washington and Lee University School of Law, and Laurence Tribe, Harvard law professor and famous constitutional scholar and commentator, filed a brief on Stevens' behalf, arguing that Section 48's prohibition of speech that depicts physical harm to animals violated the First Amendment.[7] According to these law professors, the government's request that the Supreme Court recognize an entirely new category of unprotected speech by applying a balancing approach that would prohibit speech when societal costs of the speech outweighed its attendant benefits, contravened settled principles of First Amendment jurisprudence. Although the law professors agreed that applying *Chaplinsky* to ban "well-defined" and "narrowly limited" categories of speech did not raise constitutional problems, they argued that the speech embraced by Section 48 was neither well-defined nor narrowly limited.[8] Rather, they contended that the government offered "no convincing argument why images of physical harm to animals are of only low First Amendment value."[9] In their minds, the mere fact that speech is offensive and not communicative is insufficient to render it of low social value. They emphasized that *Chaplinsky* should not be used to ban speech that society dislikes and distinguished depictions of animal cruelty from other forms of prohibited speech, including incitement, threats, and obscenity.[10]

Not only did the law professors find the government's reasoning in support of its assertion that the speech prohibited by Section 48 constitutes unprotected speech unavailing, they also claimed that the government's proposed category of low value violent speech was neither well-defined nor narrowly limited as required by *Chaplinsky*. They reiterated earlier criticisms of Section 48, asserting, for instance, that it could conceivably include images of Spanish bullfighting even though bullfighting is lawful in Spain.[11] Justice Scalia may have found this argument convincing as he commented on the potential overbreadth of Section 48 at the subsequent oral argument on the statute's validity.[12]

The law professors also argued that the Supreme Court should not create a new category of unprotected speech because while

> virtually every [other] recognized category of low value speech has long been subject to legal regulation, and most categories of low value speech were regulated at common law even before the adoption of the First Amendment . . . Section 48 was enacted in 1999, [and] no

court or legislature had ever seriously suggested [prior to 1999] that depictions of physical harm to animals could be regulated as a form of low value speech. Even today, only one state has seen fit to enact such a law, and that statute is much narrower than Section 48.[13]

According to the law professors, the government's proposed balancing approach would pose "intractable problems" because it would vest judges with "largely unbounded discretion to define what qualifies as low value expression" and burden the judiciary with the cumbersome task of weighing social costs against expression.[14] The law professors predicted that prohibition of depictions of animal cruelty would pave the way for subsequent banning of other offensive speech, such as an image of a dead fetus or a picture of a swastika. They cautioned that the First Amendment forbids banning speech due to "comparative offensiveness," that is, determining that depictions of animal cruelty should be prohibited because they are more offensive than obscenity.[15] They warned that creating a new category of speech to ban depictions of animal cruelty could ultimately chill other forms of expression, slowing or undermining the prior half-century's progression in the First Amendment arena where the Supreme Court had "consistently narrowed the scope of traditional categories of low value speech."[16]

After soundly denouncing the government's proposed balancing approach to determining new categories of unprotected speech, the law professors turned to their second primary point—that the dogfighting videos at issue in *Stevens* (and more importantly, "the vast majority of the speech covered by Section 48") are not analogous to obscenity or child pornography because they do not depict sexual conduct and do not involve physical harm to children.[17] The law professors appear to have agreed with the Third Circuit's assertion that the *Ferber* rationale did not justify upholding Section 48 because the interests implicated in preventing animal cruelty were not of the same magnitude as those involved in prohibiting child pornography. The law professors rejected the government's claim that the fact that every state and the District of Columbia bans animal cruelty indicates that its prevention constitutes a compelling interest by observing that every state also bans speeding; that alone, however, does not mean that preventing speeding constitutes a compelling interest. Interestingly, the law professors posited that the inconsistency in state anti-cruelty laws cut against a finding that preventing animal cruelty constitutes a compelling government interest.[18] The law professors opined:

Child sexual abuse is unlawful in the United States in every jurisdiction, and in all circumstances. By contrast, intentional injuries to animals are permitted in a wide range of circumstances. The most

obvious example is the food industry, which kills hundreds of millions of animals annually to provide not only sustenance, but also
delicacies. Despite legal limits on how animals are treated in fish-
eries, farms, and slaughterhouses, violence and suffering are com-
monplace. Another obvious example is sport. Hunters lawfully kill
and injure an untold number of animals every year. If we deemed
the interest in protecting animals from injury and death as truly
compelling, we would not tolerate the infliction of such suffering.
Indeed, one could hardly imagine a law allowing adults to sexually
abuse children for comparable reasons. Thus, although the interest
in protecting animals against physical injury is surely legitimate,
experience demonstrates that we do not regard it as compelling.[19]

The law professors reframed Section 48's exception for works of "serious value"
as the government's "recognition of the relative strength of the state interest."[20]
In other words, although Congress included the exception to narrow the scope
of Section 48, the law professors argued that the exception evidenced the government's realization that preventing animal cruelty is a less compelling interest than
preserving freedom of speech.[21]

The law professors concluded their criticism of the government's arguments by
contending that depictions of animal cruelty are not intrinsically related to the underlying cruelty, which would occur even absent the recording and profit-making
potential. The law professors did not explain how custom-order crush videos fit
into this equation or address assertions that recording an animal fight promotes
the crime of animal fighting by making the practice much more lucrative. They
challenged the law as overbroad because it applied without regard to whether the
depicted conduct was lawful at the time and place it occurred[22] and pointed out
that, unlike in *Ferber*, circulation of depictions of animal cruelty causes no ongo-
ing harm to the animal victims portrayed in the films.[23]

Although the law professors agreed that animal cruelty should be illegal, they
rejected the government's attempt to, in their words:

> expand the concept of low value speech and dilute the concept of
> compelling interest. *Chaplinsky* recognized a narrowly defined doc-
> trine grounded in historical experience. *Ferber* and *Ashcroft* em-
> braced a carefully crafted solution to a discrete problem that impli-
> cated both low value speech and truly compelling interests.[24]

According to the law professors, the government's "approach would unravel those
doctrines and invite an analogical stampede."[25]

Law Professors—Animal Law Scholars

First Amendment scholars were not the only academics to weigh in on the debate regarding Section 48's validity. A group of animal law professors also filed an amicus brief, primarily arguing that prevention of animal cruelty constitutes a compelling government interest.[26] The animal law professors recounted the evolution and increasing importance of animal law, stating that the fact that animal law has been or is currently taught at over 100 American law schools and that as of 2009, at least 15 states have animal law bar sections or committees evidences that preventing animal cruelty is a compelling government interest.[27] Now, as of 2013 , at least 26 states have animal law bar sections or committees.[28] Numerous journals have been devoted exclusively to animal law scholarship, including *Animal Law* at Lewis & Clark Law School, the *Journal of Animal Law* at Michigan State University College of Law, the *Journal of Animal Law & Ethics* at the University of Pennsylvania Law School,[29] the *Stanford Journal of Animal Law and Policy*, the *Journal of International Policy and Wildlife* affiliated with Stetson University College of Law, and the *Journal of Animal & Environmental Law* at the University of Louisville Louis D. Brandeis School of Law.[30]

The animal law professors professed neutrality but asked the Supreme Court to reject the conclusion of the Third Circuit that preventing animal cruelty does not constitute a compelling government interest.[31] They claimed that the Third Circuit had misconstrued *Lukumi* to indicate that the prevention of animal cruelty is not a compelling government interest, rather than properly treating the issue as one of first impression.[32] The animal law professors challenged the Third Circuit's characterization of the governmental interest as being solely about protecting animals and its alleged failure to "appreciate the magnitude of human interests implicated by the prevention of animal cruelty."[33]

The law professors emphasized that whether the prevention of animal cruelty constitutes a compelling interest is an issue of first impression because *Lukumi* did not resolve that question.[34] Nor did it involve depictions of animal cruelty or freedom of speech. As such, *Lukumi* was inapposite. They further contended that the absence of precedent acknowledging a compelling governmental interest related to animal cruelty does not demonstrate that to be compelling, an interest must implicate human, not animal, welfare.[35]

In support of their assertion that preventing animal cruelty constitutes a compelling government interest, the animal law professors cited the long-established history of animal anti-cruelty statutes, judicial opinions discussing the attendant evils of animal cruelty, and philosophical opinions regarding whether prohibiting animal cruelty serves human interests.[36] Courts have consistently recognized the

public interest in preventing inhumane treatment of animals; indeed, this belief
is so strong that it constitutes a cognizable injury for purposes of standing under
the Constitution.[37]

The animal law professors recounted numerous scientific studies, documenting
a link between animal and human violence, including child abuse/animal abuse as
well as domestic violence/animal violence. They emphasized that many serial killers had committed violence against animals before progressing to human victims
and recounted specific acts of animal cruelty committed by notorious murderers,
including David Berkowitz, Albert DeSalvo, Ted Bundy, and Jeffrey Dahmer.[38]

Of particular import was research regarding the impact of depictions of animal fighting on viewers.[39] As the animal law professors explained:

> Studies regarding the consequences of children observing animal
> abuse are particularly noteworthy due to the surprising extent to
> which children are spectators and participants in dogfighting. Pro-
> fessionals on the front lines against dogfighting report that "you now
> have 8-, 9-, 10-year-olds conducting their own dog fights. Or being
> spectators at the fights people are holding."[40]

The animal law professors emphasized that abusers use animal violence to
control victims and that as a result, states increasingly include companion animals
within protective orders in domestic violence cases as well as the coordination of
domestic abuse and animal abuse cases in an effort to earlier detect occasions of
human violence.[41] In further support of the correlation between animal and human
violence, the animal law professors pointed out that the International Association
of Chiefs of Police urges law enforcement officials to take animal cruelty reports
seriously because violence against animals provides an early opportunity to prevent future violent crimes against humans. The animal law professors opined that
perhaps because of this link, an increasing number of legislatures nationwide had
enacted felony-level anti-cruelty laws within the last two decades. Although only
7 states had such statutes in 1993, 41 states and the District of Columbia punished
at least some forms of animal abuse as a felony by 2005. By 2010, only four states
lacked felony-level anti-cruelty laws.[42] Furthermore, numerous states, including
but not limited to Oregon, Colorado, Georgia, Idaho, New York, Arizona, and
Minnesota, require veterinarians to report animal abuse.[43]

According to the animal law professors, the Third Circuit "failed to appreciate this well-documented connection" between animal and human violence, and
by too narrowly viewing the prevention of animal cruelty, erroneously concluded
that anti-cruelty efforts are only an "exceedingly worthy goal," not a compelling

government interest.[44] Rather, the animal law professors contended that preventing animal cruelty is not just a goal, "it is a well-established national public policy that government pursues to protect the interests of human beings."[45]

Viewpoints on Criminal Enforcement under Section 48

Like the constitutional and animal law scholars, attorneys general of several states and other law enforcement officials voiced their concerns during the Section 48 controversy. The Center on the Administration of Criminal Law (CACL) is based out of the New York University School of Law. In its own words, its mission is "to promote and defend good government practices in criminal matters."[46] As such, it analyzes significant criminal law issues, focusing on prosecutorial discretion.[47]

According to CACL, the Third Circuit erroneously concluded that upholding Section 48 would have necessitated the creation of an entirely new category of unprotected speech. Rather, CACL contended that Congress had so narrowly drafted Section 48 that the statute effectively covered only crime-scene photographs and videos that were subsequently exploited for commercial gain and lacked serious artistic or other redeeming social value. CACL argued that it is well-settled that speech that furthers, proposes, or abets criminal activity, does not warrant First Amendment protection.[48] Depictions of animal cruelty fall into this existing category, and as such, Section 48 is not facially invalid.

CACL also criticized the Third Circuit's facial invalidity analysis of Section 48, claiming that the Third Circuit did not determine, as is required for a statute to be struck as facially invalid, that "no set of circumstances exists in which Section 48 could be constitutionally applied, and no such finding would be remotely plausible. Nor did the District Court below apply the substantial overbreadth doctrine . . . Nonetheless, the Third Circuit struck down Section 48 on its face."[49] CACL described the Third Circuit's decision as "doctrinally incoherent and plainly erroneous."[50] It pointed out that Section 48 was not overbroad because it narrowly targeted only unlawful conduct and that even if protected speech was within the statute's embrace, prosecutorial discretion and as-applied challenges were sufficient to prevent misapplications of the statute without resort to its wholesale invalidation. According to CACL, the Third Circuit ignored well-settled law and instead relied on "fanciful hypotheticals" to invalidate the statute.[51]

Attorneys General

The attorneys general of the following 26 states filed an amicus brief on the government's behalf: Florida, Alabama, Arkansas, Arizona, California, Colorado,

Connecticut, Hawaii, Illinois, Indiana, Kentucky, Louisiana, Maryland, Michigan, Mississippi, Montana, New Hampshire, New Mexico, North Carolina, Ohio, Rhode Island, South Carolina, Texas, Utah, Virginia, and West Virginia.

They argued that the Supreme Court should reverse the Third Circuit and uphold Section 48 because the statute "vitally assists efforts to deter and enforce their own animal cruelty laws by keeping perpetrators (and downstream distributors) from advertising, selling, and profiting from depictions of their vile crimes in any market."[52] They emphasized that every state and the District of Columbia criminalize animal cruelty, animal crime task forces and initiatives have sprung up across America, and animal law academic programs proliferate, furthering awareness, detection, and prosecution of crimes relating to animal cruelty. According to the attorneys general, striking Section 48 and permitting individuals to openly profit from depictions of criminal animal cruelty would seriously undermine these efforts.[53]

The attorneys general reiterated Section 48's deterrent effect, observing that many states have found enforcement of anti-cruelty laws to be "exceptionally difficult with respect to those animal cruelty crimes most often depicted, marketed, and sold, such as animal fighting, production of 'crush videos,' and hog-dog rodeos" because sophisticated producers conceal identifying information that would lead to prosecution.[54] The attorneys general pointed out that as a result, a successful prosecution often required animal victims to be fed and housed for substantial periods of time and demand the expert analysis and testimony of forensic and veterinary professionals.[55]

The attorneys general also highlighted the devastating impact of animal cruelty on communities. They explained that serious crimes against humans, including gang activity, gambling, drug dealing, and violence, are often closely linked to animal cruelty. They observed that youth who commit animal cruelty graduate to progressively violent crimes against humans, and pop culture tends to glorify animal fighting, attracting an increasing number of young people.[56] The attorneys general also acknowledged the strong correlation between domestic and animal abuse, stating that "adults that abuse animals tend often to abuse their children. Based on the amici states' experience, relaxing societal restraints and legitimizing the activities of animal cruelty purveyors substantially threatens the well-being and mores of the next generation."[57]

In urging the Supreme Court to reverse the Third Circuit and recognize that Section 48 served a compelling government interest, the attorneys general described animal cruelty as a "serious menace" and quipped that "crime should not pay."[58]

International Society for Animal Rights

The International Society for Animal Rights (ISAR) is a not-for-profit corporation founded in 1959 to promote the "protection of animals from all forms of cruelty and suffering inflicted upon them for the demands of science, profit, sport or from neglect or indifference to their welfare or from any other cause."[59] In furtherance of that goal, ISAR engages in extensive public education.[60]

ISAR filed an amicus brief on behalf of the government, arguing that Stevens was not entitled to First Amendment protection because his acts constituted conduct, not speech.[61] Although certiorari was granted solely with respect to whether Section 48 was unconstitutional on its face, ISAR asserted that "the making, exploitation, and sale of videos depicting cruelty to animals is conduct lacking sufficient communicative elements to implicate the speech guarantee of the First Amendment."[62] Thus, the Third Circuit erroneously applied the First Amendment because Section 48 does not regulate speech or an incidental non-expressive effect of speech.[63] ISAR further contended that the protections of the First Amendment could not be invoked simply by placing depictions of animal torture and killing on videos and selling them. ISAR argued that conduct could not be labeled speech just because the person engaging in the conduct claims that he or she intends to express an idea.[64] In other words, conduct is not speech for First Amendment purposes just because it was intended to be expressive.

ISAR also maintained that the case should have been decided on an as-applied ground, instead of as a facial challenge.[65] ISAR emphasized that Stevens "was engaged in conduct, not speech, but if there were communicative elements in his sale of the videos, they were in aid of illegal commercial speech [which is unprotected by the First Amendment] and the statute which suppressed them is constitutional."[66]

ISAR also maintained that *New York v. Ferber*[67] supports the constitutionality of Section 48, namely the prevention of animal cruelty, although it did not find it necessary to rely on *Ferber* to uphold Section 48 as constitutional.[68] ISAR asserted that the Third Circuit misapplied *Ferber* because of the similar nature of the statutes in both cases and the compelling interest in protection of animals and humans.[69] Thus, although Section 48 can be upheld without reliance on *Ferber*, the similarities between humans and animals, not the differences, compel application of *Ferber*, not extension, to the instant case.[70]

Washington Legal Foundation

The Washington Legal Foundation (WLF) is a national organization that works with the government and private legal sector to "maintain balance in the courts and help our government strengthen America's free enterprise system."[71] In its own words, WLF "champions free market principles, limited and accountable government, individual rights, business civil liberties, and legal ethics."[72]

The crux of WLF's argument was that the Third Circuit erred in entertaining a facial challenge to Section 48 because First Amendment jurisprudence makes clear that a statutory facial challenge will only succeed if the challenger demonstrates that the statute is unconstitutional in all of its applications or at the very least, that it does not have a plainly legitimate sweep. WLF observed that the Third Circuit conceded that Section 48 might well have a legitimate sweep because it noted that a statute prohibiting only crush videos might withstand a First Amendment challenge. According to WLF, in light of that important concession, the Third Circuit should not have considered a facial challenge to Section 48.[73]

Furthermore, the Third Circuit expressly declined to undertake an overbreadth analysis of Section 48, recognizing that voiding a statute on overbreadth grounds is "strong medicine" that should be used "sparingly and only as a last resort."[74] WLF characterized the Third Circuit's decision to strike the statute as unconstitutional on its face as "even stronger medicine" and asked the Supreme Court to engage in its own overbreadth analysis only after the Third Circuit addressed that issue.[75] WLF further opined that Section 48 was not overbroad.[76]

Nor was Section 48 unconstitutional as applied to Stevens, at least according to WLF.[77] WLF pointed out that the animal fighting depictions that resulted in Stevens' conviction lacked redeeming social value and did not warrant First Amendment protection because Congress had reasonably determined that regulating such speech was necessary to regulate the criminal animal cruelty portrayed therein.[78]

WLF also rejected the Third Circuit's contention that according to First Amendment jurisprudence, speech is not protected when it is inextricably linked to conduct that poses a serious risk to human welfare. WLF described that assertion as "demonstrably incorrect."[79] In so doing, WLF relied upon *United States v. Williams*,[80] in which the Supreme Court held that the First Amendment does not protect speech consisting of an offer to engage in an illegal transaction. WLF applied *Williams* to argue that, likewise, an offer to engage one's dog in unlawful animal fighting does not constitute protected speech.[81] Conceivably, nor would asking someone to participate in animal cruelty for the purpose of creating a depiction of animal cruelty that could later be used for commercial gain. WLF also contended that Section 48 could not be dismissed merely because its primary beneficiaries are animals, not humans.[82]

Humane Society of the United States

The Humane Society of the United States (HSUS) filed its first amicus brief in support of the government's petition for certiorari to the Supreme Court in January of 2009 and weighed in on the government's behalf a second time in the summer of 2009 after certiorari was granted.

In its first amicus brief, the HSUS described Section 48 as a vital law enforcement tool essential to combating abhorrent acts of animal cruelty.[83] In support of its assertion that Section 48 should be upheld, the HSUS provided graphic and haunting descriptions of the specific types of animal cruelty portrayed in the depictions prohibited by Section 48. Two such descriptions were as follows:

> A woman slowly crushing to death a speckled kitten. The kitten, secured to the ground, watches and shrieks in pain as a woman thrusts the sharp point of her high-heeled shoe into its body, slams her heel into the kitten's eye socket, thrusts it into the kitten's mouth loudly fracturing its skull, and stomps repeatedly on the animal's head. During the attack, the kitten hemorrhages blood, screams blindly in pain, and is ultimately left dead in a moist pile of blood-soaked hair and bone.[84]

> An orchestrated fight to the death where tortured dogs and puppies rip the skin and ears off their opponents, and bite through each other's ears, paws, neck and genitals in a desperate attempt to survive. To avoid impending death, one dog rips out the trachea of the other, leaving the dead dog sprawled on the ground, covered in blood, with its eyes closed and paws in the air.[85]

According to the HSUS, the Third Circuit's decision to strike down Section 48 rested upon "gravely flawed reasoning and a fundamental misunderstanding of First Amendment doctrine."[86] The HSUS outlined its objections to the Third Circuit's decision as follows:

> First, and most importantly, the Third Circuit's bald pronouncement that the interest in preventing egregious acts of animal cruelty is not "compelling" is a tragic error that, if left undisturbed, will distort consideration of animal welfare issues in the lower courts, Congress, and state and local legislatures for years to come.[87]

> Second, the "speech" here is akin to categories of expression this Court has deemed unprotected by the First Amendment. The Third Circuit's decision to subject §48 to strict scrutiny evidences an unduly rigid view of this Court's precedents.[88]

Third, the Third Circuit's facial invalidation of a federal statute
in a criminal case is itself unprecedented: §48 was indisputably not
invalid in all its applications, and the overbreadth doctrine (which
the court did not even claim to apply) was wholly inapplicable.[89]

In its second amicus brief, the HSUS sought "to provide further historical perspective about [Section] 48 and animal welfare legislation in general."[90] The HSUS
elaborated on three critical reasons for overturning the Third Circuit's decision:

First, and most importantly, §48 serves a compelling government
interest in preventing cruelty to animals. Criminal statutes designed
to ensure the humane treatment of animals and to preserve public
morals are older than our Nation and reflect its deepest values.[91]

Second, the "speech" at issue is not entitled to strict scrutiny.
It is "obscene" in every sense of the word, and affording sexual obscenity very limited protection under the First Amendment while
wrapping other depraved and obscene speech in the cloak of strict
scrutiny has no basis in history or logic.[92]

Third, if §48 violates Respondent's First Amendment rights, the
proper remedy would be to vacate his conviction, period. There is
no reason to invalidate §48 *in toto* when an as-applied remedy fully
vindicates the litigant's rights.[93]

Northwest Animal Rights Network

Northwest Animal Rights Network (NARN) is an all-volunteer Seattle-based animal protection organization founded in 1986 that is dedicated to preventing animal exploitation by raising awareness of animal cruelty and suffering, primarily
in the food, entertainment, experimentation, and fashion industries.[94]

NARN argued that the factors articulated in *New York v. Ferber*[95] to find that
child pornography constitutes unprotected speech could and should be applied to
hold that depictions of animal cruelty are also undeserving of First Amendment
protection, particularly because such depictions lack redeeming social value.[96]

NARN emphasized that the state of Washington takes animal cruelty seriously
and shared the story of Pasado the donkey. The donkey resided at Kelsey Creek
Farm Park in Bellevue, Washington, and in 1992, was found beaten, strangled,
and left to die. Three individuals, ages 16, 18, and 20, and all with prior criminal
convictions, were charged with Pasado's killing. Although they initially claimed
they just wanted to "play" with Pasado, the noose found around Pasado's neck
suggested that the cruelty was premeditated and intentional.[97]

According to NARN, Pasado's killing received extensive media coverage and provoked public outrage.[98] As NARN explained, the late King County Prosecutor observed that in his fourteen years in office, "'there has never been a case that has sparked the outrage of the public as the killing of Pasado the donkey.'"[99] Pasado's death led Washington lawmakers to enact statutes criminalizing animal cruelty.[100] NARN opined that Washington passed these laws for the same reasons that Congress enacted Section 48—"broad concern for animal welfare and the well-documented link between animal abuse and other crimes and harms inflicted upon society."[101]

NARN argued that the King County Sheriff's Office trained every officer to notice and investigate animal cruelty and that, in turn, this widespread focus on animal cruelty and the dedication of resources and time to combat it demonstrates that, at least in the state of Washington, protecting animals from wanton cruelty constitutes a compelling interest.[102] NARN further pointed out that no state anti-cruelty law has been "interpreted to forbid culturally accepted commercial and recreational uses of animals."[103] Rather, NARN opined that many state anti-cruelty laws exempt, *inter alia*, hunting, fishing, scientific experimentation, and routine animal husbandry. Even absent such exemptions, no prosecutions have resulted from such activities—unless they constitute criminal animal cruelty.[104] NARN further emphasized that Section 48 had an appropriately defined scienter requirement and the speech it prohibited did not warrant First Amendment protection pursuant to *Ferber*. As such, NARN argued that Section 48 was not required to satisfy strict scrutiny.[105]

Animal Legal Defense Fund

The Animal Legal Defense Fund (ALDF) is an organization boasting in excess of 110,000 members, including many attorneys, founded in 1979 to utilize the legal system to prevent animal cruelty, to protect animals, and to advance their interests.[106]

In describing the Third Circuit's analysis of Section 48 as "simply wrong,"[107] ALDF emphasized that preventing animal cruelty is a compelling interest because every state and many foreign countries have prohibited cruelty to animals.[108] As ALDF explained, "these laws are animated by more than mere principles of moral justice for the most victimized and powerless members of our society, but also for the protection of human society in light of the proven correlation between cruelty to animals and violence to people."[109] ALDF claimed that despite these widespread prohibitions, animal cruelty continues in part because of animal cruelty depictions, namely crush videos and dogfighting depictions, which allow individuals to attend and wager on illegal animal fights remotely even though nearly every state criminalizes actual attendance.[110]

According to ALDF, Congress intended Section 48 to quash the market for such depictions, thereby ending the underlying acts of animal cruelty portrayed therein.[111] As ALDF noted, "the advertisement and sale of depictions of animal cruelty provide an economic motive for, and are an integral part of, the commission of acts of animal cruelty. The marketplace for depictions of animal cruelty economically benefits and motivates the participants in the conduct, who then provide these depictions to those who are unable or unwilling to commit the act but who nonetheless will pay to see the acts performed by others."[112] ALDF opined that Section 48 furthered a compelling interest by criminalizing depictions that are "an integral part of conduct in violation of . . . valid criminal statute[s]."[113]

ALDF further pointed out that prohibiting such depictions would combat animal cruelty because acts of cruelty are frequently committed so others can watch.[114] As ALDF observed:

> The distribution of photographs and films depicting animal cruelty is intrinsically connected to the acts of cruelty they portray. The acts of animal cruelty targeted by §48 are themselves criminal, and are committed in secret, to avoid detection by law enforcement. However, the commercial distribution of materials that §48 prohibits is by its nature a more public process that law enforcement can identify in its efforts to stop the underlying practice. If the market for cruelty videos is eliminated, the commercial motivation for the commission of those acts of cruelty will be greatly diminished. By prohibiting the marketing of these depictions, Congress is taking a permissible step toward eliminating acts of cruelty.[115]

Although ALDF first observed that "there is little, if any, dispute that the 'value' of animal cruelty is, in the language of *Ferber*, 'exceedingly modest, if not *de minimis*,'"[116] it went on to claim that Section 48 was sufficiently narrowly tailored because its exceptions clause acknowledges that some depictions of animal cruelty may contain an expressive message warranting First Amendment protection, making the law consistent with *Miller v. California*.[117] According to ALDF, for these reasons, Section 48 is constitutional.

Finally, ALDF explained that criminalizing the creation, sale in interstate commerce, or possession of depictions of animal cruelty is entirely consistent with First Amendment jurisprudence because Section 48 "seeks to regulate the criminal conduct of animal cruelty . . . not . . . protected speech. If there is some expressive content . . . §48 does not criminalize [the depiction]. . . . Only if, the only expressive content is the criminal act of animal cruelty, does §48 apply."[118]

American Society for the Prevention of Cruelty to Animals

The American Society for the Prevention of Cruelty to Animals (ASPCA), which was incorporated in 1866, is the oldest humane organization in North America and the first humane organization to be given legal authority to investigate and make arrests for animal cruelty.[119] A not-for-profit corporation with more than one million supporters, the ASPCA aims "to provide effective means for the prevention of cruelty to animals throughout the United States."[120]

The ASPCA argued that preventing animal cruelty constitutes a compelling interest because every state and the District of Columbia criminalizes animal cruelty: "It is barbaric and intolerable in a civilized society to allow the senseless suffering of defenseless beings capable of experiencing (and expressing) pain."[121] As the ASPCA opined:

> The Government clearly has a compelling interest in preventing animal cruelty due to its far-reaching and devastating consequences on animals and humans alike, the longstanding nationwide interest in its prevention, and the indisputable link between animal cruelty and other forms of serious criminal and violent behavior.[122]

The ASPCA further argued that Section 48 is narrowly tailored because it only reaches a small subcategory of speech "depicting intentional and illegal acts of animal cruelty to live animals, created solely for profit, that lack any redeeming social value and depend on criminal acts of animal torture"[123]—such speech has little, or no, redeeming social value.[124] Due to the broad exceptions clause, Section 48 does not prohibit animal cruelty depictions with expressive value.[125]

Finally, the ASPCA contended that even if the Supreme Court did not conclude that preventing animal cruelty constitutes a compelling interest, it should still reverse the holding of the Third Circuit because the Third Circuit did not apply *Chaplinsky* to determine whether the speech embraced by Section 48 warrants First Amendment protection.[126] According to the ASPCA, proper application of *Chaplinsky*, which balances the government's interest in restricting speech against the value of the speech, establishes that the speech Section 48 prohibits is unprotected.[127]

National Coalition Against Censorship and College Art Association

The National Coalition Against Censorship (NCAC) is an organization composed of religious, educational, professional, labor, and civil liberties groups, that, collectively, aim to promote "freedom of thought, inquiry and expression and oppose censorship in all its forms."[128] Founded in 1974, NCAC has, by its own account, consistently worked to preserve the First Amendment rights of artists, authors, teachers, students, librarians, and so on across America.[129] Among other things, NCAC analyzes and reports on important First Amendment cases and controversies, educates the public on First Amendment issues, assists individuals and entities in dealing with censorship, and promotes discussion regarding freedom of speech.[130]

NCAC joined forces with The College Art Association (CAA) to file an amicus brief on behalf of Stevens. CAA describes itself as an organization encompassing 14,000 practitioners and interpreters of visual art and culture, such as artists, art historians, scholars, curators, and educators, and 2,000 institutional members, including university art and art history departments, museums, libraries, and professional and commercial organizations.[131] CAA filed an amicus brief because it feared that Section 48 might deter or criminalize its members' work.[132]

NCAC and CAA contended that Section 48 prohibited, and thereby chilled, countless forms of protected speech to prevent animal cruelty—a goal that the government admitted was already being served by state and federal law.[133] They opined that by its literal terms, Section 48 criminalized depictions of people engaged in acts ranging from hunting with weapons that are allowed in some states but prohibited in others, to hunting out of season, and to bullfighting.[134] NCAC and CAA rejected the government's assertion that depictions with serious value would not be subject to prosecution because "the history of conceptual and avant-garde art . . . is replete with instances in which the public scorned work later deemed to be groundbreaking and influential."[135] They observed:

> If just one necessary but risk-averse participant in the process decides, out of an abundance of caution, not to join in the production, distribution, or display of a work that includes statutorily defined depictions of animal cruelty for fear that it might subsequently be found by a prosecutor or jury to lack "serious value," the dissemination of protected expression could be deterred. That danger flows directly from the absence of any criteria in Section 48 to guide the application of the "serious value" exception, which makes it impossible for any of these participants to determine prospectively and with any reasonable certainty whether a particular work will be found by a prosecutor or jury to violate Section 48.[136]

NCAC and CAA argued that Section 48's exceptions clause was inadequate because Section 48 did not require that the depiction's value be assessed in the context of the entire work. They claimed that when viewed in isolation and out of context, a depiction of animal cruelty could be misjudged as lacking serious value although the work within which the depiction is embedded does indeed possess such value.[137]

According to NCAC and CAA, Section 48 posed a particular threat to the stock photography industry, which does not create, sell, or possess images for any serious religious, political, scientific, educational, journalistic, historical, or artistic purposes; it creates the images exclusively for sale to third parties. As such, NCAC and CAA averred that stock images of illegal animal cruelty come within Section 48's embrace.[138]

NCAC and CAA also criticized Section 48 because it did not define the term "serious value."[139] Consequently, criminal liability under Section 48 depends on prosecutorial and juror discretion. They contended that such "unavoidable subjectivity invites not only inconsistent application of the law, but viewpoint discrimination as well."[140]

NCAC and CAA further claimed that the government's arguments in support of Section 48 conflated conduct and expression because the government's indisputable ability to prohibit acts of animal cruelty does not necessarily mean that the government may also penalize speech about or images of animal cruelty without running afoul of the Constitution.[141] NCAC and CAA claim that the "chief purpose of the First Amendment is to protect the right to express ideas that challenge social, moral, and legal norms."[142] They further contended that such protection is not confined to expression that advances the "exposition of ideas" and serves a "high purpose."[143] As such, NCAC and CAA argued that jurors should not be permitted to determine which speech is protected and which is not.[144] They urged the Supreme Court to affirm the decision of the Third Circuit, declaring Section 48 to be unconstitutional, and opined that "to conclude otherwise would eviscerate an important constitutional protection against majoritarian sentiment and governmental censorship."[145]

Safari Club International and Congressional Sportsmen's Foundation

Safari Club International (SCI) is an Arizona-based nonprofit corporation with approximately 53,000 members, which by its own account, aims to promote wildlife conservation, "protection of the hunter," and public awareness regarding hunting and its use for conservation.[146] SCI argued that Section 48 had already and if left intact, would continue to chill hunting videos and other media, which, in turn, would adversely impact SCI, its members, members of the hunting community, and hunting-related wildlife management efforts.[147]

The Congressional Sportsmen's Foundation (CSF) is a D.C.-based organization founded in 1989 that, in its own words, promotes and supports "hunting and angling for their recreational, wildlife management, and conservation benefits."[148] CSF facilitates the flow of information on hunting and fishing issues among CSF members and legislators, and utilizes hunting and fishing depictions to promote sporting activities as well as for fundraising.[149]

SCI and CSF emphasized that neither organization took an official position on crush videos or unlawful animal fighting; rather, they claimed that although Section 48 was well-intentioned, the statute was facially overbroad and as such, could chill the creation, possession, or sale of hunting media.[150] SCI and CSF averred that Section 48's plain language did not limit its reach to depictions of animal cruelty, or in the alternative, to crush videos or animal fighting media. They argued that Section 48 "criminalizes the depiction of the killing or wounding of a live animal, although legal where it is recorded, if the killing or wounding simply would be illegal under the laws of the state where the sale or possession of that depiction ultimately occurs."[151] As such, they claimed, Section 48 was not confined exclusively to depictions of illegal animal cruelty, but rather, potentially prohibited recordings of legitimate hunting activities. Furthermore, Section 48's exceptions clause did not remedy its overbreadth because many hunting depictions are produced solely for entertainment, hunter recruitment, or commercial gain and thus, lack "serious value" within the meaning of the statute.[152]

SCI and CSF also emphasized that state hunting laws vary significantly; in fact, "virtually all international hunting activities could be deemed illegal in the United States because most of the species hunted overseas cannot be legally hunted here."[153] As a result, SCI and CSF claimed that Section 48 was overbroad and thus, facially unconstitutional.

Interestingly enough, SCI and CSF suggested a way in which the Supreme Court could uphold Section 48 without endangering hunting media. They advised the Court to narrowly interpret Section 48 to require that the underlying conduct depicted be illegal for a reason related to state or federal anti-cruelty laws, not hunting laws.[154] As they explained, "if the Court cannot narrowly interpret Section 48 to its apparently intended scope, the Court should strike down the statute on this ground alone, thereby encouraging Congress to more carefully and narrowly tailor the reach of Section 48."[155]

Association of American Publishers, American Booksellers Foundation for Free Expression, Association of American University Presses, Comic Book Legal Defense Fund, Entertainment Consumers Association, Entertainment Merchants Association, Film Independent, Freedom to Read Foundation, Independent Book Publishers Association, Independent Filmmaker Project, Independent Film & Television Alliance, International Documentary Association, National Association of Recording Merchandisers, National Association of Theatre Owners, Inc., and Pen American Center

The amicus brief in support of Stevens filed by the organizations listed above opined that the Supreme Court has never approved of prohibiting depictions of violence.[156] Rather, as the esteemed Judge Richard Posner of the Seventh Circuit has observed:

> Classic literature and art, and not merely today's popular culture, are saturated with graphic scenes of violence, whether narrated or pictorial. The notion of forbidding not violence itself, but pictures of violence, is a novelty, whereas concern with pictures of graphic sexual conduct is of the essence of the traditional concern with obscenity.[157]

The amici argued that a clear distinction exists in the Supreme Court's First Amendment jurisprudence between illegal conduct and depictions of such conduct, with the notable exception of child pornography.[158] They claimed that "maintaining this crucial distinction is essential if speakers in all media are to have the freedom to grapple honestly and directly with the world around them. This freedom would be jeopardized if the Court were to adopt the [*Chaplinsky*] balancing test the Government proposes."[159]

The amici criticized the government's reliance on *Ferber*, claiming that animal cruelty depictions and the creation of the imagery are not inextricably intertwined as with child pornography.[160] The amici cautioned against the *Ferber* factors "morphing into a justification for banning depictions of any illegal or otherwise reprehensible conduct on the premise that the depictions support or encourage the conduct" and emphasized that in *Ashcroft v. Free Speech Coalition*[161] the Supreme Court declined to extend *Ferber* to ban "virtual" child pornography. For the same reasons as articulated in *Ashcroft*, the amici urged the Supreme Court to avoid extending *Ferber* to uphold Section 48.[162] According to the amici, to do otherwise would "sweep away [Supreme Court] precedents requiring that a ban on speech to prevent harm be justified by a direct and immediate connection between the speech and the harm."[163] The amici warned, "if the fact that speech plays a role in a process of conditioning were enough to permit governmental regulation, that would be the end of freedom of speech."[164] They further cautioned that although they, too, oppose animal cruelty, such antipathy does not permit Section 48 to contravene the Supreme Court's longstanding First Amendment jurisprudence.[165]

According to the amici, application of the government's balancing approach was nothing more than the government's attempt to "bootstrap" anti-cruelty statutes into a justification for banning animal cruelty depictions and persuade the Supreme Court "to abandon its extremely limited approach to defining categorical First Amendment exceptions."[166]

The amici also criticized the government for proffering "false assurances" that Section 48 only applied to crush videos and depictions of illegal fighting. However, the amici claimed that the statute was far broader on its face and that "under a plausible reading of [Section 48], the creators and distributors of illustrated books, films, or magazines that graphically depict conduct such as slaughterhouse practices, the inhumane treatment of farm animals, bullfighting, or poaching would, if the work were created, sold, or possessed with the intent to sell where such activities are illegal, be at risk of prosecution."[167]

The amici rejected the government's contention that Section 48 was not facially overbroad due to its broad exceptions clause because, according to the amici, many depictions lack serious value and the exceptions clause did not require that the work be considered as a whole.[168] Rather, according to the amici, "engrafting a 'serious value' exception onto an otherwise invalid speech restriction is a legislative tactic that could become a blunt instrument of censorship, providing a false veneer of constitutionality on a range of substantial incursions on protected speech."[169] They further averred, "the dividing line between proscribed and protected material under [Section 48] is simply too unclear, and the resulting chilling effect on protected speech too great" to withstand a facial challenge.[170]

National Rifle Association of America

The National Rifle Association of America, Inc. (NRA) is a nonprofit organization of some four million members that self-describes as America's oldest civil rights organization that aims to preserve American's constitutional right to keep and bear arms.[171] In that capacity, the NRA "educates hunters and supports their rights" and also publishes *American Hunter*, a hunting magazine with over a million readers.[172]

The NRA claimed that Section 48 was overbroad and unconstitutional because it banned hunting speech even though it was only intended to target crush videos.[173] The NRA claimed that each of the following fall within Section 48's embrace: "selling a video depicting a deer hunt to a citizen of the District of Columbia, showing a television program depicting a dove hunt to a citizen of Iowa, or selling a magazine with a photograph of a mountain lion hunt to a citizen of California."[174] As such, organizations like the NRA and many retailers could run afoul of the statute. According to the NRA, Section 48's exceptions clause would not save the statute because the average hunting video could reasonably be found by a jury to lack serious value of great importance. The NRA described Section 48 as "rarely employed and superfluous."[175]

Professional Outdoor Media Association, American Society of Media Photographers, North American Nature Photography Association, Pennsylvania Outdoor Writers Association, Southeastern Outdoor Press Association, and Texas Outdoor Writers Association

The Professional Outdoor Media Association (POMA) is an organization of outdoor writers, photographers, broadcasters, videographers, illustrators, artists, editors, producers, firms, and organizations dedicated to hunting, shooting, fishing, trapping, and other traditional outdoor sports.[176] POMA self-describes as the "premier journalists' organization in the outdoor industry" and claims to deliver pertinent information to American hunters and anglers as well as to the public at large.[177] The American Society of Media Photographers (ASMP) is an organization boasting roughly 7,000 members around the world that was founded in 1944 to protect and promote the interests of professional photographers.[178] The North American Nature Photography Association (NANPA) is a not-for-profit corporation of photographers, which aims to promote nature photography as a medium of communication, nature appreciation, and environmental protection.[179] The Pennsylvania Outdoor Writers Association (POWA) purports to be America's "largest state outdoor writer organization."[180] The Southeastern Outdoor Press Association (SEOPA) is a non-profit organization of some 500 members that professes to be America's "leading regional outdoor communicator's organization."[181] The Texas Outdoor Writers Association (TOWA) consists of Texas-based journalists and outdoor industry members and promotes "quality writing, broadcasting, photography, and teaching relating to hunting, fishing, and the outdoors."[182]

These amici argued that Section 48 was unconstitutionally overbroad because it bans "images 'where an animal is wounded or killed' even if the underlying conduct, as with lawful hunting and fishing, is legal where it occurred."[183] As such, the amici argued that the otherwise lawful conduct of outdoor photographers and journalists comes within Section 48's embrace.[184]

The amici further contended that the Supreme Court has long recognized that a statute affecting a substantial amount of lawful speech is facially invalid under the First Amendment, but most of the images that come within Section 48's embrace constitute lawful speech depicting conduct that is legal where it occurred but illegal where the image was sold. The amici described the exceptions clause as narrow because according to them, it excluded protected speech lacking "serious value" and did not apply to the work as a whole.[185] The amici criticized the serious value requirement because it would "almost always be a jury question, and one where the jury's determination is very hard to predict, thereby significantly chilling protected speech."[186]

The First Amendment Lawyers Association

The First Amendment Lawyers Association (FALA) filed a brief on behalf of Stevens, claiming that the government had never taken "such an aggressive position against the most well-established principles of First Amendment doctrine."[187]

FALA argued that the Third Circuit correctly held that Section 48 was facially unconstitutional. It explained that as a content-based law, Section 48 was presumptively invalid and could not survive strict scrutiny because it was not the least restrictive means of preventing animal cruelty. Although FALA agreed with the Third Circuit's holding that Section 48 was facially unconstitutional, it asked the Supreme Court to affirm that conclusion because the serious value exceptions clause was unconstitutionally vague.[188]

According to FALA, First Amendment jurisprudence makes clear that speech involving sadism and violence is not obscene.[189] The amici cautioned the Supreme Court not to extend the obscenity doctrine to embrace such materials.[190] The amici emphasized that obscenity is the only context in which the Supreme Court has ever calibrated First Amendment protection to the "value" of the expression as articulated.[191] FALA described the serious value standard as "impermissibly vague, because they are unavoidably subjective" and cautioned that "criminal obscenity laws defined by these amorphous criteria have resulted in abusive prosecutions, unpredictable results, and censorship by chilling effect."[192] The amici claimed that Section 48's exceptions clause imposes a burden on the defendant to establish the speech's value, which in turn, will chill lawful speech.[193] Fact-finders may rely upon subjective evaluations of the speech's worth.[194] FALA argued that in light of the vagueness of what it termed the "serious value defense," Section 48's enormous reach extended well beyond what Congress intended.[195] FALA encouraged the Supreme Court to find the statute substantially overbroad and as such, facially unconstitutional.[196] As FALA explained:

> The Court [should] consider this case in light of the . . . doctrinal and practical problems that have attended the *Miller* test. This Court has been sharply divided over the constitutionality of criminalizing a broad, vaguely defined category of "obscene" speech. The present case raises many of these same problems, particularly as the statute would criminalize depictions based in part upon a prosecutor's or jury's subjective reaction that the expression lacks "serious value."[197]

FALA highlighted what was at stake in *Stevens*, observing that this unique case provided the Supreme Court with a golden opportunity to:

> uphold the essential doctrines of its First Amendment jurisprudence at stake in this case: the strict scrutiny of content-based laws, the narrowness of exceptions to the presumptive protection the First Amendment affords all expression, and the availability of facial overbreadth and vagueness challenges to laws that would otherwise chill free expression.[198]

National Shooting Sports Foundation, Inc.

Founded in 1961, the National Shooting Sports Foundation, Inc. (NSSF) is a Connecticut-based trade association for the firearms, ammunition, hunting, and shooting sports industry boasting roughly 5,000 members, including but not limited to licensed firearms manufacturers, distributors, and retailers. NSSF aims to protect and preserve hunting and shooting sports, encourage and facilitate safe and responsible gun sale and use, educate members and the public about wildlife conservation and ethical hunting, and promote a political landscape friendly to hunting, shooting, and Americans' right to bear arms. NSSF also publishes literature relating to wildlife, hunting legislation, and hunting as a wildlife conservation tool.[199]

NSSF filed an amicus brief in support of Stevens to protect its members' interest relating to the interstate sale and purchase of "educational videos/DVDs, books, photographs, art and other images that depict traditional hunting, but that would nevertheless fit [Section 48's] description of 'animal cruelty.'"[200] According to NSSF, such materials teach hunting basics, wildlife conservation, and safe and ethical hunting practices.[201]

NSSF claimed that prior to Stevens' conviction for the sale of dogfighting videos, NSSF believed that Section 48 would only be applied to crush videos.[202] However, in the wake of *Stevens*, "small and large retailers across the country now face the prospect of criminal prosecution on a strict liability basis for the mere possession and lawful sale of traditional hunting images that—unbeknownst to those retailers—may technically violate Section 48."[203]

NSSF argued that Section 48 placed sporting goods retailers in a precarious legal position. NSSF claimed that:

> If Section 48 is upheld, retailers can protect themselves from poten-
> tial prosecution only by a) viewing in their entirety all of the mate-
> rials they carry that may contain hunting images and b) assessing
> whether those materials contain images that: (i) fall within the ambit
> of Section 48(a); (ii) meet the subjective criteria of the exception codi-
> fied at Section 48(b); (iii) violate the laws of the jurisdiction in which
> they were created; (iv) violate the laws in the jurisdiction where the
> retailers are located; or (v) violate the laws of the jurisdiction where
> the video is sold or delivered. Indeed, simply possessing those ma-
> terials for the purpose of this review could be deemed a violation of
> the statute. Even were a retailer to undertake this time consuming
> and difficult review of each item, the materials may not provide suf-
> ficient information to determine whether possession or sale would be
> lawful. For instance, a photograph in a book is unlikely to indicate
> where the photograph was taken. In light of the burdensome and
> insurmountable obstacles imposed by the plain language of Section
> 48, the only safe choice for a retailer would be to refrain from sell-
> ing hunting books, videos, DVDs and photographs, regardless of
> their legality. The chilling effect on lawful commerce in protected
> speech is manifest.[204]

As such, NSSF argued that Section 48 was unconstitutionally overbroad.[205]

In support of its assertion that Section 48 should be declared unconstitutional, NSSF emphasized the importance of hunting in American society. It pointed out that hunting injects over $66 billion into the American economy and creates approximately 593,000 jobs.[206] According to NSSF, 14.3 million Americans hunt and more than 54,000 federally licensed firearms retailers exist nationwide. Most of these retailers sell hunting depictions, often for artistic or educational purposes. NSSF referenced a single large retailer, which estimated its annual revenue from sales of hunting depictions to be roughly $25 million. NSSF contended that this "robust commerce . . . and the concomitant free speech rights—will be chilled" if Section 48 were upheld.[207]

NSSF observed that the lack of uniformity in hunting laws across the country exacerbates Section 48's chilling effect. According to NSSF, such laws "regulate minute details of hunting and can differ depending on the tract of land, type of animal, type of ammunition, type of weapon, or disability of the hunter involved."[208] NSSF demonstrated issues arising from this lack of statutory uniformity with the following example:

> California, Connecticut, Illinois and Iowa (among other States) allow hunting of whitetail deer during specified seasons, albeit with certain restrictions. California allows hunting of whitetail deer using high-powered rifles, unless the land has been designated a "condor range," in which lead ammunition is banned. Illinois and Iowa, meanwhile, permit whitetail deer to be hunted with shotguns, but prohibit hunting whitetail deer with high-powered rifles. Connecticut also permits the hunting of whitetail deer, but the type of firearm that can be used depends upon the size of the tract of land. If the tract of land hunted on is less than ten acres, the hunter must use a shotgun; if the tract is greater than ten acres, the hunter may use a high-powered rifle.[209]

The Thomas Jefferson Center for the Protection of Free Expression

Founded in 1990, the Thomas Jefferson Center for the Protection of Free Expression (Center) is a nonprofit, nonpartisan organization based in Charlottesville, Virginia, which aims to protect freedom of speech and the press. The Center stated that animal cruelty was not central to *Stevens*; rather, it claimed that the key issue was the degree to which speech on any topic disfavored by the government can be restricted.[210]

> By its plain meaning, 18 U.S.C. §48 does nothing to regulate, prohibit, or criminalize actual acts of animal cruelty; rather, the statute only criminalizes visual or audio recordings of such acts. The United States is thus forced to concede that 18 U.S.C. §48 is a content-based restriction that does not fall under any of the established categories of unprotected speech. As such, the United States seeks to save 18 U.S.C. §48 from constitutional invalidation by proposing this Court adopt an open-ended approach to First Amendment analysis: rather than requiring the government to prove that unwelcome speech falls

within an established exception to free speech, courts should consider creating a new category of unprotected expression anytime government claims it has a strong reason for wanting to suppress speech.[211]

Significantly, the Center conceded that the government's analogy of depictions of animal cruelty "to the child pornography exception is understandable because it 'is the only place in First Amendment law where the Supreme Court has accepted the idea that we can constitutionally criminalize the depiction of a crime.'"[212] However, the Center pointed out that the rationale for creating a child pornography exception reveals little support for the government's proposed exception for depictions of animal cruelty.[213]

Unlike other amici, the Center focused its brief on "the inappositeness of child pornography as a template for an animal cruelty exception to First Amendment protection."[214] In explaining why the *Ferber* factors do not "translate well to the animal cruelty realm,"[215] the Center pointed out that although children and animals are vulnerable, living creatures, American society protects children from cruelty to a greater degree than its protects animals from cruelty. According to the Center, this differential degree of protection results from the indisputable fact that in America, human interests do not equate with those of animals. As such, statutes regard animals as property and subjects them to, *inter alia*, forced sterilization, euthanasia, non-consensual confinement in zoos and circuses—acts that if perpetrated on humans would be considered immoral and unlawful.[216]

The Center claimed that there was no societal consensus regarding the humane treatment of animals; such a consensus does exist with regard to child sexual abuse.[217] According to the Center:

> The majority of Americans decline to give [the humane treatment of animals] precedence over other interests that are far less compelling than a right enshrined in the United States Constitution. . . . many Americans set aside the goal of preventing animal cruelty in order to save time and money, and to satisfy personal indulgences and tastes. . . . the varying degree to which people allow the concern for animals to actually guide their actions demonstrates that there is no societal consensus as to the proper balancing of animal and human interests.[218]

In support of this assertion, the Center argued that animal slaughter for human consumption is a lucrative and lawful industry.[219] Furthermore, the Center argued that the variance in state anti-cruelty laws and the severity of punishments for violations of such laws further undercut assertions regarding the existence of a societal consensus regarding the humane treatment of animals.[220]

The Center also argued that there was insufficient evidence that the distribution network for animal cruelty depictions must be closed to decrease their production.[221] The Center observed that two of the three depictions resulting in Stevens' conviction involved organized dog fights, which according to the Center, are usually staged for a live audience who pay admission and generate gambling revenue.[222] As such, the Center inferred that such fights would occur regardless of whether they were videotaped, and similar conclusions could be made with regard to bullfighting, cockfighting, and other animal fighting.[223]

Although the Center cited no authority in support of its assertion, it claimed that Section 48 would not dry up the market for animal cruelty depictions where the depicted acts of animal cruelty are legal.[224] The Center averred that a "potential animal abuser may only choose to engage in illegal activities when the potential for monetary gain is great, but without the risk of punishment, even a modest financial gain would encourage acts of animal cruelty for the purpose of recording them."[225]

The Center appeared to suggest that a depiction of animal cruelty has "inherent journalistic value even if it was not shot for that purpose" because they demonstrate animal behavior and animal/human interaction.[226] The Center observed that an animal cruelty depiction could be used to provide evidence helpful in prosecuting perpetrators of animal cruelty but did not explain why such a depiction would not come within Section 48's exceptions clause.[227]

The Center characterized the inclusion of the serious value component into Section 48 as indicative of a "fundamental misunderstanding of the obscenity exception's exclusive focus on erotic expression. Unlike obscenity, [Section 48] is not motivated by the sensibilities of the viewers to depictions of acts, but the harm caused by the underlying acts themselves."[228] It also criticized the exceptions clause for not requiring consideration of the work as a whole when determining whether it has serious value or that the work appeal to the prurient interest as in *Miller*.[229] According to the Center, *Miller*'s serious value requirement "effectively protects erotic expression only in conjunction with the other elements of the *Miller* test; its isolated presence in [Section 48] is far less effective in protecting valuable expression through depictions of animal cruelty."[230]

DKT Liberty Project, American Civil Liberties Union, and the Center for Democracy and Technology

Founded in 1920, the American Civil Liberties Union (ACLU) is a nationwide, nonprofit, nonpartisan organization of 500,000 members that aims to promote and preserve civil rights, including freedom of speech.[230] DKT Liberty Project was

founded in 1997 to, in its own words, "promote individual liberty against encroach-
ment by all levels of government."[232] The Center for Democracy and Technology
(CDT) is a "nonprofit public interest and Internet policy organization" that, by its
own account, "represents the public's interest in an open, decentralized Internet
reflecting constitutional and democratic values of free expression, privacy and
individual liberty."[233]

These amici argued that Section 48 was facially unconstitutional and threatened to chill a wide array of protected speech because it criminalizes possession
and publication of depictions of conduct lawful in other states or countries, as well
as speech that was made many years ago.[234] They claimed that images of Spanish
bullfighting, historical footage of cockfighting, or documentaries about clubbing
seals in Canada come within the statute's embrace.[235]

These amici made two primary arguments. First, they urged the Supreme
Court to reject the *Chaplinsky* Balancing Approach because:

> The idea that the government may restrict speech based on an as-
> sessment of its "value" is antithetical to this Court's longstanding
> recognition that speech of all kinds—including offensive, contro-
> versial, and divisive speech—is protected . . . subject to a few very
> limited exceptions that do not apply here. . . . contrary to decades
> of . . . precedents and is premised on rationales . . . that do not jus-
> tify the suppression of speech under this Court's well-established
> jurisprudence.[236]

According to the amici, acceptance of the government's proposed balancing
test would "open the door for the government to regulate a broad range of expression based on interests that the Court has long held are constitutionally insufficient to justify the suppression of speech. Under the government's approach, the
government would have virtually unfettered discretion to regulate, and criminalize, any speech it—or a local jury—determines is without serious social value."[237]

The amici characterized the government's argument that Section 48 pre-
vents attendant harms to humans resulting from animal cruelty as "tenuous"
and "impermissible" because the Supreme Court had already rejected an analogous argument that speech could be banned based on "attenuated association between expression and undesirable thoughts or behavior."[238] The amici argued that
Congress could not prohibit speech just because the speech might increase the risk
of illegal activity in the future or because it may encourage crime.[239]

The amici also averred that prevention of the erosion of public morality is not
sufficient to warrant prohibiting speech because "speech may not be prohibited

because it concerns subjects offending our sensibilities."[240] The amici also rejected the assertion that Section 48 is nothing more than an expanded obscenity test in part because Section 48's "exceptions clause is not cabined by the critical limitations that this Court has insisted must apply in the obscenity context" and its serious value component contains only one prong of the three-prong obscenity test articulated in *Miller*; all prongs must be met before speech constitutes obscenity that can be lawfully prohibited.[241]

The amici further claimed that Section 48's exceptions clause actually bolsters the conclusion that the statute is unconstitutional because it leaves the determination of whether speech has serious value up to prosecutors and juries.[242] As the amici explained, "far from curing the constitutional flaws inherent in Section 48, the possibility that prosecutors will not evenhandedly enforce the statutory terms only adds to the statute's constitutional problems. The government may not privilege some speakers over others 'through the combined operation of a general speech restriction and its exemptions.'"[243]

The amici warned that fear of prosecution under Section 48 would chill protected speech, as many individuals would rather abstain from potentially prohibited speech than risk costly and time-consuming litigation and an adverse legal outcome.[244] The amici argued that Section 48's criminal penalties made it "particularly intolerable."[245] The amici also averred that Section 48's constitutionality should not be resolved as applied because to do so would effectively reverse the presumption that content-based speech restrictions like Section 48 are unconstitutional unless they satisfy strict scrutiny, which according to the amici, Section 48 did not.[246]

Cato Institute

Founded in 1977, the Cato Institute (Cato) is a public policy research organization "dedicated to the principles of individual liberty, limited government free markets and peace."[247] Although Cato made clear that it opposes animal cruelty, it filed an amicus brief in support of Stevens.[248] Cato argued that there is no long history of censoring depictions of animal cruelty; rather, Section 48 prohibited historically lawful speech.[249] According to Cato, "that goal pose[d] an alarming threat to Americans' most basic freedom. But the greater danger . . . [was the *Chaplinsky*] balancing test that invites the judiciary to determine the 'value' of the expression and weigh it against the Government's interest, not in suppressing a depiction, but in suppressing the conduct depicted."[250] Cato argued that under such reasoning, depictions of any unlawful or immoral conduct were vulnerable to prohibition, which contravenes longstanding First Amendment jurisprudence. In fact, until Section 48's enactment in 1999, depictions of animal cruelty were considered lawful to the extent they did not fall under an existing category of unprotected speech, such as obscenity. According to Cato, "divining a new category of unprotected speech under these circumstances would mark a radical shift in this Court's First Amendment jurisprudence, one contrary to over six decades of decisions cautioning against suppressing speech based on its content."[251] Cato characterized Section 48 as a "dramatic break with both precedent and tradition [that] threatens to undermine the very principles that the First Amendment exists to protect."[252] According to Cato, Section 48 "represent[ed] not the wisdom of inherited tradition, but rather the ambition of the Federal Government to proscribe a whole new swath of previously free expression."[253]

Cato rejected the government's assertion that the speech that Section 48 targeted was substantially analogous to the existing categories of unprotected speech because the speech did not have to be sexual or prurient.[254] Cato stressed that expanding the obscenity doctrine to include images "uncongenial . . . [to] 'public morality' would eviscerate the freedom of speech."[255]

Cato further stated that the government's analogy of child pornography to depictions of animal cruelty could "only be true at an absurdly high level of generality."[256] Cato admitted that both involve "helpless victims" but emphasized the significant distinction between children and animals.[257] Cato made much of the fact that, unlike an animal victim, pornographic images could come back to haunt a child victim, thereby exacerbating the harm.[258]

Cato described the government's compelling interest argument as "a radical expansion of this Court's compelling interest jurisprudence—one that clashes with established authority of this Court and greatly enlarges the scope of the interests that might be asserted to support restrictions on speech."[259] Cato claimed that under the government's balancing approach, if the interest is compelling and the value of the speech is minimal, the speech may be prohibited.[260]

Cato also resorted to making a slippery slope argument, reasoning that the Court's acceptance of the government's proposed balancing approach could be utilized to proscribe a significant amount of currently protected speech, such as speech regarding a particular religion, depictions of torture or violence by or against American troops, racially motivated hate speech, and depictions of crime, such as the Cheech and Chong films portraying marijuana use or episodes of popular television shows like *Law & Order* or *24*.[261] Notably, Cato failed to adequately explain why such depictions would not fit within Section 48's exceptions clause.

Endangered Breed Association and American Dog Breeders Association

Founded in the 1980s, the Endangered Breed Association (EBA) is an Oklahoma non-profit corporation, which by its own account, aims "to combat breed specific legislation and the preservation of the bull breeds."[262] The American Dog Breeders Association (ADBA) was founded as a registry for the American Pit Bull Terrier in 1909 but recently expanded to become an all-breed registry. It now conducts sanctioned dog shows and weight pulls across America.[263] They claimed to have filed the brief in support of Stevens because of their shared concern that Section 48 would prohibit historical information about dog breeds and depictions of activities, such as obedience and agility trials, hunting, weight pulling contests, rodeo events, herding, and other animal-related activities.[264]

According to the amici, Section 48 did not seek to prosecute dogfighters or animal abusers; rather, it criminalized and hence, chilled speech related to hunting with dogs, rodeos, horse shows, weight pull contests, predator and vermin control, herding of livestock, and dog training.[265] By way of illustration, the amici observed that animal rights activists picket rodeos and circuses, and some jurisdictions have banned the use of live animals in such events. According to the amici, creation, possession, or sale of instructional videos utilized to train dogs to herd sheep and cattle could be criminalized by Section 48. Sometimes injury or death to animals or herding dogs may result from herding trials, and some organizations consider this activity to be cruel and inhumane. The amici also averred that videos demonstrating the use of electronic collars as a dog training tool might also be targeted by Section 48 since some consider the practice to be cruel.[266]

The amici argued that upholding Section 48 would have serious economic consequences because it would require the small businesses that earn roughly $24,000 or less per year from marketing educational depictions to retain a First Amendment attorney to first determine whether the depiction has serious value sufficient to survive scrutiny under Section 48.[267] As a result, most citizens might choose not to create, edit, possess, and sell such depictions to the public and industry's detriment. The amici contended that it was "patently unfair to the citizenry to be in a position of constantly scrutinizing laws in other jurisdictions to determine whether an educational video falls under §48 and whether they should amass expert witnesses etc. in advance of a prosecution."[268]

The amici argued that Section 48 was facially unconstitutional because it was so broad that dog trainers, hunters and sellers of any educational or instructional video regarding hunting or dog training may not know whether the depictions falls within the scope of Section 48.[269] The amici criticized Stevens' conviction because it was not based on his direct participation in dogfighting; nor were the videos resulting in his conviction prurient, that is, utilized to stimulate sexual arousal.[270]

The amici also appeared to argue that Section 48 was redundant and/or unnecessary because animal cruelty statutes and anti-dog fighting statutes, rather than Section 48, "go to the heart of the matter which is to prosecute individuals involved in dog fighting and animal cruelty."[271] Finally, the amici rejected the government's assurance that prosecutorial discretion and the exceptions clause will prevent Section 48 from chilling lawful speech.[272] As the amici explained:

> Prosecutorial discretion leads to a disparate result in the administration of justice. Our system of justice should be blind and free of any hint of bias, prejudice or favoritism. Furthermore, [Section 48] provides no guidance to prosecutors in the use of their discretionary powers so as to provide for the least restrictive restriction on the rights of free speech of the public.[273]

The Reporters Committee for Freedom of the Press, The American Society of News Editors, The Association of Alternative Newsweeklies, Citizen Media Law Project, MediaNews Group, Inc., The National Press Photographers Association, National Public Radio, Inc., The New York Times Company, The Newspaper Association of America, The Newspaper Guild-CWA, Outdoor Writers Association of America, The Radio-Television News Directors Association, The Society of Environmental Journalists, and The Society of Professional Journalists

The above named groups filed an amicus brief in support of Stevens. These amici framed the central issue as "whether the Government can criminalize the possession and dissemination of a broad range of depictions involving animals," generally, not animal cruelty.[274] They averred that Section 48 chilled the media's ability to expose animal abuse without fear of prosecution. The amici emphasized that media coverage of animal cruelty has long been recognized as valuable speech and has played an important role in ending and preventing animal abuse.[275] They also observed that media coverage helps to define the difference between animal

cruelty and acceptable treatment of animals, including articles discussing class-
room animal dissections, fox hunting, and novelty sports like donkey ball.[276] The
amici further claimed that under Section 48, possessing a photograph in the state
of Washington of a deer being killed with a crossbow in Oregon is a federal crime,
even though that type of hunting is lawful in Washington with a permit and is
only a misdemeanor in Oregon.[277]

According to the amici, "the only possible protections . . . are prosecutorial discretion and the exceptions clause in section (b)."[278] However, the amici contended
that the exceptions clause was not broad enough to protect news coverage and that
members of the media are left to rely upon prosecutorial discretion, which had
already proved to be unreliable. They argued that such depictions might not satisfy Section 48's exception for depictions having journalistic or educational value
because only works with "serious value" were included and the exceptions clause
did not require the viewer to consider the work taken as a whole. The amici took
no position as to whether preventing animal cruelty constitutes a compelling government interest.[279] They also contended that the serious value requirement would
exclude a significant amount of journalism despite longstanding First Amendment
jurisprudence that has refused to "treat news and entertainment differently in the
First Amendment context, noting that 'the line between the informing and the
entertaining is too elusive for the protection of that basic right,' because 'what is
one man's amusement, teaches another's doctrine.'"[280]

The amici also claimed that Section 48 did not protect news-gathering because
it prohibited possession of depictions of animal cruelty "no matter their intended
purpose."[281] According to the amici, reporters intentionally place depictions that
would come within Section 48's embrace in interstate or foreign commerce for
commercial gain as part of the news-gathering process. They further contended
that creation of serious journalism frequently requires the possession of source
materials that are not exempt as "serious" works, which, under their interpretation of Section 48, could pose a risk of imprisonment for the reporter.[282] Finally,
the amici criticized the government's proposed balancing approach because, in
their opinion, the test would effectively "close off the 'breathing space' that 'First
Amendment freedoms need . . . to survive.'"[283]

Notes

1.   559 U.S. 460 (2010).
2.   Brief for a Group of American Law Professors as Amicus Curiae in Support of Neither
     Party at 6, *United States v. Stevens*, 559 U.S. 460 (2010) (No. 08-769) [hereinafter Law
     Professors' Brief].

3. Brief Amicus Curiae of Endangered Breed Association and American Dog Breeders Association in Support of Respondent at 9–17, *United States v. Stevens*, 559 U.S. 460 (2010) (No. 08-769) [hereinafter EBA & ADBA Brief].
4. Ibid., 6.
5. Ibid.
6. Ibid.
7. Brief of Constitutional Law Scholars Bruce Ackerman, Jack M. Balkin, Lee C. Bollinger, Erwin Chemerinsky, Daniel A. Farber, Craig Green, Sanford Levinson, Burt Neuborne, Lucas A. Powe, Jr., Rodney A. Smolla, Geoffrey R. Stone, Laurence H. Tribe, and William W. Van Alstyne, as Amici Curiae in Support of Respondent at 5, *United States v. Stevens*, 559 U.S. 460 (2010) (No. 08-769) [hereinafter Law Scholars' Brief].
8. Ibid., 5.
9. Ibid., 4.
10. Ibid., 4–6.
11. Ibid., 5–6.
12. Transcript of Oral Argument at 37–40, *United States v. Stevens*, 559 U.S. 460 (2010) (No. 08-769).
13. Law Scholars' Brief, 6.
14. Ibid., 7–8.
15. Ibid., 8–9.
16. Ibid., 10.
17. Ibid., 15–31.
18. Ibid., 23–24.
19. Ibid., 24–25.
20. Ibid., 25.
21. Ibid., 25–26.
22. Ibid., 26.
23. Ibid., 27–28.
24. Ibid., 29.
25. Ibid.
26. Law Professors' Brief, 6.
27. Ibid., 3–5.
28. See http://aldf.org/resources/law-professional-law-student-resources/law-professionals/bar-association-animal-law-sections-and-committees/.
29. Publication of the *Journal of Animal Law & Ethics* at the University of Pennsylvania Law School has been suspended.
30. Law Professors' Brief, 5.
31. Ibid., 6.
32. *Church of the Lukumi Bablu Aye, Inc. v. City of Hialeah*, 508 U.S. 520 (1993).
33. Law Professors' Brief, at 6–7.
34. Ibid., 8.
35. Ibid., 10.
36. Ibid., 12–17.

37. Ibid., 17; *see, e.g., Animal Legal Def. Fund, Inc. v. Glickman*, 154 F.3d 426, 433, 438 (D.C. Cir. 1998) ([en] banc) (holding that plaintiff Marc Jurnove had a cognizable interest in "view[ing] animals free from . . . 'inhumane treatment'") (quoted source omitted), *cert. denied, Nat'l Ass'n for Biomedical Research v. Animal Legal Def. Fund, Inc.*, 526 U.S. 1064 (1999); *Animal Welfare Inst. v. Kreps*, 561 F.2d 1007 (D.C. Cir. 1977) (holding plaintiff organizations had an interest in seeing Cape Fur Seals not subject to inhumane treatment); *Humane Soc'y of U.S. v. Hodel*, 840 F.2d 45, 52 (D.C. Cir. 1988) (holding that Humane Society members had an interest in not viewing animal corpses on wildlife refuges); *Fund for Animals, Inc. v. Lujan*, 962 F.2d 1391, 1396 (9th Cir. 1992) (holding that members had standing due to "psychological injury they suffered from viewing the killing of the bison in Montana").

38. Law Professors' Brief, 18–33.

39. Ibid., 19–21.

40. Ibid., 21; Comments of Sergeant Steve Brownstein, Chicago's Animal Abuse Control Team, quoted in William Hageman, "A Child, A Pup, A Blood Sport; Spring Brings Rise in Dogfights Staged By Kids for Fun," *Chi. Trib.*, May 11, 2004; see also, *e.g.*, Jamey Medlin, *Pit Bull Bans and the Human Factors Affecting Canine Behavior*, 56 DePaul L. Rev. 1285, 1301 (2007) ("Perhaps most disturbing is the fact that children are often present at dogfighting matches, raising concerns about desensitizing children to violence and animal cruelty.") (quoted source omitted). Thus, dogfights expose children to organized and systematic animal abuse with far-reaching consequences.

41. Law Professors' Brief, 22–23.

42. Ibid., 27–28.

43. Ibid., 31.

44. Ibid., 33.

45. Ibid., 33–34.

46. *Center on the Administration of Criminal Law—Mission*, NYU Law, http://www.law.nyu.edu/centers/adminofcriminallaw/mission/index.htm.

47. Ibid.

48. Brief of the Center on the Administration of Criminal Law as Amicus Curiae in Support of Petitioner at 5–6, *United States v. Stevens*, 559 U.S. 460 (2010) (No. 08-769) [hereinafter CACL Brief].

49. Ibid., 6–7.

50. Ibid., 7.

51. Ibid. (quoting *United States v. Williams*, 553 U.S. 285, 301 [2008]).

52. Brief of Florida, Alabama, Arkansas, Arizona, California, Colorado, Connecticut, Hawaii, Illinois, Indiana, Kentucky, Louisiana, Maryland, Michigan, Mississippi, Montana, New Hampshire, New Mexico, North Carolina, Ohio, Rhode Island, South Caroline, Texas, Utah, Virginia, and West Virginia, as Amici Curiae in Support of Petitioner at 2, *United States v. Stevens*, 559 U.S. 460 (2010) (No. 08-769) [hereinafter A-G Brief].

53. Ibid.

54. Ibid., 2–3.

55. Ibid., 3.

56. Ibid.
57. Ibid.
58. Ibid.
59. Brief Amicus Curiae of International Society for Animal Rights in Support of Petitioner at 1-2, *United States v. Stevens*, 559 U.S. 460 (2010) (No. 08-769) [hereinafter ISAR Brief].
60. Ibid., 2.
61. Ibid., 7.
62. Ibid., 2.
63. Ibid., 7.
64. Ibid., 10.
65. Ibid., 11–12.
66. Ibid., 34.
67. 458 U.S. 747 (1982).
68. ISAR Brief, 3.
69. Ibid., 19.
70. Ibid., 34.
71. *WLF Mission*, Washington Legal Foundation, http://www.wlf.org/org/mission.asp (last visited June 13, 2012).
72. Ibid.
73. Brief Washington Legal Foundation and Allied Educational Foundation as Amici Curiae in Support of Petitioner at 7–9, *United States v. Stevens*, 559 U.S. 460 (2010) (No. 08-769) [hereinafter WLF Brief].
74. Ibid., 10.
75. Ibid., 10–11.
76. Ibid., 13.
77. Ibid.
78. Ibid., 6.
79. Ibid.
80. 553 U.S. 285 (2008).
81. WLF Brief, 18–19.
82. Ibid., 7.
83. Brief of Amicus Curiae the Humane Society of the United States in Support of Petitioner at 1 (January 2009), *United States v. Stevens*, 559 U.S. 460 (2010) (No. 08-769) [hereinafter HSUS Brief 1].
84. Ibid., 2.
85. Ibid.
86. Ibid., 3.
87. Ibid.
88. Ibid.
89. Ibid.
90. Brief of Amicus Curiae the Humane Society of the United States in Support of Petitioner at 3 (June 2009), *United States v. Stevens*, 559 U.S. 460 (2010) (No. 08-769) [hereinafter HSUS Brief 2].
91. Ibid.

92. Ibid.
93. Ibid.
94. Brief for Amicus Curiae Northwest Animal Rights Network in Support of Petitioner at 1, *United States v. Stevens*, 559 U.S. 460 (2010) (No. 08-769) [hereinafter NARN Brief].
95. 458 U.S. 747 (1982).
96. NARN Brief, 16.
97. Ibid., 11.
98. Ibid.
99. Ibid., 12.
100. Ibid.
101. Ibid.
102. Ibid., 13.
103. Ibid., 17.
104. Ibid., 17–18.
105. Ibid., 23.
106. Brief Amicus Curiae of Animal Legal Defense Fund in Support of Petitioner at 1, *United States v. Stevens*, 559 U.S. 460 (2010) (No. 08-769) [hereinafter ALDF Brief].
107. Ibid., 3.
108. Ibid., 2.
109. Ibid., 3–4.
110. Ibid., 2.
111. Ibid.
112. Ibid., 4.
113. Ibid., 2 (quoting *Ferber*, 458 U.S. at 762).
114. Ibid.
115. Ibid., 4.
116. Ibid.
117. Ibid., 3; 413 U.S. 15 (1973).
118. Ibid., 5.
119. Brief of Amicus Curiae the American Society for the Prevention of Cruelty to Animals In Support of Petitioner at 1, *United States v. Stevens*, 559 U.S. 460 (2010) (No. 08-769) [hereinafter ASPCA Brief].
120. Ibid.
121. Ibid., 2.
122. Ibid.
123. Ibid.
124. Ibid., 25.
125. Ibid., 26.
126. Ibid., 2–3.
127. Ibid., 3.
128. "Who We Are," *National Coalition Against Censorship* (NCAC), http://www.ncac.org/who-we-are (last visited June 14, 2012).
129. Brief of the National Coalition Against Censorship and the College Art Association

as Amici Curiae in Support of Respondent at 1, *United States v. Stevens*, 559 U.S. 460 (2010) (No. 08-769) [hereinafter NCAC & CAA Brief].
130. Ibid.
131. Ibid., 2.
132. Ibid.
133. Ibid., 3.
134. Ibid.
135. Ibid.
136. Ibid., 5.
137. Ibid., 3–4.
138. Ibid., 4.
139. Ibid.
140. Ibid.
141. Ibid., 5.
142. Ibid.
143. Ibid.
144. Ibid., 6.
145. Ibid.
146. Brief of Amici Curiae Safari Club International and Congressional Sportsmen's Foundation in Support of Respondent at 1-2, *United States v. Stevens*, 559 U.S. 460 (2010) (No. 08-769) [hereinafter SCI & CSF Brief].
147. Ibid., 2.
148. Ibid.
149. Ibid., 2–3.
150. Ibid., 3.
151. Ibid., 4.
152. Ibid., 4–5.
153. Ibid., 5.
154. Ibid., 5–6.
155. Ibid., 6.
156. Brief of Amici Curiae Association of American Publishers, Inc., American Booksellers Foundation for Free Expression, Association of American University Presses, Comic Book Legal Defense Fund, Entertainment Consumers Association, Entertainment Merchants Association, Film Independent, Freedom to Read Foundation, Independent Book Publishers Association, Independent Filmmaker Project, Independent Film & Television Alliance, International Documentary Association, National Association of Recording Merchandisers, National Association of Theatre Owners, Inc., and Pen American Center in Support of Respondent at 2, *United States v. Stevens*, 559 U.S. 460 (2010) (No. 08-769) [hereinafter AAP et al. Brief].
157. Ibid.
158. Ibid.
159. Ibid.
160. Ibid., 3.

161. 535 U.S. 234 (2002).

162. AAP et al. Brief, 3.

163. Ibid.

164. Ibid., 4 (quoting *American Booksellers Ass'n, Inc. v. Hudnut*, 771 F.2d 323, 330 (7th Cir. 1985)).

165. Ibid., 4.

166. Ibid.

167. Ibid., 5.

168. Ibid.

169. Ibid., 6.

170. Ibid., 5.

171. Brief of Amicus Curiae National Rifle Association of America, Inc. in Support of Respondent at 1, *United States v. Stevens*, 559 U.S. 460 (2010) (No. 08-769) [hereinafter NRA Brief].

172. Ibid., 1–2.

173. Ibid., 2.

174. Ibid.

175. Ibid., 3.

176. Brief of Professional Outdoor Media Association, American Society of Media Photographers, North American Nature Photography Association, Pennsylvania Outdoor Writers Association, Southeastern Outdoor Press Association, and Texas Outdoor Writers Association as Amici Curiae in Support of Respondent at 1, *United States v. Stevens*, 559 U.S. 460 (2010) (No. 08-769) [hereinafter POMA et al. Brief].

177. Ibid.

178. Ibid.

179. Ibid., 2.

180. Ibid.

181. Ibid.

182. Ibid., 3.

183. Ibid.

184. Ibid.

185. Ibid., 4.

186. Ibid.

187. Brief of First Amendment Lawyers Association as Amicus Curiae in Support of Respondent at 4, *United States v. Stevens*, 559 U.S. 460 (2010) (No. 08-769) [hereinafter FALA Brief].

188. Ibid., 4–5.

189. Ibid., 5.

190. Ibid.

191. Ibid.

192. Ibid., 6.

193. Ibid.

194. Ibid.

195. Ibid.

196. Ibid., 4–5.

197. Ibid., 8.

198. Ibid., 7.
199. Brief of the National Shooting Sports Foundation, Inc. as Amicus Curiae in Support of Respondent at 1-2, *United States v. Stevens*, 559 U.S. 460 (2010) (No. 08-769) [hereinafter NSSF Brief].
200. Ibid., 2.
201. Ibid.
202. Ibid., 3.
203. Ibid.
204. Ibid., 3–4.
205. Ibid., 4.
206. Ibid., 5.
207. Ibid.
208. Ibid., 8.
209. Ibid., 8–9.
210. Amicus Curiae Brief of the Thomas Jefferson Center for the Protection of Free Expression in Support of Respondent at 1, *United States v. Stevens*, 559 U.S. 460 (2010) (No. 08-769) [hereinafter Center's Brief].
211. Ibid., 1–2.
212. Ibid., 2 (quoting *United States v. Stevens*, 533 F. 3d 218, 226 [3d Cir. 2008]).
213. Ibid.
214. Ibid., 3.
215. Ibid., 4 (quoting *Stevens*, 533 F. 3d at 226 [3d Cir. 2008]).
216. Ibid., 5.
217. Ibid., 10.
218. Ibid., 10–11.
219. Ibid., 11.
220. Ibid., 12–13.
221. Ibid., 17.
222. Ibid.
223. Ibid., 17–18.
224. Ibid., 18.
225. Ibid.
226. Ibid., 19.
227. Ibid.
228. Ibid., 24.
229. Ibid.
230. Ibid., 25.
231. Brief of the DKT Liberty Project, the American Civil Liberties Union, and the Center for Democracy and Technology, as Amici Curiae in Support of Respondent at 1, *United States v. Stevens*, 559 U.S. 460 (2010) (No. 08-769) [hereinafter DKT et al. Brief].
232. Ibid.
233. Ibid., 2.
234. Ibid.
235. Ibid.

236. Ibid., 3.
237. Ibid., 9–10.
238. Ibid., 11.
239. Ibid.
240. Ibid., 12 (quoting *Ashcroft v. Free Speech Coalition*, 535 U.S. 234, 245 [2002]).
241. Ibid., 14.
242. Ibid.
243. Ibid., 21–22.
244. Ibid., 20–21.
245. Ibid., 21.
246. Ibid., 3–4.
247. "About Cato," *Cato Institute*, http://www.cato.org/about.php (last visited June 15, 2012).
248. Brief for the Cato Institute as Amicus Curiae in Support of Respondent at 1, *United States v. Stevens*, 559 U.S. 460 (2010) (No. 08-769) [hereinafter Cato Brief].
249. Ibid., 1–2.
250. Ibid., 2.
251. Ibid., 5.
252. Ibid., 6.
253. Ibid., 14.
254. Ibid.
255. Ibid.
256. Ibid.
257. Ibid., 14–15.
258. Ibid., 15.
259. Ibid., 18.
260. Ibid., 20.
261. Ibid., 22–27.
262. EBA & ADBA Brief, 1.
263. Ibid.
264. Ibid., 2.
265. Ibid.
266. Ibid., 7–9.
267. Ibid., 13.
268. Ibid., 12.
269. Ibid.
270. Ibid., 9.
271. Ibid., 14.
272. Ibid., 17.
273. Ibid.
274. Brief Amici Curiae of the Reporters Committee for Freedom of the Press and Thirteen News Media Organizations in Support of Respondent at 1, *United States v. Stevens*, 559 U.S. 460 (2010) (No. 08-769).
275. Ibid., 4–5.

276. Ibid., 7–8.
277. Ibid., 9–10.
278. Ibid., 12.
279. Ibid., 2 n.2.
280. Ibid., 16 (quoting *Winters v. New York*, 333 U.S. 507, 510 (1948)).
281. Ibid., 3.
282. Ibid., 19–20.
283. Ibid., 3 (quoting *N.A.A.C.P. v. Button*, 371 U.S. 415, 433 (1963)).

CHAPTER 7

Oral Argument: The Last Stand

When a party disagrees with the outcome of a trial court decision, the party can appeal the decision to the appellate court in an appropriate circuit. On appeal, the parties can present their cases with briefing and oral argument or "on the briefs," in which the parties waive the right to oral argument and have the case decided on the briefs alone. As explained earlier, an oral argument is an attorney's oral presentation before a court.[1]

Oral argument can focus the court on hub issues, fill gaps in the briefing, and answer outstanding questions that are troubling the judges and their law clerks. Occasionally attorneys even raise new issues or arguments for the first time at argument, although this practice is highly frowned upon and in most, if not all cases, new arguments will not be considered.[2] In many cases, the oral argument is the attorney's last chance to prevail, and especially in a close case, an effective oral argument can tip the scales in a party's favor. Within a day or two after an oral argument in the Supreme Court, the justices hold a conference and vote.[3]

The time allotted for oral argument has shrunk throughout the history of the Supreme Court. In 1848, the Supreme Court permitted four hours of argument per side; by 1871, only two hours was allowed. In 1970, Chief Justice Warren Burger convinced his fellow justices to limit argument to 30 minutes per side.[4] In some appellate circuits, such as the Federal Circuit, argument time is cut further still, permitting each side only 15 minutes of argument, including rebuttal time.[5]

Oral arguments at the Supreme Court usually occur within four months after a petition for certiorari is granted. Beginning the first Monday in October, the Supreme Court hears arguments on Mondays through Wednesdays every two weeks until the end of April. When certiorari is granted after February, the case is docketed for the next judicial term.[6]

Judges differ in their preparation for oral argument.[7] Some judges review the briefing and appendices on their own; others heavily depend upon comprehensive bench memoranda prepared by law clerks, detailing the arguments, controlling law, and relevant facts. Preparation varies markedly judge-by-judge and even case-by-case. For instance, a judge might not require any bench memorandum to be written on a simple case suitable for an affirmance without opinion, while he or she would require a comprehensive memorandum on a complex case where reversal is recommended.

Supreme Court justices also differ in their oral argument preparation techniques and strategies. Former Chief Justice Earl Warren did not find oral arguments very persuasive, but Justice Felix Frankfurter asked countless questions at argument. By contrast, Justice Thomas' silence at argument has become legendary, almost as well known as Justice Scalia's infamous hypotheticals and wry humor on the bench. Like their brethren in appellate circuits, Supreme Court justices often utilize bench memoranda drafted by law clerks. These memos identify the key facts, hub issues, and possible questions.[8] Most justices meet with their law clerks about each case in advance of oral argument, and law clerks may discuss their thoughts regarding disposition of the case. Of course, justices vary in the weight, if any, afforded to such opinions.

Justices also differ in their approach to questioning. Some ask few or no questions; others barrage the attorneys with one question after another. One justice may ask a pointed question, such as whether any controlling authority exists as to a particular question. Other justices pose complex hypotheticals divorced from the factual realities of the case.

The tone and tenor of oral arguments vary with the composition of the Court. In the 70s and 80s under the Burger Court, few justices asked questions.[9] By contrast, the justices of the Rehnquist Court, with the notable exception of Justice Thomas, more aggressively asked questions. Today, Justice Scalia is well known for his witty hypotheticals.[10] Justice Kennedy is known to occasionally help attorneys by clarifying their questions to his fellow justices.

The cases on appeal to the Supreme Court are quite different than those on appeal in appellate circuits, primarily because the Supreme Court selects the cases it will hear; there is no appeal as of right. Typically, it chooses only interesting and often controversial cases that pose exceptionally important questions, usually involving the interpretation of the Constitution or federal law. For certiorari to be granted, at least four out of the nine justices must vote to take the case.[11]

Prior to the argument, each side has submitted a legal brief—a written legal argument outlining each party's points of law. The justices have read these briefs prior to argument and are thoroughly familiar with the case, its facts, and the legal positions that each party is advocating.[12] At oral argument, each party's attorney presents his or her position to the Court and answers questions posed by the justices.

On the first Monday in October, the Court usually hears two one-hour arguments per day, at 10 a.m. and 11 a.m.; afternoon sessions are scheduled as necessary. The Court hears argument on Mondays, Tuesdays, and Wednesdays in two-week intervals through late April. The Court's website posts the argument calendar under the "Oral Arguments" link. Between sessions, the justices write opinions, decide which cases to hear, and prepare for the next argument session. The Court grants review in approximately 75–100 of the more than 10,000 petitions filed each term. No one knows when the Court will issue an opinion in an argued case; there is no set time period in which the Court must make a decision. However, all cases argued during a court term are decided before the summer recess.[13]

During argument week, the justices discuss the cases and take a preliminary vote on each case. If the Chief Justice is in the majority, he chooses the opinion's author. He may write the opinion himself or assign it to another justice in the majority. If the Chief Justice is in the minority, the most senior justice in the majority determines who will write the opinion.[14]

"Oral arguments are open to the public, but seating is limited and on a first-come, first-seated basis."[15] Two lines generally form—one for those who wish to attend an entire argument and another much shorter line for those who simply wish to briefly observe the Court in session.[16] Seating for the first argument begins at 9:30 a.m. and seating for the brief observation begins at 10 a.m.[17]

When the session begins, the marshal will announce the entrance and seating of the justices with the following distinctive call: "Oyez! Oyez! Oyez! All persons having business before the Honorable, the Supreme Court of the United States, are admonished to draw near and give their attention, for the Court is now sitting. God save the United States, and this Honorable Court."[18]

The justices enter the courtroom through three different entrances located behind the bench. The chief justice and two senior associate justices enter through the center entrance, and three associate justices enter through each side entrance. Justices sit in order of seniority with the chief justice in the middle, and the other justices alternating from left to right, ending with the most junior associate justice on the far right.[19] The Chief Justice announces the number and name of the case and asks the appellant's counsel to proceed.

To the left of the bench sits the Clerk of the Supreme Court or his representative. Among other things, the clerk provides justices with materials regarding the case when the justices request additional documents and notifies court personnel when an opinion may be publicly released. He also swears in attorneys who are newly admitted to the Supreme Court Bar.[20]

On the right sits the marshal or his representative. The marshal calls the Court to order, maintains proper courtroom decorum, tapes the argument, and times each argument to ensure that each attorney does not exceed 30 minutes. The marshal's aides sit behind the justices and carry messages between the justices and/or members of the justices' staff.[21]

The attorneys scheduled to argue sit at tables facing the bench. During the argument, the arguing attorney will stand behind a lectern placed directly in front of the Chief Justice. Two lights adorn the lectern. When the white light turns on, that signals that the attorney has five minutes remaining. The red light indicates that the attorney has utilized the allotted time.[22]

In some instances, attorneys can more easily predict how the justices will vote based on commentary from the justices in prior opinions. In other cases, however, there is no way of predicting the votes and of course, justices are free to change their minds to some extent. A justice who dissented on one ground five years earlier could change his or her position years later, reaching a decision that goes in an entirely different direction.

The Counsel

In *United States v. Stevens*, Neal Katyal argued the case for the United States. He served as acting solicitor general after President Obama nominated then-Solicitor General Elena Kagan to serve on the U.S. Supreme Court.[23] The government could not have asked for a better spokesman. Katyal is a legal superstar.

Katyal's parents—an engineer and a pediatrician—emigrated from India to Chicago before he was born.[24] A strong student and top teen debater, Katyal attended Loyola Academy in Chicago and then spent a month at the Dartmouth Debate Institute. He decided to return to Dartmouth for his undergraduate work.[25]

After obtaining bachelor's degrees in Asian studies and government at Dartmouth University in 1991, Katyal obtained his law degree at Yale. While in law school, he interned in Vice President Al Gore's legal office and in the Office of the Solicitor General. After graduating from Yale, he worked for a summer under the chief justice of the Supreme Court, John Roberts, who was then a Supreme Court litigator at Hogan & Hartson.[26]

Next, Katyal clerked for the Honorable Guido Calabresi of the United States Court of Appeals for the Second Circuit and then the Honorable Justice Stephen G. Breyer of the Supreme Court. In 1997, Katyal became a law professor at Georgetown University Law Center. He also worked in the Deputy Attorney General's Office at the Department of Justice where he served as special assistant to Deputy Attorney General Eric Holder and later an adviser for national security affairs. There, he dealt mainly with issues of terrorism and "the constitutionality and legality of military operations in Kosovo and Iraq."[27] He also worked in private practice, where he focused on appellate and complex litigation, including patent, securities, criminal, tort, employment, and constitutional issues.[28]

In 2009, President Obama asked Katyal to serve as acting solicitor general until he replaced the newly appointed Justice Elena Kagan who had formerly held that role. As acting solicitor general, Katyal represented the federal government in all appellate matters.[29]

Even before arguing on behalf of the government in *U.S. v Stevens*, Katyal already had extensive experience handling cases before the Supreme Court. He successfully advocated for the constitutionality of the Voting Rights Act of 1965, defended former Attorney General John Ashcroft against allegations of purported abuses in the war on terror, and unanimously prevailed against eight states that sued America's leading power plants for contributing to global warming.[30] Katyal was a member of Al Gore's legal team and wrote briefs and petitions in preparation for *Bush v. Gore*. In 2003, he wrote a brief on behalf of presidents of law schools advocating for affirmative action in *Grutter v. Bollinger*. However, he is best known for his 2006 Supreme Court victory deeming Guantanamo Bay military tribunals unconstitutional.[31] Not yet fifty years old, Katyal has orally argued seventeen cases in the Supreme Court in addition to countless others in lower courts. He also argued an important case in the U.S. Court of Appeals for the Federal Circuit regarding whether certain aspects of the human genome were patentable.[32]

In addition to his extensive government experience, Katyal was one of the youngest tenured law professors in the history of the Georgetown University Law Center.[33] He has published dozens of scholarly articles and op-ed pieces in law reviews, the New York Times, and the Washington Post.[34] He has testified before committees of both the U.S. House of Representatives and the U.S. Senate.[35]

Not surprisingly, Katyal has received countless awards recognizing his impressive professional achievements. In 2011, he received the Edmund Randolph Award—the highest award a civilian can receive from the U.S. Department of Justice. That same year, Chief Justice Roberts appointed Katyal to the Advisory Committee on Federal Appellate Rules. Katyal has been named "One of the 40 Most Influential Lawyers of the Last Decade Nationwide" by the *National Law Journal*; "One of the 90 Greatest Washington Lawyers over the Last 30 Years" by the *Legal Times*; "Lawyer of the Year" by *Lawyers USA*;[36] and "One of the 30 best advocates before the Supreme Court," according to the *Washingtonian* magazine.[37]

Attorneys prepare for oral arguments in different ways. Katyal explained that in anticipation for one of his arguments in front of the Supreme Court, he listed 15 to 20 of the most intimidating people he knew, including law school deans and prominent practitioners, and flew around the country practicing his oral argument in front of them.[38] When asked how he keeps his competitive edge, Katyal intimated that he "work[s] harder than most anyone and . . . vest[s] [his] junior lawyers with tremendous amounts of responsibility . . . I'm very, very careful about who I work with."[39]

Katyal has been open about what it takes to succeed during an oral argument in the "Marble Temple." He explained:

> People think you want your lawyer to be some fancy orator who's beautiful with words. But actually you want your lawyer to know how the justices think and can answer 50 or 60 questions in a half hour. There's no room for a script. It's all rapid-fire back and forth. If you make one false move, your case and, indeed, your career can be over. It's a real challenging place, but it's also the most fun a lawyer could have.[40]

Stevens' counsel—Patricia Millett—is equally impressive. Recently appointed to the United States Court of Appeals for the D.C. Circuit, Millett graduated from Harvard Law School and was formerly a partner at Akin Gump—one of the world's most prestigious law firms. Millett has argued at least thirty cases before the Supreme Court and countless others in lower courts.[41]

From August 1996 to September 2007, Millett served as an assistant to the Solicitor General. She has received the Attorney General's Distinguished Service Award and the Environmental and Natural Resources Division Special Commendation for Assistance and Support in the Activities of the Division.[42]

Prior to her employment with the Office of the Solicitor General, Millett worked in the Department of Justice's Civil Division where she briefed and argued more than 20 cases in various courts. She also clerked for the late Judge Thomas Tang on the U.S. Court of Appeals for the Ninth Circuit and worked in the litigation department of a Washington, D.C., law firm. She is admitted to the bar in the District of Columbia.[43]

Millett's legal prowess has been consistently recognized and rewarded. *Washingtonian* magazine named her one of Washington's 100 Most Powerful Women and described her as "a persuasive writer and an eloquent arguer."[44] *Washingtonian* also named Millett to its 2011 list of "Washington's Best Lawyers" for her Supreme Court work.[45] She was also named by the *National Law Journal* as one of "Washington's Most Influential Women Lawyers," and by *Am Law Litigation Daily* as "Litigator of the Week," for her successful, closely watched and highly publicized argument before the Second Circuit in the matter of *Securities and Exchange Commission v. Galleon Group, et al.* One of her Supreme Court briefs is featured in Ross Guberman's book, *Point Made: How to Write Like the Nation's Top Advocates.*

Millett is or has been a member of the Supreme Court Fellows Commission (by appointment of the Chief Justice), a fellow of the American Academy of Appellate Lawyers, a board member of the Dwight D. Opperman Institute of Judicial Administration at New York University Law School, a member of the Outside Advisory Board for the Georgetown University Law Center's Supreme Court Institute, a member of the Board of Trustees of the Lawyers Committee for Civil Rights, and a master in the Edward Coke Appellate Inn of Court.[46]

Oral Argument

The Supreme Court commenced oral argument in *U.S. v. Stevens* at 10:03 a.m. on Tuesday, October 6, 2009.[47] As counsel for the petitioner, the United States, Katyal went first. Katyal began his presentation by stating that the Third Circuit erred in striking Section 48 down on its face without first applying a substantial overbreadth analysis.[48] However, in his view, Supreme Court precedent made clear that such a law should not be struck unless it is substantially overbroad, and Section 48 was not.[49]

Next, Katyal began to outline the four critical features of Section 48 that would warrant upholding it. Before he even explained the third feature, however, Justice Sotomayor asked him what record evidence supported his assertion that the statute only applied to commercial messages that, according to Congress, drove the market for animal cruelty.[50] Justice Scalia asked Katyal to define "for profit commercial market," and in response, Katyal explained that the term referred broadly to "anything that is sold."[51]

Chief Justice Roberts then asked the question that would arguably become the crux of the decision: "what is your test for determining which categories of speech are unprotected by the First Amendment?" Katyal responded that if a compelling interest existed in regulating a means of production and the underlying content was not targeted, then the depiction could be regulated as long as there are alternative mechanisms for expression.[52] In support of his assertion, he relied upon *New York v. Ferber*,[53] a Supreme Court case determining that the First Amendment does not protect child pornography.[54] Justice Ginsburg likened *Stevens* to an earlier case—*American Booksellers Association v. Hudnut*[55]—that involved a civil suit arising from the depiction of women as sexual objects enjoying pain.[56] The Seventh Circuit held that an attempt to sue purveyors of those depictions violated the First Amendment, and the Supreme Court had summarily affirmed. Katyal distinguished *Stevens* on the ground that here, the law does not target the communicative element of the depictions because animal cruelty can be shown so long as live animals are not used. Chief Justice Roberts pointed out that one must look to the content of the depiction to determine if it falls into a statutory exemption,[57] but Katyal countered, "Congress carved a broad exemption in Section 48 precisely to make sure that expressive messages aren't swept up."[58] However, he admitted that "the line will sometimes be difficult to draw."[59] After Katyal emphasized that in *Osborne v. Ohio*,[60] the Supreme Court approved a child pornography statute that exempted bona fide artistic, educational, and certain other uses for the material, Justice Scalia implied that child pornography is different because it constitutes obscenity, but animal cruelty depictions do not. In keeping with his reputation for hypotheticals, Justice Scalia asked whether Section 48 would prohibit a bullfighting aficionado from creating depictions promoting bullfighting.[61] Anticipating other hypotheticals, Katyal preempted those arguments and effectively utilized his limited time by disposing of them all at once:

> We believe that Section 48 will have as-applied constitutional challenges that will be inferred from case to case. But . . . in *United States v. Williams*,[62] [the Court said] that we should be careful about that endless stream of fanciful hypotheticals precisely because the test under substantial overbreadth, which knocks an entire act of Congress out on its face, is that there must be a realistic danger that the statute will be applied in . . . the manner the hypothetical suggests.[63]

With respect to your bullfighting hypothetical, there is no realistic danger. . . . [Congress] explicitly exempted Spanish bullfighting and said that is the paradigmatic case of what is educational and
artistic and the like.[64]

Justice Breyer jumped in, asking how people were expected to know whether
hunting activities, humane slaughter, or even stuffing geese for pate de foie gras
violated the law. Justice Kennedy seemed unconvinced that prosecutorial restraint
was enough to save the statute. In response to Justice Ginsburg's question implying
that she did not understand why dogfighting and cockfighting would be covered
but bullfighting would not, Katyal explained that the former two types of animal
fighting are illegal in all 50 states. He also emphasized that not all dogfighting
videos would violate Section 48, only those that did not fall into one of the statute's categorical exemptions.[65]

Turning to the specific statutory language, Justice Scalia asked Katyal "how
do you limit 'killed' to cruel?"[66] Although Katyal stated that the term "kill" was
subject to various meanings because there are various ways to kill cruelly,[67] Justice
Scalia seemed unconvinced. He responded, "You don't have a single case in which
an absolutely clear word like 'kill' is given a more narrow meaning because of other
words that are different from that word."[68] Justice Breyer joined in, suggesting
that the statute should have said "cruelly kill" or "cruelly wound" rather than just
"wound" or "kill." He continued, suggesting that Congress should draft a statute
specifically about crush videos or dogfighting rather than a general one prohibiting depictions of animal cruelty. Katyal countered that Section 48's exemption
borrowed language from the *Miller* obscenity test but went further than *Miller*.[69]

The hypotheticals raised during the argument seemed endless, and few tied
closely to the realities of the case before the Court. Although Section 48 only regulated depictions of animal cruelty involving live animals, Justice Scalia compared
the depictions of animal cruelty prohibited by Section 48 to horror films depicting
torture.[70] Justice Alito asked whether under a different statute gladiatorial fights
to the death could be broadcast on TV around the world.[71]

Justice Ginsburg then focused the argument on an important jurisdictional
issue; the statute prohibits a video of conduct that is illegal in the state where the
depiction is created, sold, or possessed regardless if the conduct was legal where
it occurred.[72] One of the videos resulting in Stevens' conviction was of dogfighting in Japan, where the practice is legal.

Justice Ginsburg also distinguished *Ferber* because child pornography involved the simultaneous abuse of the child portrayed, but Justice Ginsburg ap-

peared to believe that the dog fight would occur whether Stevens filmed it or not. Katyal pointed out that Stevens sent his dogs to Japan to fight and that under *Ferber*, Congress can prohibit a depiction of the idea if it can be communicated in an alternative, non-violative way, such as a simulated fight or by writing a book.[73] Katyal concluded by pointing out that the "statute has nothing to do with the offense of the message. It has to do with trying to dry up an underlying market for animal cruelty."[74]

When Katyal's time expired, Millett approached the lectern. She began her argument by observing that prohibiting Stevens from selling real footage of dog fights but allowing animal rights organizations seeking to ban the practice to use real images of such fights "puts the government's censorial thumb on the scale of public debate."[75] She quickly noted, however, that a "properly drawn law" could regulate unprotected speech like obscenity.[76] She went further, observing that "a statute that says the patently offensive intentional torture and killing of an animal . . . designed to appeal to the prurient interest of the purpose of producing the image. . . . would satisfy strict scrutiny."[77] Millett also speculated that a properly drawn statute could prohibit an image taken legally abroad.[78]

Justice Breyer raised the question of whether Congress could find a category of things that do not communicate but rather appeal to the instinct of sadism.[79] Millett opined that the only way to save the statute was to effectively rewrite it, which is not the Court's job and exceeds its proper role in construing statutes. Millett also emphasized that the legislative history of Section 48 focused only on crush videos, but Congress wrote it broadly enough to apply to other things such as animal fighting videos.[80]

Chief Justice Roberts warned Millett that the language in *Ferber* cut against Stevens: "'the evil to be restricted so overwhelmingly outweighs the expressive interest at stake.'"[81] While Chief Justice Roberts referred to this language as a "test,"[82] Millett stated that the language was not a test but rather "a description of the types of categories that by history and tradition had been outside the First Amendment and the rationale for why *Ferber* came in."[83] Millett also distinguished *Stevens* from *Ferber* in the following ways: (i) there has been no finding that creating the image is the primary or sole motive for creating these images and (ii) you do not dry up the market by having a sweeping value exception. Millett stated that the government had to prove that the images cause the harm in order to prevail.[84]

Justice Stevens wondered whether Section 48 would prohibit depictions of hunting if it involved killing in Washington, D.C., where hunting is prohibited.

Millett responded that it would depend on if the depiction had serious value, but entertainment value, standing alone, would not be enough.[85] Although Justice Scalia seemed concerned about the chilling effect that Section 48 might have on hunting television shows,[86] Justice Alito emphasized that in the decade of the statute's existence there had been no decrease in hunting videos and shows; the only effect was drying up the crush video market. Millett opined that this lacked relevance because if the Outdoor Channel consulted her, she would have to conclude that their shows fall within the statute's embrace.[87]

As to overbreadth, Millett speculated that 2,000 crush videos might be prohibited, but the statute also embraced hundreds of thousands of other images that were not crush videos.[88] Justice Ginsburg asked Millett if there was any evidence that Section 48 had led to a drying up of the market for animal fighting videos.[89] Millett responded, "none whatsoever."[90]

Justice Alito quipped, "what about people . . . who like to see human sacrifices? Suppose that is legally taking place someplace in the world. I mean, people here would probably love to see it. Live, pay per view, you know, on the human sacrifice channel."[91]

When Justice Breyer opined that these depictions might appeal to people's worst instincts,[92] Justice Scalia remarked "it's not up to the government to decide what are people's worst instincts."[93] Millett seemed hesitant to say that Congress could ban a human sacrifice channel.[94]

Katyal had reserved three minutes for rebuttal. Rebuttal provides the attorney who goes first with a very brief opportunity to respond to the arguments made by opposing counsel. Katyal first addressed the concerns raised during Millett's presentation. "When the statute is not aimed at the communicative impact of the message . . . but rather is aimed at reducing underlying acts of exploitation, that is an area [in] which Congress has great leeway."[95] Ironically, after peppering Katyal with hypotheticals during his presentation, Justice Scalia observed that nobody was doing human sacrifice. Katyal noted that there had been no prosecutions for crush videos because the market had dried up so quickly after Section 48's enactment.[96] Katyal also returned to Justice Stevens' questions about hunting. He explained that Section 48 did not cover hunting unless it was illegal under existing animal cruelty laws.[97]

Chief Justice Roberts thanked both counsel for their "able presentation[s]," and the argument concluded at 11:06 a.m.[98]

Notes

1. *See* Daniel Oran, *Oran's Dictionary of the Law,* (New York: Delmar Cengage Learning, 2007), 371.

2. *See People v. Harris,* 10 Cal. App. 4th 672, 686 (Cal. Ct. App. 1992) ("contentions raised for the first time at oral argument are disfavored and may be rejected solely on the ground of their untimeliness.").

3. David M. O'Brien, *Storm Center: The Supreme Court in American Politics* (New York: W.W. Norton & Company, Inc., 2011), 250.

4. Ibid.

5. *See* Fed. Cir. I.O.P. 7 (2008) ("It is the court's policy that 15 minutes per side be the normal time allocation . . .").

6. O'Brien, *Storm Center,* 252.

7. Ibid., 258.

8. Ibid.; see also David M. O'Brien, *Judges on Judging: Views from the Bench* (4th ed.; Thousand Oaks, CA: CQ Press, 2013).

9. O'Brien, *Storm Center,* 258.

10. Ibid., 259.

11. "Visitor's Guide to Oral Argument," Supreme Court of the United States, accessed June 26, 2012, http://www.supremecourt.gov/visiting/visitorsguidetooralargument.aspx.

12. Ibid.

13. Ibid.

14. Ibid.

15. Ibid.

16. Ibid.

17. Ibid.

18. O'Brien, *Storm Center,* 116.

19. Supreme Court, "Visitor's Guide to Oral Argument."

20. Ibid.

21. Ibid.

22. Ibid.

23. "Who Runs Gov: Neal Katyal," *Washington Post,* accessed June 27, 2012, http://www.washingtonpost.com/politics/neal-katyal/gIQAOxnx9O_topic.html.

24. Ibid.

25. Ibid.

26. Ibid.

27. Ibid.

28. "Neal Katyal," Hogan Lovells, accessed June 27, 2012, http://www.hoganlovells.com/neal-katyal/.

29. "Who Runs Gov: Neal Katyal."

30. Lovells, "Neal Katyal."

31. "Who Runs Gov: Neal Katyal."

32. Lovells, "Neal Katyal."

33. Vandana Sinha, "Executive Profile—Neal Katyal," *Washington Business Journal,* last modified October 25, 2011, http://www.bizjournals.com/washington/print-edition/2011/10/21/neal-katyal.html?page=all.

34. Lovells, "Neal Katyal."

35. Ibid.

36. Ibid.

37. "Who Runs Gov: Neal Katyal."

38. Sinha, "Executive Profile."

39. Ibid.

40. Ibid.

41. "Patricia Ann Millett," Akin Gump Strauss Hauer & Feld LLP, accessed June 27, 2012, http://www.akingump.com/pmillett/.

42. Ibid.

43. Ibid.

44. Ibid.

45. Ibid.

46. Ibid.

47. Transcript of Oral Argument at 1, *United States v. Stevens*, 559 U.S. 460 (2010) (No. 08-769).

48. Ibid., 3.

49. Ibid., 5–6.

50. Ibid., 3–4.

51. Ibid., 5.

52. Ibid., 6.

53. 102 S. Ct. 3348 (1982).

54. Transcript of Oral Argument, 6.

55. 771 F. 2d 323 (7th Cir. 1985), aff'd mem., 475 U.S. 1001 (1986).

56. Transcript of Oral Argument, 6–7.

57. Ibid., 7–8.

58. Ibid., 9.

59. Ibid.

60. 110 S. Ct. 1691 (1990).

61. Transcript of Oral Argument, 9–11.

62. 128 S. Ct. 1830 (2008).

63. Transcript of Oral Argument, 11.

64. Ibid., 11–12.

65. Ibid., 12–16.

66. Ibid., 17.

67. Ibid., 18.

68. Ibid., 19.

69. Ibid., 19–21.

70. Ibid., 21–22.

71. Ibid., 23.

72. Ibid., 22.

73. Ibid., 24–26.

74. Ibid., 27.

75. Ibid., 27.
76. Ibid., 28.
77. Ibid., 29.
78. Ibid., 30–31.
79. Ibid., 32.
80. Ibid., 33–34.
81. Ibid., 34.
82. Ibid.
83. Ibid., 35.
84. Ibid., 35–36.
85. Ibid., 36–37.
86. Ibid., 37.
87. Ibid., 39–40.
88. Ibid., 42.
89. Ibid., 43–44.
90. Ibid., 44.
91. Ibid., 46.
92. Ibid., 49.
93. Ibid., 50-51.
94. Ibid., 52.
95. Ibid., 55–56.
96. Ibid., 56.
97. Ibid., 58.
98. Ibid., 60.

CHAPTER 8

The Supreme Court Speaks

On April 20, 2010, the Supreme Court affirmed the decision of the Third Circuit, declaring Section 48 unconstitutional.[1] Writing for the eight-member majority, Chief Justice John Roberts noted that as a content-based regulation, Section 48 is presumptively invalid, and the United States did not successfully rebut that presumption. Although the majority conceded that restricting certain categories of speech is consistent with the First Amendment, it emphasized that the depictions of animal cruelty embraced by Section 48 neither constitute a new category of unprotected speech nor fall into existing categories of unprotected speech. The majority reached this conclusion in part because it saw no evidence of a tradition of prohibiting such depictions as exists for criminalizing the underlying animal cruelty portrayed.[2]

After concluding that the videos at issue warranted First Amendment protection, the majority determined that Section 48 was substantially overbroad.[3] A law may be invalidated as overbroad where a "substantial number of its applications are unconstitutional, judged in relation to the statute's plainly legitimate sweep."[4] The majority concluded that Section 48 was overbroad because its definition of *depiction of animal cruelty* did not require the conduct portrayed to be cruel and included the terms *wounded* and *killed*, which could reach a wide array of conduct not intended to come within Section 48's embrace.[5] In addition, because Section 48 applied to any depiction of conduct unlawful in the state where the depiction was created, sold, or possessed, the majority reasoned that depictions of legal conduct could violate the law if sold in another state where the same conduct was unlawful. As such, the majority observed that Section 48 could apply to the sale of hunting depictions within the District of Columbia where hunting is banned because such depictions are not typically educational or instructional.[6] The majority emphasized that Section 48 "draws no distinction based on the reason the intentional killing of animal is made illegal, and includes, for example, the humane slaughter of a stolen cow."[7]

Although the majority admitted that Section 48 borrowed the "serious value" language of *Miller v. California*, it clarified that serious value was not a general precondition that, standing alone, could save a statute. It further noted that the First Amendment protected much speech that lacked serious value but still fell within Section 48's embrace. According to the majority, despite the government's assertions to the contrary, Section 48's "exceptions clause simply has no adequate reading that results in the statute's banning only the depictions the government would like to ban."[8] Nor did the government's assurance that it would only apply Section 48 to the narrow subset of depictions for which it was intended save the statute.[9] However, in striking down Section 48, the majority did not decide whether a narrowly tailored statute limited to crush videos or depictions of *extreme* animal cruelty would be constitutional.

In his lengthy dissent, Justice Samuel Alito argued, among other things, that the question presented was whether Section 48 was unconstitutional as applied to the facts of the case. According to Justice Alito, the majority had unnecessarily resorted to the "'strong medicine' of the overbreadth doctrine" that generally "should be administered only as 'a last resort'" to declare Section 48 unconstitutional.[10] Justice Alito criticized the majority's reliance on "fanciful hypotheticals" to find Section 48 overbroad.[11] He observed that "when a federal court is dealing with a federal statute challenged as overbroad, it should, of course, construe the statute to avoid constitutional problems, if the statute is subject to such a limiting instruction;"[12]— a doctrine that, according to Justice Alito, the majority failed to follow when interpreting Section 48.[13] Justice Alito insisted that, despite the majority's contentions to the contrary, portrayals of lawful hunting are beyond Section 48's embrace as clearly stated in legislative debate on the law.[14] Such depictions would also fall within Section 48's broad exceptions clause.[15] Justice Alito emphasized that "invalidation for overbreadth is appropriate only if the challenged statute suffers from substantial overbreadth—judged not just in absolute terms, but in relation to the statute's 'plainly legitimate sweep.'"[16] Applying the *Ferber* Approach to depictions of animal cruelty, he determined that such depictions constitute unprotected speech.[17] Justice Alito would have vacated the decision and ordered the Third Circuit to determine whether the dogfighting videos at issue were constitutionally protected.[18]

The complete decision is excerpted below and analyzed in the subsequent chapter. Chief Justice Roberts delivered the majority opinion in which Justices Stevens, Scalia, Kennedy, Thomas, Ginsburg, Breyer, and Sotomayor joined. Justice Alito filed a dissenting opinion.

SUPREME COURT OF THE UNITED STATES

No. 08–769

UNITED STATES, PETITIONER v. ROBERT J. STEVENS

ON WRIT OF CERTIORARI TO THE UNITED STATES COURT OF APPEALS FOR THE THIRD CIRCUIT

[April 20, 2010]

CHIEF JUSTICE ROBERTS delivered the opinion of the Court.

Congress enacted 18 U. S. C. §48 to criminalize the commercial creation, sale, or possession of certain depictions of animal cruelty. The statute does not address underlying acts harmful to animals, but only portrayals of such conduct. The question presented is whether the prohibition in the statute is consistent with the freedom of speech guaranteed by the First Amendment.

I

Section 48 establishes a criminal penalty of up to five years in prison for anyone who knowingly "creates, sells, or possesses a depiction of animal cruelty," if done "for commercial gain" in interstate or foreign commerce. §48(a).[1] A depiction of "animal cruelty" is defined as one "in which a living

---

1.   The statute reads in full:
    "§48. Depiction of animal cruelty "
    CREATION, SALE, OR POSSESSION.—Whoever knowingly creates, sells, or possesses a depiction of animal cruelty with the intention of placing that depiction in interstate or foreign commerce for commercial gain, shall be fined under this title or imprisoned not more than 5 years, or both.
    "(b) EXCEPTION.—Subsection (a) does not apply to any depiction that has serious religious, political, scientific, educational, journalistic, historical, or artistic value.
    "(c) DEFINITIONS.—In this section—
    "(1) the term 'depiction of animal cruelty' means any visual or auditory depiction, including any photograph, motion-picture film, video recording, electronic image, or sound recording of conduct in which a living animal is intentionally maimed, mutilated, tortured, wounded, or killed, if such conduct is illegal under Federal law or the law of the State in which the creation, sale, or possession takes place, regardless of whether the maiming, mutilation, torture, wounding, or killing took place in the State; and

animal is intentionally maimed, mutilated, tortured, wounded, or killed," if that conduct violates federal or state law where "the creation, sale, or possession takes place." §48(c)(1). In what is referred to as the "exceptions clause," the law exempts from prohibition any depiction "that has serious religious, political, scientific, educational, journalistic, historical, or artistic value." §48(b).

The legislative background of §48 focused primarily on the interstate market for "crush videos." According to the House Committee Report on the bill, such videos feature the intentional torture and killing of helpless animals, including cats, dogs, monkeys, mice, and hamsters. H. R. Rep. No. 106–397, p. 2 (1999) (hereinafter H. R. Rep.). Crush videos often depict women slowly crushing animals to death "with their bare feet or while wearing high heeled shoes," sometimes while "talking to the animals in a kind of dominatrix patter" over "[t]he cries and squeals of the animals, obviously in great pain." *Ibid.* Apparently these depictions "appeal to persons with a very specific sexual fetish who find them sexually arousing or otherwise exciting." *Id.,* at 2–3. The acts depicted in crush videos are typically prohibited by the animal cruelty laws enacted by all 50 States and the District of Columbia. See Brief for United States 25, n. 7 (listing statutes). But crush videos rarely disclose the participants' identities, inhibiting prosecution of the underlying conduct. See H. R. Rep., at 3; accord, Brief for State of Florida et al. as *Amici Curiae* 11.

This case, however, involves an application of §48 to depictions of animal fighting. Dogfighting, for example, is unlawful in all 50 States and the District of Columbia, see Brief for United States 26, n. 8 (listing statutes), and has been restricted by federal law since 1976. Animal Welfare Act Amendments of 1976, §17, 90 Stat. 421, 7 U. S. C. §2156. Respondent Robert J. Stevens ran a business, "Dogs of Velvet and Steel," and an associated Web site, through which he sold videos of pit bulls engaging in dogfights and attacking other animals. Among these videos were Japan Pit Fights and Pick-A-Winna: A Pit Bull Documentary, which include contemporary footage of dogfights in Japan (where such conduct is allegedly legal) as well as footage of American

---

"(2) the term 'State' means each of the several States, the District of Columbia, the Commonwealth of Puerto Rico, the Virgin Islands, Guam, American Samoa, the Commonwealth of the Northern Mariana Islands, and any other commonwealth, territory, or possession of the United States."

dogfights from the 1960's and 1970's.[2] A third video, Catch Dogs and Country Living, depicts the use of pit bulls to hunt wild boar, as well as a "gruesome" scene of a pit bull attacking a domestic farm pig. 533 F. 3d 218, 221 (CA3 2008) (en banc). On the basis of these videos, Stevens was indicted on three counts of violating §48.

Stevens moved to dismiss the indictment, arguing that §48 is facially invalid under the First Amendment. The District Court denied the motion. It held that the depictions subject to §48, like obscenity or child pornography, are categorically unprotected by the First Amendment. 2:04–cr–00051–ANB (WD Pa., Nov. 10, 2004), App. to Pet. for Cert. 65a–71a. It went on to hold that §48 is not substantially overbroad, because the exceptions clause sufficiently narrows the statute to constitutional applications. Id., at 71a–75a. The jury convicted Stevens on all counts, and the District Court sentenced him to three concurrent sentences of 37 months' imprisonment, followed by three years of supervised release. App. 37.

The en banc Third Circuit, over a three-judge dissent, declared §48 facially unconstitutional and vacated Stevens's conviction. 533 F. 3d 218. The Court of Appeals first held that §48 regulates speech that is protected by the First Amendment. The Court declined to recognize a new category of unprotected speech for depictions of animal cruelty, id., at 224, and n. 6, and rejected the Government's analogy between animal cruelty depictions and child pornography, id., at 224–232.

The Court of Appeals then held that §48 could not survive strict scrutiny as a content-based regulation of protected speech. Id., at 232. It found that the statute lacked a compelling government interest and was neither narrowly tailored to preventing animal cruelty nor the least restrictive means of doing so. Id., at 232–235. It therefore held §48 facially invalid.

In an extended footnote, the Third Circuit noted that §48 "might also be unconstitutionally overbroad," because it "potentially covers a great deal of constitutionally protected speech" and "sweeps [too] widely" to be limited only by prosecutorial discretion. Id., at 235, n. 16. But the Court of Appeals declined to rest its analysis on this ground.

We granted certiorari. 556 U.S. (2009).

---

2. The Government contends that these dogfights were unlawful at the time they occurred, while Stevens disputes the assertion. Reply Brief for United States 25, n.14 (hereinafter Reply Brief); Brief for Respondent 44, n.18.

II

The Government's primary submission is that §48 necessarily complies with the Constitution because the banned depictions of animal cruelty, as a class, are categorically unprotected by the First Amendment. We disagree.

The First Amendment provides that "Congress shall make no law . . . abridging the freedom of speech." "[A]s a general matter, the First Amendment means that government has no power to restrict expression because of its message, its ideas, its subject matter, or its content." *Ashcroft* v. *American Civil Liberties Union*, 535 U. S. 564, 573 (2002) (internal quotation marks omitted). Section 48 explicitly regulates expression based on content: The statute restricts "visual [and] auditory depiction[s]," such as photographs, videos, or sound recordings, depending on whether they depict conduct in which a living animal is intentionally harmed. As such, §48 is "'presumptively invalid,' and the Government bears the burden to rebut that presumption." *United States* v. *Playboy Entertainment Group, Inc.*, 529 U. S. 803, 817 (2000) (quoting *R. A. V.* v. *St. Paul*, 505 U. S. 377, 382 (1992); citation omitted).

"From 1791 to the present," however, the First Amendment has "permitted restrictions upon the content of speech in a few limited areas," and has never "include[d] a freedom to disregard these traditional limitations." *Id.*, at 382–383. These "historic and traditional categories long familiar to the bar," *Simon & Schuster, Inc.* v. *Members of N. Y. State Crime Victims Bd.*, 502 U. S. 105, 127 (1991) (KENNEDY, J., concurring in judgment)—including obscenity, *Roth* v. *United States*, 354 U. S. 476, 483 (1957), defamation, *Beauharnais* v. *Illinois*, 343 U. S. 250, 254–255 (1952), fraud, *Virginia Bd. of Pharmacy* v. *Virginia Citizens Consumer Council, Inc.*, 425 U. S. 748, 771 (1976), incitement, *Brandenburg* v. *Ohio*, 395 U. S. 444, 447–449 (1969) (*per curiam*), and speech integral to criminal conduct, *Giboney* v. *Empire Storage & Ice Co.*, 336 U. S. 490, 498 (1949)—are "well-defined and narrowly limited classes of speech, the prevention and punishment of which have never been thought to raise any Constitutional problem." *Chaplinsky* v. *New Hampshire*, 315 U. S. 568, 571–572 (1942).

The Government argues that "depictions of animal cruelty" should be added to the list. It contends that depictions of "illegal acts of animal cruelty" that are "made, sold, or possessed for commercial gain" necessarily "lack expressive value," and may accordingly "be regulated as *unprotected* speech." Brief for United States 10 (emphasis added). The claim is not just that Congress may regulate depictions of animal cruelty subject to the First Amendment, but

that these depictions are outside the reach of that Amendment altogether—
that they fall into a "'First Amendment Free Zone.'" *Board of Airport Comm'rs
of Los Angeles* v. *Jews for Jesus, Inc.*, 482 U. S. 569, 574 (1987).

As the Government notes, the prohibition of animal cruelty itself has a
long history in American law, starting with the early settlement of the Colonies.
Reply Brief 12, n. 8; see, *e.g.,* The Body of Liberties §92 (Mass. Bay Colony
1641), reprinted in American Historical Documents 1000–1904, 43 Harvard
Classics 66, 79 (C. Eliot ed. 1910) ("No man shall exercise any Tirranny or
Crueltie towards any bruite Creature which are usuallie kept for man's use").
But we are unaware of any similar tradition excluding *depictions* of animal
cruelty from "the freedom of speech" codified in the First Amendment, and
the Government points us to none.

The Government contends that "historical evidence" about the reach of
the First Amendment is not "a necessary prerequisite for regulation today,"
Reply Brief 12, n. 8, and that categories of speech may be exempted from the
First Amendment's protection without any long-settled tradition of subjecting that speech to regulation. Instead, the Government points to Congress's
"'legislative judgment that . . . depictions of animals being intentionally tortured and killed [are] of such minimal redeeming value as to render [them]
unworthy of First Amendment protection,'" Brief for United States 23 (quoting
533 F. 3d, at 243(Cowen, J., dissenting)), and asks the Court to uphold the ban
on the same basis. The Government thus proposes that a claim of categorical
exclusion should be considered under a simple balancing test: "Whether a
given category of speech enjoys First Amendment protection depends upon
a categorical balancing of the value of the speech against its societal costs."
Brief for United States 8; see also *id.,* at 12.

As a free-floating test for First Amendment coverage, that sentence is
startling and dangerous. The First Amendment's guarantee of free speech
does not extend only to categories of speech that survive an ad hoc balancing of relative social costs and benefits. The First Amendment itself reflects a
judgment by the American people that the benefits of its restrictions on the
Government outweigh the costs. Our Constitution forecloses any attempt to
revise that judgment simply on the basis that some speech is not worth it.
The Constitution is not a document "prescribing limits, and declaring that
those limits may be passed at pleasure." *Marbury* v. *Madison*, 1 Cranch 137,
178 (1803).

To be fair to the Government, its view did not emerge from a vacuum. As the Government correctly notes, this Court has often *described* historically unprotected categories of speech as being "'of such slight social value as a step to truth that any benefit that may be derived from them is clearly outweighed by the social interest in order and morality.'" *R. A. V., supra*, at 383 (quoting *Chaplinsky, supra*, at 572). In *New York* v. *Ferber*, 458 U. S. 747 (1982), we noted that within these categories of unprotected speech, "the evil to be restricted so overwhelmingly outweighs the expressive interests, if any, at stake, that no process of case-by-case adjudication is required," because "the balance of competing interests is clearly struck," *id.,* at 763–764. The Government derives its proposed test from these descriptions in our precedents. See Brief for United States 12–13.

But such descriptions are just that—descriptive. They do not set forth a test that may be applied as a general matter to permit the Government to imprison any speaker so long as his speech is deemed valueless or unnecessary, or so long as an ad hoc calculus of costs and benefits tilts in a statute's favor.

When we have identified categories of speech as fully outside the protection of the First Amendment, it has not been on the basis of a simple cost-benefit analysis. In *Ferber*, for example, we classified child pornography as such a category, 458 U. S., at 763. We noted that the State of New York had a compelling interest in protecting children from abuse, and that the value of using children in these works (as opposed to simulated conduct or adult actors) was *de minimis. Id.,* at 756–757, 762. But our decision did not rest on this "balance of competing interests" alone. *Id.,* at 764. We made clear that *Ferber* presented a special case: The market for child pornography was "intrinsically related" to the underlying abuse, and was therefore "an integral part of the production of such materials, an activity illegal throughout the Nation." *Id.,* at 759, 761. As we noted, "'[i]t rarely has been suggested that the constitutional freedom for speech and press extends its immunity to speech or writing used as an integral part of conduct in violation of a valid criminal statute.'" *Id.,* at 761–762 (quoting *Giboney, supra*, at 498). *Ferber* thus grounded its analysis in a previously recognized, long-established category of unprotected speech, and our subsequent decisions have shared this understanding. See *Osborne* v. *Ohio*, 495 U. S. 103, 110 (1990) (describing *Ferber* as finding "persuasive" the argument that the advertising and sale of child pornography was "an integral part" of its unlawful production (internal quotation marks omitted)); *Ashcroft* v. *Free Speech Coalition*, 535 U. S. 234, 249–250 (2002) (noting that distribution and sale "were intrinsically related to the sexual abuse of children," giving the speech at issue "a proximate link to the crime from which it came" (internal quotation marks omitted)).

Our decisions in *Ferber* and other cases cannot be taken as establishing a freewheeling authority to declare new categories of speech outside the scope of the First Amendment. Maybe there are some categories of speech that have been historically unprotected, but have not yet been specifically identified or discussed as such in our case law. But if so, there is no evidence that "depictions of animal cruelty" is among them. We need not foreclose the future recognition of such additional categories to reject the Government's highly manipulable balancing test as a means of identifying them.

III

Because we decline to carve out from the First Amendment any novel exception for §48, we review Stevens's First Amendment challenge under our existing doctrine.

A

Stevens challenged §48 on its face, arguing that any conviction secured under the statute would be unconstitutional. The court below decided the case on that basis, 533 F. 3d, at 231, n. 13, and we granted the Solicitor General's petition for certiorari to determine "whether 18 U. S. C. 48 is facially invalid under the Free Speech Clause of the First Amendment," Pet. for Cert. i.

To succeed in a typical facial attack, Stevens would have to establish "that no set of circumstances exists under which [§48] would be valid," *United States* v. *Salerno*, 481 U. S. 739, 745 (1987), or that the statute lacks any "plainly legitimate sweep," *Washington* v. *Glucksberg*, 521 U. S. 702, 740, n. 7 (1997) (STEVENS, J., concurring in judgments) (internal quotation marks omitted). Which standard applies in a typical case is a matter of dispute that we need not and do not address, and neither *Salerno* nor *Glucksberg* is a speech case. Here the Government asserts that Stevens cannot prevail because §48 is plainly legitimate as applied to crush videos and animal fighting depictions. Deciding this case through a traditional facial analysis would require us to resolve whether these applications of §48 are in fact consistent with the Constitution.

In the First Amendment context, however, this Court recognizes "a second type of facial challenge," whereby a law may be invalidated as overbroad if "a substantial number of its applications are unconstitutional, judged in relation to the statute's plainly legitimate sweep." *Washington State Grange* v. *Washington State Republican Party*, 552 U. S. 442, 449, n. 6 (2008) (internal quotation marks omitted). Stevens argues that §48 applies to common depictions of ordinary and lawful activities, and that these depictions constitute the vast majority of materials subject to the statute. Brief for Respondent 22–25. The Government makes no effort to defend such a broad ban as constitutional. Instead, the Government's entire defense of §48 rests on interpreting the statute as narrowly limited to specific types of "extreme" material. Brief for United States 8. As the parties have presented the issue, therefore, the constitutionality of §48 hinges on how broadly it is construed. It is to that question that we now turn.[3]

B

As we explained two Terms ago, "[t]he first step in overbreadth analysis is to construe the challenged statute; it is impossible to determine whether a statute reaches too far without first knowing what the statute covers." *United States* v. *Williams*, 553 U. S. 285, 293 (2008). Because §48 is a federal statute, there is no need to defer to a state court's authority to interpret its own law.

We read §48 to create a criminal prohibition of alarming breadth. To begin with, the text of the statute's ban on a "depiction of animal cruelty" nowhere requires that the depicted conduct be cruel. That text applies to "any . . . depiction" in which "a living animal is intentionally maimed, mutilated, tor-

---

3   The dissent contends that because there has not been a ruling on the validity of the statute as applied to Stevens, our consideration of his facial overbreadth claim is premature. Post, at 1, and n.1, 2–3 (opinion of ALITO, J.). Whether or not that conclusion follows, here no as-applied claim has been preserved. Neither court below construed Stevens's briefs as adequately developing a separate attack on a defined subset of the statute's applications (say, dogfighting videos). See 533 F. 3d 218, 231, n.13 (CA3 2008) (en banc) ("Stevens brings a facial challenge to the statute"); App. to Pet. for Cert. 65a, 74a. Neither did the Government, see Brief for United States in No. 05–2497 (CA3), p. 28 (opposing "the appellant's facial challenge"); accord, Brief for United States 4. The sentence in Stevens's appellate brief mentioning his unrelated sufficiency-of-the-evidence challenge hardly developed a First Amendment as-applied claim. See post, at 1, n.1. Stevens's constitutional argument is a general one. And unlike the challengers in Washington State Grange, Stevens does not "rest on factual assumptions . . . that can be evaluated only in the context of an as-applied challenge." 552 U. S., at 444.

tured, wounded, or killed." §48(c)(1). "[M]aimed, mutilated, [and] tortured" convey cruelty, but "wounded" or "killed" do not suggest any such limitation.

The Government contends that the terms in the definition should be read to require the additional element of "accompanying acts of cruelty." Reply Brief 6; see also Tr. of Oral Arg. 17–19. (The dissent hinges on the same assumption. See *post,* at 6, 9.) The Government bases this argument on the definiendum, "depiction of animal cruelty," cf. *Leocal* v. *Ashcroft,* 543 U. S. 1, 11 (2004), and on "'the commonsense canon of *noscitur a sociis.*'" Reply Brief 7 (quoting *Williams,* 553 U. S., at 294). As that canon recognizes, an ambiguous term may be "given more precise content by the neighboring words with which it is associated." *Ibid.* Likewise, an unclear definitional phrase may take meaning from the term to be defined, see *Leocal, supra,* at 11 (interpreting a "'substantial risk'" of the "us[e]" of "physical force" as part of the definition of "'crime of violence'").

But the phrase "wounded . . . or killed" at issue here contains little ambiguity. The Government's opening brief properly applies the ordinary meaning of these words, stating for example that to "'kill' is 'to deprive of life.'" Brief for United States 14 (quoting Webster's Third New International Dictionary 1242 (1993)). We agree that "wounded" and "killed" should be read according to their ordinary meaning. Cf. *Engine Mfrs. Assn.* v. *South Coast Air Quality Management Dist.,* 541 U. S. 246, 252 (2004). Nothing about that meaning requires cruelty.

While not requiring cruelty, §48 does require that the depicted conduct be "illegal." But this requirement does not limit §48 along the lines the Government suggests. There are myriad federal and state laws concerning the proper treatment of animals, but many of them are not designed to guard against animal cruelty. Protections of endangered species, for example, restrict even the humane "wound[ing] or kill[ing]" of "living animal[s]." §48(c)(1). Livestock regulations are often designed to protect the health of human beings, and hunting and fishing rules (seasons, licensure, bag limits, weight requirements) can be designed to raise revenue, preserve animal populations, or prevent accidents. The text of §48(c) draws no distinction based on the reason the intentional killing of an animal is made illegal, and includes, for example, the humane slaughter of a stolen cow.[4]

4   The citations in the dissent's appendix are beside the point. The cited statutes stand for the proposition that hunting is not covered by animal cruelty laws. But the reach of §48 is, as we have explained, not restricted to depictions of conduct that violates a law specifically directed at animal cruelty. It simply requires that the depicted conduct be "illegal." §48(c)(1). The Government implicitly admits

What is more, the application of §48 to depictions of illegal conduct extends to conduct that is illegal in only a single jurisdiction. Under subsection (c)(1), the depicted conduct need only be illegal in "the State in which the creation, sale, or possession takes place, regardless of whether the . . . wounding . . . or killing took place in [that] State." A depiction of entirely lawful conduct runs afoul of the ban if that depiction later finds its way into another State where the same conduct is unlawful. This provision greatly expands the scope of §48, because although there may be "a broad societal consensus" against cruelty to animals, Brief for United States 2, there is substantial disagreement on what types of conduct are properly regarded as cruel. Both views about cruelty to animals and regulations having no connection to cruelty vary widely from place to place.

In the District of Columbia, for example, all hunting is unlawful. D. C. Munic. Regs., tit. 19, §1560 (2009). Other jurisdictions permit or encourage hunting, and there is an enormous national market for hunting-related depictions in which a living animal is intentionally killed. Hunting periodicals have circulations in the hundreds of thousands or millions, see Mediaweek, Sept. 29, 2008, p. 28, and hunting television programs, videos, and Web sites are equally popular, see Brief for Professional Outdoor Media Association et al. as *Amici Curiae* 9–10. The demand for hunting depictions exceeds the estimated demand for crush videos or animal fighting depictions by several orders of magnitude. Compare *ibid.* and Brief for National Rifle Association of America, Inc., as *Amicus Curiae* 12 (hereinafter NRA Brief) (estimating that hunting magazines alone account for $135 million in annual retail sales) with Brief for United States 43–44, 46 (suggesting $1 million in crush video sales per year, and noting that Stevens earned $57,000 from his videos). Nonetheless, because the statute allows each jurisdiction to export its laws to the rest of the country, §48(a) extends to *any* magazine or video depicting lawful hunting, so long as that depiction is sold within the Nation's Capital.

Those seeking to comply with the law thus face a bewildering maze of regulations from at least 56 separate jurisdictions. Some States permit hunting with crossbows, Ga. Code Ann. §27–3–4(1) (2007); Va. Code Ann. §29.1–519(A)(6) (Lexis 2008 Cum. Supp.), while others forbid it, Ore. Admin. Reg.

---

as much, arguing that "instructional videos for hunting" are saved by the statute's exceptions clause, not that they fall outside the prohibition in the first place. Reply Brief 6.

635–065–0725 (2009), or restrict it only to the disabled, N. Y. Envir. Conserv. Law Ann. §11–0901(16) (West 2005). Missouri allows the "canned" hunting of ungulates held in captivity, Mo. Code Regs. Ann., tit. 3, 10–9.560(1), but Montana restricts such hunting to certain bird species, Mont. Admin. Rule 12.6.1202(1)(2007). The sharp-tailed grouse may be hunted in Idaho, but not in Washington. Compare Idaho Admin. Code §13.01.09.606 (2009) with Wash. Admin. Code §232–28–342 (2009).

The disagreements among the States—and the "commonwealth[s], territor[ies], or possession[s] of the United States," 18 U. S. C. §48(c)(2)—extend well beyond hunting. State agricultural regulations permit different methods of livestock slaughter in different places or as applied to different animals. Compare, *e.g.,* Fla. Stat. §828.23(5) (2007)(excluding poultry from humane slaughter requirements) with Cal. Food & Agric. Code Ann. §19501(b) (West 2001) (including some poultry). California has recently banned cutting or "docking" the tails of dairy cattle, which other States permit. 2009 Cal. Legis. Serv. Ch. 344 (S. B. 135) (West). Even cockfighting, long considered immoral in much of America, see *Barnes* v. *Glen Theatre, Inc.,* 501 U. S. 560, 575 (1991) (SCALIA, J., concurring in judgment), is legal in Puerto Rico, see 15 Laws P. R. Ann. §301 (Supp. 2008); *Posadas de Puerto Rico Associates* v. *Tourism Co. of P. R.,* 478 U. S. 328, 342 (1986), and was legal in Louisiana until 2008, see La. Stat. Ann. §14:102.23 (West) (effective Aug. 15, 2008). An otherwise-lawful image of any of these practices, if sold or possessed for commercial gain within a State that happens to forbid the practice, falls within the prohibition of §48(a).

C

The only thing standing between defendants who sell such depictions and five years in federal prison—other than the mercy of a prosecutor—is the statute's exceptions clause. Subsection (b) exempts from prohibition "any depiction that has serious religious, political, scientific, educational, journalistic, historical, or artistic value." The Government argues that this clause substantially narrows the statute's reach: News reports about animal cruelty have "journalistic" value; pictures of bullfights in Spain have "historical" value; and instructional hunting videos have "educational" value. Reply Brief 6. Thus, the Government argues, §48 reaches only crush videos, depictions of animal fighting (other than Spanish bullfighting, see Brief for United States 47–48), and perhaps other depictions of "extreme acts of animal cruelty." *Id.,* at 41.

The Government's attempt to narrow the statutory ban, however, requires an unrealistically broad reading of the exceptions clause. As the Government reads the clause, any material with "redeeming societal value," id., at 9, 16, 23, "'at least some minimal value,'" Reply Brief 6 (quoting H. R. Rep., at 4), or anything more than "scant social value," Reply Brief 11, is excluded under §48(b). But the text says "serious" value, and "serious" should be taken seriously. We decline the Government's invitation— advanced for the first time in this Court—to regard as "serious" anything that is not "scant." (Or, as the dissent puts it, "'trifling.'" Post, at 6.) As the Government recognized below, "serious" ordinarily means a good bit more. The District Court's jury instructions required value that is "significant and of great import," App. 132, and the Government defended these instructions as properly relying on "a commonly accepted meaning of the word 'serious,'" Brief for United States in No. 05–2497 (CA3), p. 50.

Quite apart from the requirement of "serious" value in §48(b), the excepted speech must also fall within one of the enumerated categories. Much speech does not. Most hunting videos, for example, are not obviously instructional in nature, except in the sense that all life is a lesson. According to Safari Club International and the Congressional Sportsmen's Foundation, many popular videos "have primarily entertainment value" and are designed to "entertai[n] the viewer, marke[t] hunting equipment, or increas[e] the hunting community." Brief for Safari Club International et al. as Amici Curiae 12. The National Rifle Association agrees that "much of the content of hunting media . . . is merely recreational in nature." NRA Brief 28. The Government offers no principled explanation why these depictions of hunting or depictions of Spanish bullfights would be inherently valuable while those of Japanese dogfights are not. The dissent contends that hunting depictions must have serious value because hunting has serious value, in a way that dogfights presumably do not. Post, at 6–8. But §48(b) addresses the value of the depictions, not of the underlying activity. There is simply no adequate reading of the exceptions clause that results in the statute's banning only the depictions the Government would like to ban.

The Government explains that the language of §48(b) was largely drawn from our opinion in Miller v. California, 413 U. S. 15 (1973), which excepted from its definition of obscenity any material with "serious literary, artistic, political, or scientific value," id., at 24. See Reply Brief 8, 9, and n. 5. According to the Government, this incorporation of the *Miller* standard into §48 is therefore surely enough to answer any First Amendment objection. Reply Brief 8–9.

In *Miller* we held that "serious" value shields depictions of sex from regulation as obscenity. 413 U. S., at 24–25. Limiting *Miller*'s exception to "serious" value ensured that"'[a] quotation from Voltaire in the flyleaf of a book [would] not constitutionally redeem an otherwise obscene publication.'" *Id.*, at 25, n. 7 (quoting *Kois* v. *Wisconsin*, 408 U. S. 229, 231 (1972) (*per curiam*)). We did not, however, determine that serious value could be used as a general precondition to protecting *other* types of speech in the first place. *Most* of what we say to one another lacks "religious, political, scientific, educational, journalistic, historical, or artistic value" (let alone serious value), but it is still sheltered from government regulation. Even "'[w]holly neutral futilities . . . come under the protection of free speech as fully as do Keats' poems or Donne's sermons.'" *Cohen* v. *California*, 403 U. S. 15, 25 (1971) (quoting *Winters* v. *New York*, 333 U. S. 507, 528 (1948) (Frankfurter, J., dissenting); alteration in original).

Thus, the protection of the First Amendment presumptively extends to many forms of speech that do not qualify for the serious-value exception of §48(b), but nonetheless fall within the broad reach of §48(c).

D

Not to worry, the Government says: The Executive Branch construes §48 to reach only "extreme" cruelty, Brief for United States 8, and it "neither has brought nor will bring a prosecution for anything less," Reply Brief 6–7. The Government hits this theme hard, invoking its prosecutorial discretion several times. See *id.*, at 6–7, 10, and n. 6, 19, 22. But the First Amendment protects against the Government; it does not leave us at the mercy of *noblesse oblige.* We would not uphold an unconstitutional statute merely because the Government promised to use it responsibly. Cf. *Whitman* v. *American Trucking Assns., Inc.*, 531 U. S. 457, 473 (2001).

This prosecution is itself evidence of the danger in putting faith in government representations of prosecutorial restraint. When this legislation was enacted, the Executive Branch announced that it would interpret §48 as covering only depictions "of wanton cruelty to animals designed to appeal to a prurient interest in sex." See Statement by President William J. Clinton upon Signing H. R. 1887, 34 Weekly Comp. Pres. Doc. 2557 (Dec. 9, 1999). No one suggests that the videos in this case fit that description. The Government's assurance that it will apply §48 far more restrictively than its language provides is pertinent only as an implicit acknowledgment of the potential constitutional problems with a more natural reading.

Nor can we rely upon the canon of construction that "ambiguous statutory language [should] be construed to avoid serious constitutional doubts." *FCC* v. *Fox Television Stations, Inc.*, 556 U. S. ___, ___ (2009) (slip op., at 12). "[T]his Court may impose a limiting construction on a statute only if it is 'readily susceptible' to such a construction." *Reno* v. *American Civil Liberties Union*, 521 U. S. 844, 884 (1997). We "'will not rewrite a . . . law to conform it to constitutional requirements,'" *id.*, at 884–885 (quoting *Virginia* v. *American Booksellers Assn., Inc.*, 484 U. S. 383, 397 (1988); omission in original), for doing so would constitute a "serious invasion of the legislative domain," *United States* v. *Treasury Employees*, 513 U. S. 454, 479, n. 26 (1995), and sharply diminish Congress's "incentive to draft a narrowly tailored law in the first place," *Osborne*, 495 U. S., at 121. To read §48 as the Government desires requires rewriting, not just reinterpretation.

* * *

Our construction of §48 decides the constitutional question; the Government makes no effort to defend the constitutionality of §48 as applied beyond crush videos and depictions of animal fighting. It argues that those particular depictions are intrinsically related to criminal conduct or are analogous to obscenity (if not themselves obscene), and that the ban on such speech is narrowly tailored to reinforce restrictions on the underlying conduct, prevent additional crime arising from the depictions, or safeguard public mores. But the Government nowhere attempts to extend these arguments to depictions of any other activities—depictions that are presumptively protected by the First Amendment but that remain subject to the criminal sanctions of §48.

Nor does the Government seriously contest that the presumptively impermissible applications of §48 (properly construed) far outnumber any permissible ones. However "growing" and "lucrative" the markets for crush videos and dogfighting depictions might be, see Brief for United States 43, 46 (internal quotation marks omitted), they are dwarfed by the market for other depictions, such as hunting magazines and videos, that we have determined to be within the scope of §48. See *supra*, at 13–14. We therefore need not and do not decide whether a statute limited to crush videos or other depictions of extreme animal cruelty would be constitutional. We hold only that §48 is not so limited but is instead substantially overbroad, and therefore invalid under the First Amendment.

The judgment of the United States Court of Appeals for the Third Circuit is affirmed.

It is so ordered.

SUPREME COURT OF THE UNITED STATES

No. 08–769

UNITED STATES, PETITIONER *v.* ROBERT J. STEVENS

ON WRIT OF CERTIORARI TO THE UNITED STATES COURT OF APPEALS FOR THE THIRD CIRCUIT

[April 20, 2010]

JUSTICE ALITO, dissenting.

The Court strikes down in its entirety a valuable statute, 18 U. S. C. §48, that was enacted not to suppress speech, but to prevent horrific acts of animal cruelty—in particular, the creation and commercial exploitation of "crush videos," a form of depraved entertainment that has no social value. The Court's approach, which has the practical effect of legalizing the sale of such videos and is thus likely to spur a resumption of their production, is unwarranted. Respondent was convicted under §48 for selling videos depicting dogfights. On appeal, he argued, among other things, that §48 is unconstitutional as applied to the facts of this case, and he highlighted features of those videos that might distinguish them from other dogfight videos brought to our attention.[5] The Court of Appeals—incorrectly, in my view—declined to decide whether §48 is unconstitutional as applied to respondent's videos and instead reached out to hold that the statute is facially invalid. Today's decision does not en-

---

5   Respondent argued at length that the evidence was insufficient to prove that the particular videos he sold lacked any serious scientific, educational, or historical value and thus fell outside the exception in §48(b). See Brief for Appellant in No. 05–2497 (CA3), pp. 72–79. He added that, if the evidence in this case was held to be sufficient to take his videos outside the scope of the exception, then "this case presents . . . a situation" in which "a constitutional violation occurs." Id., at 71. See also id., at 47 ("The applicability of 18 U. S. C. §48 to speech which is not a crush video or an appeal to some prurient sexual interest constitutes a restriction of protected speech, and an unwarranted violation of the First Amendment's free speech guarantee"); Brief for Respondent 55 ("Stevens' speech does not fit within any existing category of unprotected, prosecutable speech"); id., at 57 ("[T]he record as a whole demonstrates that Stevens' speech cannot constitutionally be punished"). Contrary to the Court, ante, at 10–11, n. 3 (citing 533 F. 3d 218, 231, n. 13 (CA3 2008) (en banc)), I see no suggestion in the opinion of the Court of Appeals that respondent did not preserve an as applied challenge.

dorse the Court of Appeals' reasoning, but it nevertheless strikes down §48 using what has been aptly termed the "strong medicine" of the overbreadth doctrine, *United States* v. *Williams*, 553 U. S. 285, 293 (2008) (internal quotation marks omitted), a potion that generally should be administered only as "a last resort." *Los Angeles Police Dept.* v. *United Reporting Publishing Corp.*, 528 U. S. 32, 39 (1999) (internal quotation marks omitted).

Instead of applying the doctrine of overbreadth, I would vacate the decision below and instruct the Court of Appeals on remand to decide whether the videos that respondent sold are constitutionally protected. If the question of overbreadth is to be decided, however, I do not think the present record supports the Court's conclusion that §48 bans a substantial quantity of protected speech.

I

A party seeking to challenge the constitutionality of a statute generally must show that the statute violates the party's own rights. *New York* v. *Ferber*, 458 U. S. 747, 767 (1982). The First Amendment overbreadth doctrine carves out a narrow exception to that general rule. See *id.*, at 768; *Broadrick* v. *Oklahoma*, 413 U. S. 601, 611–612 (1973). Because an overly broad law may deter constitutionally protected speech, the overbreadth doctrine allows a party to whom the law may constitutionally be applied to challenge the statute on the ground that it violates the First Amendment rights of others. See, *e.g.*, *Board of Trustees of State Univ. of N. Y.* v. *Fox*, 492 U. S. 469, 483 (1989) ("Ordinarily, the principal advantage of the overbreadth doctrine for a litigant is that it enables him to benefit from the statute's unlawful application *to someone else*"); see also *Ohralik* v. *Ohio State Bar Assn.*, 436 U. S. 447, 462, n. 20 (1978) (describing the doctrine as one "under which a person may challenge a statute that infringes protected speech even if the statute constitutionally might be applied to him").

The "strong medicine" of overbreadth invalidation need not and generally should not be administered when the statute under attack is unconstitutional as applied to the challenger before the court. As we said in *Fox, supra,* at 484–485, "[i]t is not the usual judicial practice, . . . nor do we consider it generally desirable, to proceed to an overbreadth issue unnecessarily—that is, before it is determined that the statute would be valid as applied." Accord, *New York State Club Assn., Inc.* v. *City of New York*, 487 U. S. 1, 11 (1988); see also *Broadrick, supra,* at 613; *United Reporting Publishing Corp., supra,* at 45 (STEVENS, J., dissenting).

I see no reason to depart here from the generally preferred procedure of considering the question of overbreadth only as a last resort.[6] Because the Court has addressed the overbreadth question, however, I will explain why I do not think that the record supports the conclusion that §48, when properly interpreted, is overly broad.

II

The overbreadth doctrine "strike[s] a balance between competing social costs." *Williams,* 553 U. S., at 292. Specifically, the doctrine seeks to balance the "harmful effects" of "invalidating a law that in some of its applications is perfectly constitutional" against the possibility that "the threat of enforcement of an overbroad law [will] dete[r] people from engaging in constitutionally protected speech." *Ibid.* "In order to maintain an appropriate balance, we have vigorously enforced the requirement that a statute's overbreadth be *substantial,* not only in an absolute sense, but also relative to the statute's plainly legitimate sweep." *Ibid.*

In determining whether a statute's overbreadth is substantial, we consider a statute's application to real-world conduct, not fanciful hypotheticals. See, *e.g., id.,* at 301– 302; see also *Ferber, supra,* at 773; *Houston* v. *Hill,* 482 U. S. 451, 466–467 (1987). Accordingly, we have repeatedly emphasized that an overbreadth claimant bears the burden of demonstrating, "from the text of [the law] *and from actual fact,*" that substantial overbreadth exists. *Virginia* v. *Hicks,* 539 U. S. 113, 122 (2003) (quoting *New York State Club Assn., supra,* at 14; emphasis added; internal quotation marks omitted; alteration in original). Similarly, "there must be a *realistic danger* that the statute itself will significantly compromise recognized First Amendment protections of parties not before the Court for it to be facially challenged on overbreadth grounds." *Members of City Council of Los Angeles* v. *Taxpayers for Vincent,* 466 U. S. 789, 801 (1984) (emphasis added).

III

In holding that §48 violates the overbreadth rule, the Court declines to decide whether, as the Government maintains, §48 is constitutional as applied to

6   For the reasons set forth below, this is not a case in which the challenged statute is unconstitutional in all or almost all of its applications.

two broad categories of depictions that exist in the real world: crush videos and depictions of deadly animal fights. See *ante*, at 10, 19. Instead, the Court tacitly assumes for the sake of argument that §48 is valid as applied to these depictions, but the Court concludes that §48 reaches too much protected speech to survive. The Court relies primarily on depictions of hunters killing or wounding game and depictions of animals being slaughtered for food. I address the Court's examples below.

A

I turn first to depictions of hunting. As the Court notes, photographs and videos of hunters shooting game are common. See *ante*, at 13–14. But hunting is legal in all 50 States, and §48 applies only to a depiction of conduct that is illegal in the jurisdiction in which the depiction is created, sold, or possessed. §§48(a), (c). Therefore, in all 50 States, the creation, sale, or possession for sale of the vast majority of hunting depictions indisputably falls outside §48's reach.

Straining to find overbreadth, the Court suggests that §48 prohibits the sale or possession in the District of Columbia of any depiction of hunting because the District—undoubtedly because of its urban character—does not permit hunting within its boundaries. *Ante*, at 13. The Court also suggests that, because some States prohibit a particular type of hunting (*e.g.*, hunting with a crossbow or "canned" hunting) or the hunting of a particular animal (*e.g.*, the "sharp-tailed grouse"), §48 makes it illegal for persons in such States to sell or possess for sale a depiction of hunting that was perfectly legal in the State in which the hunting took place. See *ante*, at 12–14.

The Court's interpretation is seriously flawed. "When a federal court is dealing with a federal statute challenged as overbroad, it should, of course, construe the statute to avoid constitutional problems, if the statute is subject to such a limiting construction." *Ferber*, 458 U. S., at 769, n.24. See also *Williams, supra*, at 307 (STEVENS, J., concurring) ("[T]o the extent the statutory text alone is unclear, our duty to avoid constitutional objections makes it especially appropriate to look beyond the text in order to ascertain the intent of its drafters").

Applying this canon, I would hold that §48 does not apply to depictions of hunting. First, because §48 targets depictions of "animal cruelty," I would interpret that term to apply only to depictions involving acts of animal cruelty

The Supreme Court Speaks

as defined by applicable state or federal law, not to depictions of acts that
happen to be illegal for reasons having nothing to do with the prevention of
animal cruelty. See *ante*, at 12–13 (interpreting "[t]he text of §48(c)"to ban
a depiction of "the humane slaughter of a stolen cow"). Virtually all state
laws prohibiting animal cruelty either expressly define the term "animal" to
exclude wildlife or else specifically exempt lawful hunting activities,[7] so the
statutory prohibition set forth in §48(a) may reasonably be interpreted not
to reach most if not all hunting depictions.

Second, even if the hunting of wild animals were otherwise covered
by §48(a), I would hold that hunting depictions fall within the exception
in §48(b) for depictions that have "serious" (*i.e.*, not "trifling"[8]) "scientific,"
"educational," or "historical" value. While there are certainly those who find
hunting objectionable, the predominant view in this country has long been
that hunting serves many important values, and it is clear that Congress
shares that view. Since 1972, when Congress called upon the President to
designate a National Hunting and Fishing Day, see S. J. Res. 117, 92d Cong.,
2d Sess. (1972), 86 Stat. 133, Presidents have regularly issued proclamations
extolling the values served by hunting. See Presidential Proclamation No.
8421, 74 Fed. Reg. 49305 (Pres. Obama 2009) (hunting and fishing are "age-
less pursuits" that promote "the conservation and restoration of numerous
species and their natural habitats"); Presidential Proclamation No. 8295, 73
Fed. Reg. 57233 (Pres. Bush 2008) (hunters and anglers "add to our heritage
and keep our wildlife populations healthy and strong," and "are among our
foremost conservationists"); Presidential Proclamation No. 7822, 69 Fed. Reg.
59539 (Pres. Bush 2004) (hunting and fishing are "an important part of our
Nation's heritage," and "America's hunters and anglers represent the great

7   See Appendix, infra (citing statutes); B. Wagman, S. Waisman, & P. Frasch, Animal
     Law: Cases and Materials 92 (4th ed. 2010) ("Most anticruelty laws also include
     one or more exemptions," which often "exclud[e] from coverage (1) whole classes
     of animals, such as wildlife or farm animals, or (2) specific activities, such as
     hunting"); Note, Economics and Ethics in the Genetic Engineering of Animals,
     19 Harv. J. L. & Tech. 413, 432 (2006) ("Not surprisingly, state laws relating to
     the humane treatment of wildlife, including deer, elk, and waterfowl, are virtually
     non-existent").

8   Webster's Third New International Dictionary 2073 (1976); Random House
     Dictionary of the English Language 1303 (1966). While the term "serious" may
     also mean "weighty" or "important," ibid., we should adopt the former definition
     if necessary to avoid unconstitutionality.

spirit of our country"); Presidential Proclamation No.4682, 44 Fed. Reg. 53149 (Pres. Carter 1979) (hunting promotes conservation and an appreciation of "healthy recreation, peaceful solitude and closeness to nature"); Presidential Proclamation No. 4318, 39 Fed. Reg. 35315 (Pres. Ford 1974) (hunting furthers "appreciation and respect for nature" and preservation of the environment). Thus, it is widely thought that hunting has "scientific" value in that it promotes conservation, "historical" value in that it provides a link to past times when hunting played a critical role in daily life, and "educational" value in that it furthers the understanding and appreciation of nature and our country's past and instills valuable character traits. And if hunting itself is widely thought to serve these values, then it takes but a small additional step to conclude that depictions of hunting make a non-trivial contribution to the exchange of ideas. Accordingly, I would hold that hunting depictions fall comfortably within the exception set out in §48(b).

I do not have the slightest doubt that Congress, in enacting §48, had no intention of restricting the creation, sale, or possession of depictions of hunting. Proponents of the law made this point clearly. See H. R. Rep. No. 106–397, p. 8 (1999) (hereinafter H. R. Rep.) ("[D]epictions of ordinary hunting and fishing activities do not fall within the scope of the statute"); 145 Cong. Rec. 25894 (Oct. 19,1999) (Rep. McCollum) ("[T]he sale of depictions of legal activities, such as hunting and fishing, would not be illegal under this bill"); *id.*, at 25895 (Rep. Smith) ("[L]et us be clear as to what this legislation will not do. It will in no way prohibit hunting, fishing, or wildlife videos"). Indeed, even *opponents* acknowledged that §48 was not intended to reach ordinary hunting depictions. See *ibid.* (Rep. Scott); *id.*, at 25897 (Rep. Paul).

For these reasons, I am convinced that §48 has no application to depictions of hunting. But even if §48 did impermissibly reach the sale or possession of depictions of hunting in a few unusual situations (for example, the sale in Oregon of a depiction of hunting with a crossbow in Virginia or the sale in Washington State of the hunting of a sharp-tailed grouse in Idaho, see *ante*, at 14), those isolated applications would hardly show that §48 bans a substantial amount of protected speech.

B

Although the Court's overbreadth analysis rests primarily on the proposition that §48 substantially restricts the sale and possession of hunting depictions, the Court cites a few additional examples, including depictions of methods of slaughter and the docking of the tails of dairy cows. See *ante*, at 14–15.

Such examples do not show that the statute is substantially overbroad, for two reasons. First, as explained above, §48 can reasonably be construed to apply only to depictions involving acts of animal cruelty as defined by applicable state or federal law, and anti-cruelty laws do not ban the sorts of acts depicted in the Court's hypotheticals. See, *e.g.*, Idaho Code §25–3514 (Lexis 2000) ("No part of this chapter [prohibiting cruelty to animals] shall be construed as interfering with or allowing interference with . . . [t]he humane slaughter of any animal normally and commonly raised as food or for production of fiber . . . [or] [n]ormal or accepted practices of . . . animal husbandry"); Kan. Stat. Ann. § 21–4310(b) (2007) ("The provisions of this section shall not apply to . . . with respect to farm animals, normal or accepted practices of animal husbandry, including the normal and accepted practices for the slaughter of such animals"); Md. Crim. Law Code Ann. §10–603 (Lexis 2002) (sections prohibiting animal cruelty "do not apply to . . . customary and normal veterinary and agricultural husbandry practices, including dehorning, castration, tail docking, and limit feeding").

Second, nothing in the record suggests that any one has ever created, sold, or possessed for sale a depiction of the slaughter of food animals or of the docking of the tails of dairy cows that would not easily qualify under the exception set out in §48(b). Depictions created to show proper methods of slaughter or tail-docking would presumably have serious "educational" value, and depictions created to focus attention on methods thought to be inhumane or otherwise objectionable would presumably have either serious "educational" or "journalistic" value or both. In short, the Court's examples of depictions involving the docking of tails and humane slaughter do not show that §48 suffers from any overbreadth, much less substantial overbreadth.

The Court notes, finally, that cockfighting, which is illegal in all States, is still legal in Puerto Rico, *ante*, at 15 and I take the Court's point to be that it would be impermissible to ban the creation, sale, or possession in Puerto Rico of a depiction of a cockfight that was legally staged in Puerto Rico.[9] But

---

9   Since the Court has taken pains not to decide whether §48 would be unconstitutional as applied to graphic dogfight videos, including those depicting fights occurring in countries where dogfighting is legal, I take it that the Court does not intend for its passing reference to cockfights to mean either that all depictions of cockfights, whether legal or illegal under local law, are protected by the First

assuming for the sake of argument that this is correct, this veritable sliver of unconstitutionality would not be enough to justify striking down §48 *in toto*.

In sum, we have a duty to interpret §48 so as to avoid serious constitutional concerns, and §48 may reasonably be construed not to reach almost all, if not all, of the depictions that the Court finds constitutionally protected. Thus, §48 does not appear to have a large number of unconstitutional applications. Invalidation for overbreadth is appropriate only if the challenged statute suffers from *substantial* overbreadth—judged not just in absolute terms, but in relation to the statute's "plainly legitimate sweep." *Williams*, 553 U. S., at 292. As I explain in the following Part, §48 has a substantial core of constitutionally permissible applications.

IV

A

1

As the Court of Appeals recognized, "the primary conduct that Congress sought to address through its passage [of §48] was the creation, sale, or possession of 'crush videos.'" 533 F. 3d 218, 222 (CA3 2008) (en banc). A sample crush video, which has been lodged with the Clerk, records the following event:

> "[A] kitten, secured to the ground, watches and shrieks in pain
> as a woman thrusts her high-heeled shoe into its body, slams
> her heel into the kitten's eye socket and mouth loudly fractur-
> ing its skull, and stomps repeatedly on the animal's head. The
> kitten hemorrhages blood, screams blindly in pain, and is ulti-
> mately left dead in a moist pile of blood-soaked hair and bone."
> Brief for Humane Society of United States as *Amicus Curiae* 2
> (hereinafter Humane Society Brief).

It is undisputed that the *conduct* depicted in crush videos may constitutionally be prohibited. All 50 States and the District of Columbia have enacted statutes prohibiting animal cruelty. See 533 F. 3d, at 223, and n. 4 (citing statutes); H. R. Rep., at 3. But before the enactment of §48, the underlying conduct depicted in crush videos was nearly impossible to prosecute. These videos, which "often appeal to persons with a very specific sexual fetish," *id.*,

---

Amendment or that it is impermissible to ban the sale or possession in the States of a depiction of a legal cockfight in Puerto Rico.

at 2, were made in secret, generally without a live audience, and "the faces of the women inflicting the torture in the material often were not shown, nor could the location of the place where the cruelty was being inflicted or the date of the activity be ascertained from the depiction." *Id.*, at 3. Thus, law enforcement authorities often were not able to identify the parties responsible for the torture. See Punishing Depictions of Animal Cruelty and the Federal Prisoner Health Care Co-Payment Act of 1999: Hearing before the Subcommittee on Crime of the House Committee on the Judiciary, 106th Cong., 1st Sess., p. 1 (1999) (hereinafter Hearing on Depictions of Animal Cruelty). In the rare instances in which it was possible to identify and find the perpetrators, they "often were able to successfully assert as a defense that the State could not prove its jurisdiction over the place where the act occurred or that the actions depicted took place within the time specified in the State statute of limitations." H. R. Rep., at 3; see also 145 Cong. Rec. 25896 (Rep. Gallegly) ("[I]t is the prosecutors from around this country, Federal prosecutors as well as State prosecutors, that have made an appeal to us for this"); Hearing on Depictions of Animal Cruelty 21 ("If the production of the video is not discovered during the actual filming, then prosecution for the offense is virtually impossible without a cooperative eyewitness to the filming or an undercover police operation"); *id.*, at 34–35 (discussing example of case in which state prosecutor "had the defendant telling us he produced these videos," but where prosecution was not possible because the State could not prove where or when the tape was made).

In light of the practical problems thwarting the prosecution of the creators of crush videos under state animal cruelty laws, Congress concluded that the only effective way of stopping the underlying criminal conduct was to prohibit the commercial exploitation of the videos of that conduct. And Congress' strategy appears to have been vindicated. We are told that "[b]y 2007, sponsors of §48 declared the crush video industry dead. Even overseas Websites shut down in the wake of §48. Now, after the Third Circuit's decision [facially invalidating the statute], crush videos are already back online." Humane Society Brief 5 (citations omitted).

2

The First Amendment protects freedom of speech, but it most certainly does not protect violent criminal conduct, even if engaged in for expressive purposes. Crush videos present a highly unusual free speech issue because they are so closely linked with violent criminal conduct. The videos record the commission of violent criminal acts, and it appears that these crimes are committed for the sole purpose of creating the videos. In addition, as noted above, Congress was presented with compelling evidence that the only way of preventing these crimes was to target the sale of the videos. Under these circumstances, I cannot believe that the First Amendment commands Congress to step aside and allow the underlying crimes to continue.

The most relevant of our prior decisions is *Ferber*, 458 U. S. 747, which concerned child pornography. The Court there held that child pornography is not protected speech, and I believe that *Ferber*'s reasoning dictates a similar conclusion here.

In *Ferber*, an important factor—I would say the most important factor— was that child pornography involves the commission of a crime that inflicts severe personal injury to the "children who are made to engage in sexual conduct for commercial purposes.'" *Id.*, at 753 (internal quotation marks omitted). The *Ferber* Court repeatedly described the production of child pornography as child "abuse," "molestation," or "exploitation." See, *e.g., id.*, at 749 ("In recent years, the exploitive use of children in the production of pornography has become a serious national problem"); *id.*, at 758, n. 9 ("Sexual molestation by adults is often involved in the production of child sexual performances"). As later noted in *Ashcroft* v. *Free Speech Coalition*, 535 U. S. 234, 249 (2002), in *Ferber* "[t]he production of the work, not its content, was the target of the statute." See also 535 U.S., at 250 (*Ferber* involved "speech that itself is the record of sexual abuse").

Second, *Ferber* emphasized the fact that these underlying crimes could not be effectively combated without targeting the distribution of child pornography. As the Court put it, "the distribution network for child pornography must be closed if the production of material which requires the sexual exploitation of children is to be effectively controlled." 458 U. S., at 759. The Court added:

"[T]here is no serious contention that the legislature was unjustified in believing that it is difficult, if not impossible, to halt the exploitation of children by pursuing only those who produce the photographs and movies. . . . The most expeditious if not the only practical method of law enforcement may be to dry up the market for this material by imposing severe criminal penalties on persons selling, advertising, or otherwise promoting the product." *Id.*, at 759–760.

See also *id.*, at 761 ("The advertising and selling of child pornography provide an economic motive for and are thus an integral part of the production of such materials").

Third, the *Ferber* Court noted that the value of child pornography "is exceedingly modest, if not *de minimis*," and that any such value was "overwhelmingly outweigh[ed]" by "the evil to be restricted." *Id.*, at 762–763.

All three of these characteristics are shared by §48, as applied to crush videos. First, the conduct depicted in crush videos is criminal in every State and the District of Columbia. Thus, any crush video made in this country records the actual commission of a criminal act that inflicts severe physical injury and excruciating pain and ultimately results in death. Those who record the underlying criminal acts are likely to be criminally culpable, either as aiders and abettors or conspirators. And in the tight and secretive market for these videos, some who sell the videos or possess them with the intent to make a profit may be similarly culpable. (For example, in some cases, crush videos were commissioned by purchasers who specified the details of the acts that they wanted to see performed. See H. R. Rep., at 3; Hearing on Depictions of Animal Cruelty 27). To the extent that §48 reaches such persons, it surely does not violate the First Amendment.

Second, the criminal acts shown in crush videos cannot be prevented without targeting the conduct prohibited by §48—the creation, sale, and possession for sale of depictions of animal torture with the intention of realizing a commercial profit. The evidence presented to Congress posed a stark choice: Either ban the commercial exploitation of crush videos or tolerate a continuation of the criminal acts that they record. Faced with this evidence, Congress reasonably chose to target the lucrative crush video market.

Finally, the harm caused by the underlying crimes vastly outweighs any minimal value that the depictions might conceivably be thought to possess. Section 48 reaches only the actual recording of acts of animal torture; the statute does not apply to verbal descriptions or to simulations. And, unlike the child pornography statute in *Ferber* or its federal counterpart, 18 U. S. C. §2252, §48(b) provides an exception for depictions having any "serious religious, political, scientific, educational, journalistic, historical, or artistic value."

It must be acknowledged that §48 differs from a child pornography law in an important respect: preventing the abuse of children is certainly much more important than preventing the torture of the animals used in crush videos. It was largely for this reason that the Court of Appeals concluded that *Ferber* did not support the constitutionality of §48. 533 F. 3d, at 228 ("Preventing cruelty to animals, although an exceedingly worthy goal, simply does not implicate interests of the same magnitude as protecting children from physical and psychological harm"). But while protecting children is unquestionably *more* important than protecting animals, the Government also has a compelling interest in preventing the torture depicted in crush videos.

The animals used in crush videos are living creatures that experience excruciating pain. Our society has long banned such cruelty, which is illegal throughout the country. In *Ferber*, the Court noted that "virtually all of the States and the United States have passed legislation proscribing the production of or otherwise combating 'child pornography,'" and the Court declined to "second-guess [that] legislative judgment."[10] 458 U. S., at 758. Here, likewise, the Court of Appeals erred in second-guessing the legislative judgment about the importance of preventing cruelty to animals.

Section 48's ban on trafficking in crush videos also helps to enforce the criminal laws and to ensure that criminals do not profit from their crimes. See 145 Cong. Rec. 25897 (Oct. 19, 1999) (Rep. Gallegly) ("The state has an interest in enforcing its existing laws. Right now, the laws are not only being violated, but people are making huge profits from promoting the violations"); *id.,* at 10685 (May 24, 1999) (Rep. Gallegly) (explaining that he introduced the House version of the bill because "criminals should not profit from [their] illegal acts"). We have already judged that taking the profit out of crime is a compelling interest. See *Simon & Schuster, Inc.* v. *Members of N. Y. State Crime Victims Bd.,* 502 U. S. 105, 119 (1991).

In short, *Ferber* is the case that sheds the most light on the constitutionality of Congress' effort to halt the production of crush videos. Applying the principles set forth in *Ferber,* I would hold that crush videos are not protected by the First Amendment.

---

10   In other cases, we have regarded evidence of a national consensus as proof that a particular government interest is compelling. See Simon & Schuster, Inc. v. Members of N. Y. State Crime Victims Bd., 502 U. S. 105, 118 (1991) (State's compelling interest "in ensuring that victims of crime are compensated by those who harm them" evidenced by fact that"[e]very State has a body of tort law serving exactly this interest"); Roberts v. United States Jaycees, 468 U. S. 609, 624–625 (1984) (citing state laws prohibiting discrimination in public accommodations as evidence of the compelling governmental interest in ensuring equal access).

B

Application of the *Ferber* framework also supports the constitutionality of §48 as applied to depictions of brutal animal fights. (For convenience, I will focus on videos of dogfights, which appear to be the most common type of animal fight videos.)

First, such depictions, like crush videos, record the actual commission of a crime involving deadly violence. Dogfights are illegal in every State and the District of Columbia, Brief for United States 26–27, and n. 8 (citing statutes), and under federal law constitute a felony punishable by imprisonment for up to five years, 7 U. S. C.§2156 *et seq.* (2006 ed. and Supp. II), 18 U. S. C. §49 (2006ed., Supp. II).

Second, Congress had an ample basis for concluding that the crimes depicted in these videos cannot be effectively controlled without targeting the videos. Like crush videos and child pornography, dogfight videos are very often produced as part of a "low-profile, clandestine industry," and "the need to market the resulting products requires a visible apparatus of distribution." *Ferber,* 458 U. S., at 760. In such circumstances, Congress had reasonable grounds for concluding that it would be "difficult, if not impossible, to halt" the underlying exploitation of dogs by pursuing only those who stage the fights. *Id.*, at 759–760; see 533 F. 3d, at 246 (Cowen, J., dissenting) (citing evidence establishing "the existence of a lucrative market for depictions of animal cruelty," including videos of dogfights, "which in turn provides a powerful incentive to individuals to create [such] videos").

The commercial trade in videos of dogfights is "an integral part of the production of such materials," *Ferber, supra,* at 761. As the Humane Society explains, "[v]ideotapes memorializing dogfights are integral to the success of this criminal industry" for a variety of reasons. Humane Society Brief 5. For one thing, some dogfighting videos are made "solely for the purpose of selling the video (and not for a live audience)." *Id.*, at 9. In addition, those who stage dogfights profit not just from the sale of the videos themselves, but from the gambling revenue they take in from the fights; the videos "encourage [such] gambling activity because they allow those reluctant to attend actual fights for fear of prosecution to still bet on the outcome." *Ibid.*; accord, Brief for Center on the Administration of Criminal Law as *Amicus Curiae* 12 ("Selling videos of dogfights effectively abets the underlying crimes by providing a market for dogfighting while allowing actual dogfights to remain underground"); *ibid.* ("These videos are part of a 'lucrative market' where videos are produced by a 'bare-boned, clandestine staff' in order to permit the actual location of dogfights and the perpetrators of these underlying criminal activities to go undetected" (citations omitted)). Moreover, "[v] ideo documentation is vital to the criminal enterprise because it provides *proof* of a dog's fighting prowess—proof demanded by potential buyers and critical to the underground market." Humane Society Brief 9. Such recordings may also serve as "'training' videos for other fight organizers." *Ibid.* In short, because videos depicting live dogfights are essential to the success of the criminal dogfighting subculture, the commercial sale of such videos helps to fuel the market for, and thus to perpetuate the perpetration of, the criminal conduct depicted in them.

Third, depictions of dogfights that fall within §48's reach have by definition no appreciable social value. As noted, §48(b) exempts depictions having any appreciable social value, and thus the mere inclusion of a depiction of a live fight in a larger work that aims at communicating an idea or a message with a modicum of social value would not run afoul of the statute.

Finally, the harm caused by the underlying criminal acts greatly outweighs any trifling value that the depictions might be thought to possess. As the Humane Society explains:

"The abused dogs used in fights endure physical torture and emotional manipulation throughout their lives to predispose them to violence; common tactics include feeding the animals hot peppers and gunpowder, prodding them with sticks, and electrocution. Dogs are conditioned never to give up a fight, even if they will be gravely hurt or killed. As a result, dogfights inflict horrific injuries on the participating animals, including lacerations, ripped ears, puncture wounds and broken bones. Losing dogs are routinely refused treatment, beaten further as 'punishment' for the loss, and executed by drowning, hanging, or incineration." *Id.*, at 5–6 (footnotes omitted).

For these dogs, unlike the animals killed in crush videos, the suffering lasts for years rather than minutes. As with crush videos, moreover, the statutory ban on commerce in dogfighting videos is also supported by compelling governmental interests in effectively enforcing the Nation's criminal laws and preventing criminals from profiting from their illegal activities. See *Ferber, supra,* at 757–758; *Simon & Schuster,* 502 U. S., at 119.

In sum, §48 may validly be applied to at least two broad real-world categories of expression covered by the statute: crush videos and dogfighting videos. Thus, the statute has a substantial core of constitutionally permissible applications. Moreover, for the reasons set forth above, the record does not show that §48, properly interpreted, bans a substantial amount of protected speech in absolute terms. *A fortiori,* respondent has not met his burden of demonstrating that any impermissible applications of the statute are "substantial" in relation to its "plainly legitimate sweep." *Williams,* 553 U. S., at 292. Accordingly, I would reject respondent's claim that §48 is facially unconstitutional under the overbreadth doctrine.

* * *

For these reasons, I respectfully dissent.

Appendix to opinion of ALITO, J.

APPENDIX

As the following chart makes clear, virtually all state laws prohibiting animal cruelty either expressly define the term "animal" to exclude wildlife or else specifically exempt lawful hunting activities.

Alaska	Alaska Stat. §11.61.140(c)(4) (2008) ("It is a defense to a prosecution under this section that the conduct of the defendant ... was necessarily incidental to lawful fishing, hunting or trapping activities")
Arizona	Ariz. Rev. Stat. Ann. §§13–2910(C)(1), (3) (West Supp. 2009) ("This section does not prohibit or restrict ... [t]he taking of wildlife or other activities permitted by or pursuant to title 17 ... [or] [a]ctivities regulated by the Arizona game and fish department or the Arizona department of agriculture")

Arkansas	Ark. Code Ann. §5–62–105(a) (Supp. 2009) ("This subchapter does not prohibit any of the following activities: . . . (9) Engaging in the taking of game or fish through hunting, trapping, or fishing, or engaging in any other activity authorized by Arkansas Constitution, Amendment 35, by §15–41–101 et seq., or by any Arkansas State Game and Fish Commission regulation promulgated under either Arkansas Constitution, Amendment 35, or statute")
California	Cal. Penal Code Ann. §599c (West 1999) ("No part of this title shall be construed as interfering with any of the laws of this state known as the 'game laws,' . . . or to interfere with the right to kill all animals used for food")
Colorado	Colo. Rev. Stat. Ann. §18–9–201.5(2) (2009) ("In case of any conflict between this part 2 [prohibiting cruelty to animals] or section 35–43–126, [Colo. Rev. Stat.], and the wildlife statutes of the wildlife commission, as established in title 33, [Colo.Rev.Stat.], or to prohibit any conduct therein authorized or permitted")
Connecticut	Conn. Gen.Stat. § 53–247(b) (2009) ("Any person who maliciously and intentionally maims, mutilates, tortures, wounds or kills an animal shall be fined not more than five thousand dollars or imprisoned not more than five years or both. The provisions of this subsection shall not apply to . . . any person . . . while lawfully engaged in the taking of wildlife")
Delaware	Del. Code Ann., Tit. 11, § 1325(f) (2007) ("This section shall not apply to the lawful hunting or trapping of animals as provided by law")
Florida	Fla. Stat. § 828.122(9)(b) (2007) ("This section shall not apply to . . . [a]ny person using animals to pursue or take wildlife or to participate in any hunting regulated or subject to being regulated by the rules and regulations of the Fish and Wildlife Conservation Commission")

Georgia	Ga. Code Ann. § 16–12–4(e) (2007) ("The provisions of this Code section shall not be construed as prohibiting conduct which is otherwise permitted under the laws of this state or of the United States, including, but not limited to . . . hunting, trapping, fishing, [or] wildlife management")
Hawaii	Haw. Rev. Stat. § 711–1108.5(1) (2008 Cum. Supp.) ("A person commits the offense of cruelty to animals in the first degree if the person intentionally or knowingly tortures, mutilates, or poisons or causes the torture, mutilation, or poisoning of any pet animal or equine animal resulting in serious bodily injury or death of the pet animal or equine animal")
Idaho	Idaho Code § 25–3515 (Lexis 2000) ("No part of this chapter shall be construed as interfering with, negating or preempting any of the laws or rules of the department of fish and game of this state . . . or to interfere with the right to kill, slaughter, bag or take all animals used for food")
Illinois	Ill. Comp. Stat., ch. 510, § 70/13 (West 2006) ("In case of any alleged conflict between this Act . . . and the 'Wildlife Code of Illinois' or 'An Act to define and require the use of humane methods in the handling, preparation for slaughter, and slaughter of livestock for meat or meat products to be offered for sale', . . . the provisions of those Acts shall prevail"), § 70/3.03(b)(1) ("For the purposes of this Section, 'animal torture' does not include any death, harm, or injury caused to any animal by . . . any hunting, fishing, trapping, or other activity allowed under the Wildlife Code, the Wildlife Habitat Management Areas Act, or the Fish and Aquatic Life Code" (footnotes omitted))

Indiana	Ind. Code § 35–46–3–5(a) (West 2004) (subject to certain exceptions not relevant here, "this chapter [prohibiting "Offenses Relating to Animals"] does not apply to . . . [f]ishing, hunting, trapping, or other conduct authorized under [Ind. Code §]14–22")
Iowa	Iowa Code § 717B.2(5) (2009) ("This section [banning 'animal abuse'] shall not apply to . . . [a] person taking, hunting, trapping, or fishing for a wild animal as provided in chapter 481A"), § 717B.3A(2)(e) ("This section [banning 'animal torture'] shall not apply to . . . [a] person taking, hunting, trapping, or fishing for a wild animal as provided in chapter 481A")
Kansas	Kan. Stat. Ann. § 21–4310(b)(3) (2007) ("The provisions of this section shall not apply to . . . killing, attempting to kill, trapping, catching or taking of any animal in accordance with the provisions of chapter 32 [Wildlife, Parks and Recreation] or chapter 47 [Livestock and Domestic Animals] of the Kansas Statutes Annotated")
Kentucky	Ky. Rev. Stat. Ann. §§ 525.130(2)(a), (e) (Lexis 2008) ("Nothing in this section shall apply to the killing of animals . . . [p]ursuant to a license to hunt, fish, or trap . . . [or][f]or purposes relating to sporting activities"), § 525.130(3) ("Activities of animals engaged in hunting, field trials, dog training other than training a dog to fight for pleasure or profit, and other activities authorized either by a hunting license or by the Department of Fish and Wildlife shall not constitute a violation of this section")
Louisiana	La. Rev. Stat. Ann. § 14:102.1(C)(1) (West Supp.2010) ("This Section shall not apply to . . . [t]he lawful hunting or trapping of wildlife as provided by law")
Maine	Me. Rev. Stat. Ann., Tit. 17, § 1031(1)(G) (West Supp.2009) (providing that hunting and trapping an animal is not a form of prohibited animal cruelty if "permitted pursuant to" parts of state code regulating the shooting of large game, inland fisheries, and wildlife)

Maryland	Md. Crim. Law Code Ann. § 10–603(3) (Lexis 2002) ("Sections 10–601 through 10–608 of this subtitle do not apply to . . . an activity that may cause unavoidable physical pain to an animal, including . . . hunting, if the person performing the activity uses the most humane method reasonably available")
Michigan	Mich. Comp. Laws Ann. §§ 750.50(11)(a), (b) (West Supp. 2009) ("This section does not prohibit the lawful killing or other use of an animal, including . . . [f]ishing . . . [h]unting, [or] trapping [as regulated by state law]"), § 750.50b(9)(a), (b) ("This section does not prohibit the lawful killing of an animal pursuant to . . . [f]ishing . . . [h]unting, [or] trapping [as regulated by state law]")
Missouri	Mo. Rev. Stat. § 578.007(3) (2000) ("The provisions of sections 578.005 to 578.023 shall not apply to . . . [h]unting, fishing, or trapping as allowed by" state law)
Montana	Mont. Code Ann. § 45–8–211(4)(d) (2009) ("This section does not prohibit . . . lawful fishing, hunting, and trapping activities")
Nebraska	Neb. Rev. Stat. § 28–1013(4) (2008) (exempting "[c]ommonly accepted practices of hunting, fishing, or trapping")
Nevada	Nev. Rev. Stat. §§ 574.200(1), (3) (2007) (provisions of Nevada law banning animal cruelty "do not . . . [i]nterfere with any of the fish and game laws . . . [or] the right to kill all animals and fowl used for food")
New Hampshire	N.H. Rev. Stat. Ann. § 644:8(II) (West Supp.2009) ("In this section, 'animal' means a domestic animal, a household pet or a wild animal in captivity")
New Jersey	N.J. Stat. Ann. § 4:22–16(c) (West 1998) ("Nothing contained in this article shall be construed to prohibit or interfere with . . . [t]he shooting or taking of game or game fish in such manner and at such times as is allowed or provided by the laws of this State")

New Mexico	N.M. Stat. Ann. § 30–18–1(I)(1) (Supp. 2009) ("The provisions of this section do not apply to . . . fishing, hunting, falconry, taking and trapping")
New York	N.Y. Agric. & Mkts. Law Ann. § 353–a(2) (West 2004) ("Nothing contained in this section shall be construed to prohibit or interfere in any way with anyone lawfully engaged in hunting, trapping, or fishing")
North Carolina	N.C. Gen. Stat. Ann. § 14–360(c)(1) (Lexis 2009) ("[T]his section shall not apply to . . . [t]he lawful taking of animals under the jurisdiction and regulation of the Wildlife Resources Commission . . .")
North Dakota	N.D. Cent. Code Ann. § 36–21.1–01(5)(a) (Lexis Supp.2009) ("'Cruelty' or 'torture' . . . does not include . . . [a]ny activity that requires a license or permit under chapter 20.1–03 [which governs gaming and other licenses]")
Oregon	Ore. Rev. Stat. § 167.335 (2007) ("Unless gross negligence can be shown, the provisions of [certain statutes prohibiting animal cruelty] do not apply to . . . (7)[l]awful fishing, hunting and trapping activities")
Pennsylvania	18 Pa. Cons. Stat. § 5511(a)(3)(ii) (2008) ("This subsection [banning killing, maiming, or poisoning of domestic animals or zoo animals] shall not apply to . . . the killing of any animal or fowl pursuant to . . . The Game Law"), § 5511(c)(1) ("A person commits an offense if he wantonly or cruelly illtreats, overloads, beats, otherwise abuses any animal, or neglects any animal as to which he has a duty of care")
Rhode Island	R.I. Gen. Laws § 4–1–3(a) (Lexis 1998) (prohibiting "[e]very owner, possessor, or person having the charge or custody of any animal" from engaging in certain acts of unnecessary cruelty), §§ 4–1–5(a), (b) (prohibiting only "[m]alicious" injury to or killing of animals and further providing that "[t]his section shall not apply to licensed hunters during hunting season or a licensed business killing animals for human consumption")

South Carolina	S.C. Code Ann. § 47-1-40(C) (Supp. 2009) ("This section does not apply to . . . activity authorized by Title 50 [consisting of laws on Fish, Game, and Watercraft]")
South Dakota	S.D. Codified Laws § 40-1-17 (2004) ("The acts and conduct of persons who are lawfully engaged in any of the activities authorized by Title 41 [Game, Fish, Parks and Forestry] . . . and persons who properly kill any animal used for food and sport hunting, trapping, and fishing as authorized by the South Dakota Department of Game, Fish and Parks, are exempt from the provisions of this chapter")
Tennessee	Tenn. Code Ann. § 39-14-201(1) (2010 Supp.) ("'Animal' means a domesticated living creature or a wild creature previously captured"), § 39-14-201(4) ("[N]othing in this part shall be construed as prohibiting the shooting of birds or game for the purpose of human food or the use of animate targets by incorporated gun clubs")
Texas	Tex. Penal Code Ann. § 42.092(a)(2) (West Supp. 2009) ("'Animal' means a domesticated living creature, including any stray or feral cat or dog, and a wild living creature previously captured. The term does not include an uncaptured wild living creature or a livestock animal"), § 42.092(f)(1)(A) ("It is an exception to the application of this section that the conduct engaged in by the actor is a generally accepted and otherwise lawful . . . form of conduct occurring solely for the purpose of or in support of . . . fishing, hunting, or trapping")
Utah	Utah Code Ann. § 76-9-301(1)(b)(ii)(D) (Lexis 2008) ("'Animal' does not include . . . wildlife, as defined in Section 23-13-2, including protected and unprotected wildlife, if the conduct toward the wildlife is in accordance with lawful hunting, fishing, or trapping practices or other lawful practices"), § 76-9-301(9)(C) ("This section does not affect or prohibit . . . the lawful hunting of, fishing for, or trapping of, wildlife")

Vermont	Vt. Stat. Ann., Tit. 13, § 351b(1) (2009) ("This subchapter shall not apply to . . . activities regulated by the department of fish and wildlife pursuant to Part 4 of Title 10")
Virginia	Va. Code Ann. § 3.2–6570D (Lexis 2008) ("This section shall not prohibit authorized wildlife management activities or hunting, fishing or trapping [as regulated by state law]")
Washington	Wash. Rev. Code § 16.52.180 (2008) ("No part of this chapter shall be deemed to interfere with any of the laws of this state known as the 'game laws' . . . or to interfere with the right to kill animals to be used for food")
West Virginia	W. Va. Code Ann. § 61–8–19(f) (Lexis Supp. 2009) ("The provisions of this section do not apply to lawful acts of hunting, fishing, [or] trapping")
Wisconsin	Wis. Stat. § 951.015(1) (2007–2008) ("This chapter may not be interpreted as controverting any law regulating wild animals that are subject to regulation under ch. 169 [regulating, among other things, hunting], [or] the taking of wild animals")
Wyoming	Wyo. Stat. Ann. § 6–3–203(m)(iv) (2009) ("Nothing in subsection (a), (b) or (n) of this section shall be construed to prohibit . . . [t]he hunting, capture or destruction of any predatory animal or other wildlife in any manner not otherwise prohibited by law")

Notes

1. *United States v. Stevens*, 130 S. Ct. 1577, 1592 (2010).
2. Ibid., 1580–86.
3. Ibid., 1592.
4. Ibid., 1587 (quoting *Washington State Grange v. Washington State Republican Party*, 552 U.S. 422, 449, n.6 (2008)).
5. Ibid., 1588; Barbara Grzincic, *Commentary: It Takes a Rifle, Not a Shotgun, to Target Animal Cruelty Videos*, Daily Rec. (Baltimore, MD), April 20, 2010 (During the oral argument, Justice Scalia asked, "How do you limit 'killed?!' . . . 'Kill' has one meaning, which is 'kill!'").
6. *Stevens*, 130 S. Ct. at 1589.
7. Ibid., 1580.

8. Ibid., 1581.
9. Ibid., 1591–92.
10. Ibid., 1592–93 (Alito, J., dissenting).
11. Ibid., 1594 (Alito, J., dissenting).
12. Ibid., 1595 (Alito, J., dissenting) (quoting *New York v. Ferber*, 458 U.S. 747, 769 (1982).
13. *Stevens*, 130 S. Ct. at 1594–96 (Alito, J., dissenting).
14. Ibid., 1596 (citing H.R. Rep. No. 106-397, p.8 (1999) ("[D]epictions of ordinary hunting and fishing activities do not fall within the scope of the statute."); *see, e.g.*, 145 Cong. Rec. 25894 (Oct. 19, 1999) (Rep. McCollum) ("[T]he sale of depictions of legal activities, such as hunting and fishing, would not be illegal under this bill."); *id.* at 25895 (Rep. Smith) ("[L]et us be clear as to what this legislation will not do. It will in no way prohibit hunting, fishing, or wildlife videos.").
15. *Stevens*, 130 S. Ct. at 1595 (Alito, J., dissenting).
16. Ibid., 1597 (Alito, J., dissenting) (quoting *United States v. Williams*, 553 U.S. 285, 292 [2008)).
17. Ibid., 1598–602 (Alito, J., dissenting).
18. Ibid., 1593 (Alito, J., dissenting).

CHAPTER 9

Analyzing the Decision

The First Amendment, which states in pertinent part, "Congress shall make no law . . . abridging the freedom of speech,"[1] aims to prevent governmental restrictions on what is "seen, spoken, read, or heard."[2] While it is beyond dispute that freedom of speech is an important right worth protecting, it is equally accepted that freedom of speech is not absolute.[3] The constitutionality of regulating protected speech hinges on the distinction between *content-based* and *content-neutral* restrictions.[4] Since content-neutral restrictions are less likely to chill unpopular speech, they warrant less judicial scrutiny. By contrast, content-based restrictions are presumptively invalid and warrant heightened scrutiny because they "implicate censorship."[5] To survive strict scrutiny, a content-based restriction must be narrowly tailored to achieve a compelling government interest.[6]

Some speech is categorically excluded from First Amendment protection. As the Supreme Court articulated in *Chaplinsky v. New Hampshire*:

> There are certain well-defined and narrowly limited classes of speech, the prevention and punishment of which has never been thought to raise any Constitutional problem. These include the lewd and obscene, the profane, the libelous and the insulting or 'fighting' words—those which by their very utterance inflict injury or tend to incite an immediate breach of the peace. It has been well observed that such utterances are no essential part of any exposition of ideas, and are of such slight social value as a step to truth that any benefit that may be derived from them is clearly outweighed by the social interest in order and morality.[7]

It is no surprise then that the Supreme Court's decision that depictions of illegal dogfighting constitute protected speech provoked a heated debate. Although the Court eloquently articulated its reasons for striking Section 48, the discussion that follows will examine several less-explored counterarguments under which the Court could perhaps have upheld the law. Some argue that Stevens' conviction arose from non-expressive conduct, not speech protected by the First Amendment. The government and many *amici* argued that depictions of animal cruelty fall into existing categories of unprotected speech or the Court should have created a new category of unprotected speech to encompass such depictions. Other legal scholars claim that the Court failed to properly apply well-established principles of statutory construction in determining that Section 48 was unconstitutional.

As the International Society of Animal Rights (ISAR) has pointed out, Stevens' conviction arose from his attempted *sale* of depictions of animal cruelty. It was that conduct that provoked his conviction. By selling depictions of illegal animal fighting, he profited[8] and arguably promoted the crime of dogfighting.[9] According to ISAR, Stevens should not have been permitted to retrospectively label his conduct as expression in order to reverse his conviction and profit from his purported promotion of crime.

As ISAR observed, the Court was not required to "accept the view that an apparently limitless variety of conduct can be labeled 'speech' whenever the person engaging in the conduct intends thereby to express an idea."[10] One could argue that the majority did not adequately address the threshold question of whether Stevens' conduct contained sufficient expressive elements to implicate the First Amendment. If not, then the sale was not entitled to First Amendment review.[11] For this reason, ISAR argued that the Third Circuit's decision could have been reversed without invalidating Section 48.

In *Stevens*, the majority rejected both the government and the Third Circuit's approaches to determining whether depictions of animal cruelty constitute protected speech but failed to adequately clarify what factors should be examined to make that determination. The government urged the Court to balance "the governmental interest in restricting the speech against the value of the speech" in determining whether speech warrants First Amendment protection (*Chaplinsky* Balancing Test or *Chaplinsky* Approach).[12] In rejecting that approach, the majority stated that "[t]he First Amendment's guarantee of free speech does not extend only to categories of speech that survive an ad hoc balancing of relative social costs and benefits"[13] but admitted that the government's "view did not emerge from a vacuum."[14] The majority explained that *descriptions* of factors that make a category of speech unprotected do not give rise to a general test and then appeared to endorse the application of a "competing interests plus" test that, among other things, weighs a state's interest in preventing speech against the speech's redeeming value.[15]

The majority ultimately determined that depictions of animal cruelty constitute protected speech in part because there is no "long history in American law" prohibiting them.[16] However, this argument loses strength when one considers that perhaps no long legal history exists because depictions of animal cruelty are of recent origin. The primary mechanism through which the animal cruelty depiction industry operates—the Internet—is also in its relative infancy. Production of such depictions has been so clandestine that few people, including legislators, knew of its existence. When Congress did become aware of the depictions, it acted quickly to prohibit them. As Professor Nadine Strossen explained:

> *Stevens*'s strict reliance on history and tradition constitutes an unusual twist on such sources of constitutional interpretation even in the specific context of identifying categorical exemptions from First Amendment protection. Typically, a judge who invokes history and tradition in this context does so in support of limiting First Amendment protection. That is exactly the purpose for which the key *Chaplinsky* passage itself invoked history and tradition: *Chaplinsky*'s specific holding was to reject a First Amendment challenge to a conviction for expressing provocative religious and political opinions because of the historically enshrined "fighting words" exception to free speech. Therefore, it is noteworthy that the *Stevens* Court turns that typical use of history and tradition on its head, and converts it into a criterion that forestalls limits on First Amendment protection.[17]

By comparison, the Third Circuit rejected the *Chaplinsky* Approach and instead applied the *Ferber* Approach in determining whether depictions of animal cruelty constitute protected speech.[18] Justice Alito also utilized the *Ferber* Approach but reached the opposite conclusion.[19]

In *New York v. Ferber*, the Court announced five "reasons" it was "persuaded that the States are entitled to greater leeway in the *regulation of pornographic depictions of children*."[20] Taken together, the Court's use of the word *reasons* and of the phrase "regulation of pornographic depictions of children" suggest that the *Ferber* factors were not intended to create a new test to determine whether speech is protected.[21] In fact, the Court even refers to the *Ferber* factors as a "test for child pornography,"[22] further indicating that the factors are inapplicable to other types of speech, such as depictions of animal cruelty, that do not consist of child pornography. According to the government, the Third Circuit's inexplicable rejection of the *Chaplinsky* Approach and its misapplication of *Ferber* seriously misconstrued the Court's First Amendment jurisprudence.[23]

However, the majority also rejected the *Ferber* Approach, noting, "our decisions in *Ferber* and other cases cannot be taken as establishing a freewheeling authority to declare new categories of speech outside the scope of the First Amendment."[24] The majority did not foreclose the possibility that new and additional categories of unprotected speech may be identified in the future but failed to clarify exactly how it or other courts can make that determination without running afoul of precedent or the Constitution. This lack of clarity threatens to perpetuate additional misapplications of *Ferber*, *Chaplinsky*, and other First Amendment cases.

Furthermore, as Strossen observed, the majority recast the child pornography at issue in *Ferber* as illustrative of "'a previously recognized, long-established category of unprotected, speech,' rather than a newly minted category, [giving] Ferber . . . only [a] limited capacity to serve as a springboard for judicial recognition of additional categories of unprotected expression, which is how the U.S. government and other proponents of Section 48 had invoked it."[25] As such, after *Stevens*, *Ferber* likely cannot serve as a basis to create new categories of unprotected speech; rather, it can only identify new subsets of speech historically excepted from First Amendment protection.[26]

Rather than declaring Section 48 unconstitutional, the Court could have applied either the *Chaplinsky* Approach or the *Ferber* Approach to create a new category of unprotected speech or held that depictions of animal cruelty fall into existing categories of unprotected speech. Instead, as Strossen observed, *Stevens* is the latest in a line of decisions "contracting government power to enforce content-based regulations of expression, even when those regulations receive overwhelming support from elected officials and the general public, and even when the expression conveys ideas or depicts actions that most people consider offensive or wrongful."[27]

According to others, the Court could also have upheld Section 48 by creating a categorical exclusion for low value violent speech, including but perhaps not limited to depictions of animal cruelty. The Court last ruled on content-based restrictions on violent speech in the 1948 case—*Winters v. New York*—which involved the obscenity prosecution of a magazine that included "police reports and accounts of criminal deeds."[28] Although that law was invalidated, the Court nowhere indicated that all content-based restrictions on violent speech are unconstitutional.[29] Rather, as one commentator noted, at least some scientific evidence supports the creation of such an exclusion.[30]

Frequent exposure to violent speech can cause what some psychologists term *mean world syndrome* ("an overly bleak view of society" associated with "higher degrees of fear and distrust") as well as symptomatic fear and anxiety characterized by depression, insomnia, nightmares, and post-traumatic stress disorder symptoms, all of which decrease productivity and incur significant healthcare costs.[31] Recurring exposure may desensitize viewers as evidenced by research indicating that viewers of media violence are less willing to assist victims; one commentator predicts that this could increase crime rates by decreasing intervention and police cooperation.[32]

Low value violent speech may also offend unwilling or unintended viewers.[33] As one commentator explained, in *FCC v. Pacifica Foundation*, a radio station broadcast a comedian's offensive and graphic monologue; a man who was driving with his young child sued, and the Court held that restricting offensive speech is permissible where the speech invades the privacy of unwilling listeners.[34]

Perhaps the strongest justification for excluding low value violent speech from First Amendment protection is the tremendous harm its production necessitates. Dogfighting and crush videos, for instance, not only exacerbate the harm of unlawful acts of animal cruelty but are often the cause. A dogfight might be held so that owners can film dogs' fighting styles and thus increase stud fees, side bets, purses, or sale prices. Likewise, made-to-order crush videos require an animal to be slaughtered according to a viewer's sadistic specifications; in such instances, the depiction is the direct cause of the animal cruelty. In *Ferber*, the Court held that child pornography constitutes unprotected speech in part because its subsequent distribution exacerbates the harm to victims.[35] The same harmful production rationale applies to depictions of animal cruelty because, in the case of snuff videos, their production requires an innocent victim to be slowly and painfully tortured to death or, in the case of depictions of animal fighting, victims must endure a lifetime of abuse.[36]

Others argue that Section 48 did not warrant First Amendment review because the depictions of animal cruelty it targeted fall into existing categories of unprotected speech, such as obscenity.[37] In describing the scope of Section 48, former President Clinton noted that it would "be limited to material 'designed to appeal to the prurient interest in sex'"—wording borrowed from the obscenity test the Court articulated in *Miller v. California*.[38]

According to First Amendment obscenity jurisprudence, speech is obscene if: (i) an "'average person, applying contemporary community standards' would find that the work, taken as a whole, appeals to the prurient interest"; (ii) "the work depicts or describes, in a patently offensive way, sexual conduct specifically defined by the applicable state law"; and (iii) "the work, taken as a whole, lacks serious literary, artistic, political, or scientific value."[39]

Because obscenity does not contribute to an "essential part of any exposition of ideas, and [is] of . . . slight social value," it does not warrant First Amendment protection.[40] Like the materials that obscenity bans prohibit, the depictions of animal cruelty criminalized by Section 48 are patently offensive, lack redeeming social value, and with regard to crush videos, appeal to depraved sexual fetishes.[41] Crush videos arguably constitute obscenity because they lack redeeming social value, are objectively offensive to the average person applying contemporary community standards, and appeal to the prurient interest of viewers who fantasize that they are being tortured by the dominatrix in the video.[42] As one detective explained, crush video viewers "have foot fetishes . . . want to be the animal as it is crushed . . . [and] enjoy seeing and hearing the bones break."[43] For similar reasons, depictions of bestiality also constitute obscenity.

While opponents of Section 48 argue that obscenity does not embrace non-sexual images, such as videos of illegal animal fighting, at least some historical evidence and case law suggest otherwise.[44] According to one commentator, nearly all federal obscenity prosecutions involve violent pornography or child pornography, and "if pornography without violence is not considered obscene, perhaps it is the violent content, more than the sexual content, which people find patently offensive."[45]

Likewise, some legal scholars support the expansion of obscenity to include depictions of animal cruelty.[46] A description of several crush videos from the Humane Society of the United States (HSUS) explains why. "High Heel Hell Part III: The Ritual" involves a partially nude actress who uses spiked heels to trample five large rabbits to death and then drags their bloody corpses into the shape of a cross. In "Kitten Torture and Crush," a sadistic actress repeatedly burns a caged kitten with cigarettes and a cigarette lighter. As if this torture were not enough, the actress then rips the dying, charred kitten from its cage and proceeds to tear it limb from limb with her high heel.[47] Another depiction shows dogs hunting a pig that is confined to a pen. With no chance of escape from its impending death, the pig runs back and forth frantically seeking an escape. The maddened dogs leap inside the pen, cornering the pig and ripping chunks of flesh from its back, arms, and legs; the pig is slowly eaten alive.[48] Although snuff videos may, at least at first glance, appear to be inherently worse than depictions of unlawful animal fighting, one must consider that while a snuff video requires a victim to suffer a tortuous death, participants in animal fighting must suffer a lifetime of abuse and ultimately, a painful death—either by the jaws of an opponent or by their owners who may electrocute them if they lose or allow them to die from untreated wounds.

How could such depictions possess redeeming social value? And what reasonable person would not be offended by such gruesome images? Such depictions of animal brutality could only appeal to the basest human beings and undoubtedly violate "community norms"[49] as demonstrated by the fact that a jury determined that the videos at issue in *Stevens* lacked redeeming social value.[50]

Survey evidence and common sense further support the assertion that depictions of animal cruelty violate community norms.[51] According to a 2004 Edge Research survey, 67% of participants stated that preventing animal cruelty was "very important" to them; 13% ranked the issue as "somewhat important"; 18% ranked it as "important"; and only 2% indicated that the issue was "not important."[52] Public outrage surrounding the infamous Michael Vick dogfighting ring and other recent prosecutions further demonstrates that most Americans object to animal cruelty.[53] Not surprisingly, *People*'s coverage of the story of two juveniles who murdered seventeen cats and injured twelve others provoked more reader email than any news event except Princess Di's untimely death.[54] In another poignant illustration of public sentiment, when a man tossed a dog into traffic, members of his outraged community donated $120,000 to track him down.[55] Other indicia of public support for animal cruelty prevention include the popularity of television shows highlighting anti-cruelty efforts, the existence of Animal Law courses at many law schools, the creation of Animal Law bar association committees, the widespread establishment of Animal Cruelty Task Forces, and the fact that states increasingly assign felony status to animal cruelty offenses.[56]

Public sentiment also extends to depictions of animal cruelty. For example, in 1997 four teenagers were prosecuted for "burning and bludgeoning" a dog. They videotaped the murder for their own use before it was used on an episode of *Panorama* titled "The Cruelty Connection."[57] The case prosecutor reportedly "received over 5,000 letters in support of her pursuit of the case."[58]

Not only do depictions of animal cruelty offend community norms, but also they lack redeeming social value. Just as traditional forms of obscenity appeal only to base prurient interests rather than communicating socially valuable information, customized crush videos portraying scantily clad women crushing kittens to death or abused dogs tearing off each other's limbs in forced death matches convey nothing but meaningless death and gore.[59]

Taken together, the history of obscenity laws and the layman's definition of obscenity support the conclusion that depictions of animal cruelty are obscene and, thus, undeserving of First Amendment protection.[60] It comes as no surprise then that the findings accompanying the revised Crush Act state that many crush videos constitute obscenity.[61] As such, if one agrees that the societal interest in preserving and promoting public mores outweighs whatever expressive sole content, if any, such depictions convey, then the majority could have upheld Section 48 because it merely prohibited the sale, creation, or possession of unprotected speech.

Furthermore, the depictions of animal cruelty that Section 48 targeted arguably constitute incitement and thus do not warrant First Amendment protection. States may lawfully forbid speech advocating the use of force or violating the law where the speech is directed to incite or produce imminent lawless action and is likely to incite or produce such action (incitement).[62] Because the depictions of animal cruelty that Section 48 prohibited are predicated on illegal acts of vicious animal cruelty without which they cannot be produced, this extremely narrow exception arguably applies to at least some of the speech that Section 48 targeted. To create a crush video a filmmaker solicits an actress to commit a crime of animal cruelty and conspires with her to choreograph and film the brutality—a film he later sells for profit again and again. As such, the depictions arguably constitute speech that incites and produces the imminent crimes of solicitation to commit animal cruelty, conspiracy to commit animal cruelty, aiding and abetting the commission of animal cruelty, and the commission of animal cruelty to the extent such crimes exist in the relevant jurisdiction.[63] In the case of made-to-order crush videos, a purchaser specifies, among other things, the details of the torture method and duration, nature of the victim, and perhaps even the killer's attire; the purchase necessitates the commission of each of the aforementioned crimes. Not surprisingly, the findings accompanying the Crush Act state, "serious criminal acts of extreme animal cruelty are integral to the creation, sale, distribution, advertising, marketing, and exchange of animal crush videos."[64]

Section 48 only targeted the commercial trafficking of images that lack serious value but memorialize (and incite) crime for commercial gain.[65] First Amendment jurisprudence permits prohibitions on speech that proposes, abets, or constitutes a crime. This is why states lawfully criminalize speech that constitutes fraud, perjury, or solicitation.[66] Just as those laws coexist harmoniously with the First Amendment, so too, could Section 48.

Critics of Stevens argue that the decision makes crime pay by permitting filmmakers to profit from their facilitation of crime.[67] Dogfighting videos arguably make crime more profitable because such videos evidence a dog's champion status, showcase its fighting style to potential buyers, and increase side bets, purses, entry fees, sale prices, and stud fees.[68] Clearly then, the creation and commercial distribution of depictions of animal cruelty generate interest and participation in the crimes of animal fighting and animal cruelty, either facilitating, or worse yet, provoking their commission.

However, some commentators argue that the incitement doctrine covered only a small subset of the depictions that Section 48 reached and failed to consider the value of the speech.[69] More importantly, in *Ashcroft v. Free Speech Coalition*, the Court held that the government may not "prohibit speech because it increases the chance that an unlawful act will be committed at some 'indefinite future time' because 'the mere tendency of speech to encourage unlawful acts is not a sufficient reason for banning it.'"[70] As such, a finding that depictions of animal cruelty may promote future criminal acts likely would have been insufficient, standing alone, to save Section 48; nor will it render the Crush Act invulnerable to constitutional challenges.

A strong argument also exists that depictions of animal cruelty constitute unprotected speech under *Ferber*. The *Ferber* Court upheld a statute prohibiting persons from knowingly promoting sexual performances by minors under the age of 16 by distributing depictions of such performances.[71] The Court articulated five reasons that states may prohibit child pornography: (i) the State has a compelling interest in regulating it; (ii) the speech is "intrinsically related" to the underlying crime depicted; (iii) advertising and selling the speech provides an economic motive for, and is thus integral to, its production; (iv) the possibility that any material of serious value would be prohibited under the newly created category of unprotected speech is "exceedingly modest, if not, de minimis"; and (v) banning full categories of speech is an acceptable approach in First Amendment law and was appropriate under the circumstances.[72]

The Third Circuit held that the depictions of animal cruelty targeted by Section 48 failed to satisfy the *Ferber* factors primarily because of the inherent differences between children and animals.[73] A flaw in this argument is that the Court has never explicitly stated that a compelling interest must involve the welfare of humans rather than animals.[74] As Justice Alito explained, "while protecting children is unquestionably more important than protecting animals, the Government also has a compelling interest in preventing the torture depicted in crush videos. . . . The statutory ban on commerce in dogfighting videos is also supported by compelling governmental interests in effectively enforcing the Nation's criminal laws and preventing criminals from profiting from their illegal activities."[75] Preventing cruelty to animals and to children are not mutually exclusive interests. In fact, ASPCA founders Henry Bergh and Elbridge Gerry were personally involved in the 1873 Mary Ellen case, the first successful child abuse prosecution, and went on to found the Society for the Prevention of Cruelty to Children eight years after the formation of the ASPCA.[76]

Although the majority indicated that the *Ferber* factors do not establish a new general test to determine whether a category of speech is protected, Justice Alito and the Third Circuit disagreed. The next section of the chapter will address each of the five *Ferber* factors in turn. Doing so is necessary because while the majority rejected the *Ferber* Approach, the Third Circuit and Justice Alito utilized it, albeit to reach very different conclusions. An exploration of the *Ferber* factors, therefore, is necessary to explore how the Court could and perhaps should have invoked the *Ferber* Approach to uphold Section 48.

The first *Ferber* factor is especially significant because the majority did not hold that preventing animal cruelty fails to constitute a compelling government interest. In fact, the majority avoided addressing this issue completely by striking the statute on overbreadth grounds. For this reason, animal rights groups considered *Stevens* a small victory of sorts. Had the majority determined that preventing animal cruelty does not constitute a compelling interest, *Stevens* could have undone, or at least imperiled, the last century's progress in the area of animal rights as well as other animal rights legislation. In the wake of *Stevens*, the question of whether preventing animal cruelty constitutes a compelling government interest is perhaps the most important consideration because, as will be discussed in a subsequent chapter, the new Crush Act has allegedly "fixed" the overbreadth problems observed by the majority. Assuming the overbreadth problems have truly been corrected, then the first challenge to the new Crush Act may require the Court, if it grants certiorari, to definitively resolve whether preventing animal cruelty constitutes a compelling government interest.

In the absence of controlling precedent to the contrary, preventing animal cruelty constitutes a compelling government interest because anti-cruelty efforts exist nationwide and serve a variety of laudable social goals, including but not limited to protecting property interests, preventing emotional and physical harm to humans, identifying and preventing interpersonal violence, and decreasing the likelihood of future crimes against humans and animals, including interpersonal violence, drug and weapons trafficking, and gambling. Accordingly, the findings in the Crush Act confirm that preventing intentional acts of extreme animal cruelty constitutes a compelling government interest.

The Court has never held that preventing animal cruelty does not constitute a compelling government interest. Nor did *Stevens* resolve that question. Prior to *Stevens*, the issue was before the Court only once, in *Lukumi*.[77] The Third Circuit interpreted *Lukumi* to indicate that preventing animal cruelty fails to constitute a compelling government interest;[78] however, the *Lukumi* Court never explicitly ruled on the issue.[79]

In *Lukumi*, the Court invalidated a law banning animal sacrifice that had been enacted to burden the exercise of a religion: Santeria.[80] A Santerian church leased land in Hialeah, Florida, with the intent of openly practicing its religion, which involved animal sacrifice; in response, Hialeah enacted ordinances aimed at prohibiting ritualized animal sacrifice.[81] The church sued, alleging a violation of its constitutional rights. The district court upheld the ordinances and found that preventing cruelty to animals was a compelling interest; the Eleventh Circuit affirmed. The Court declared the ordinances unconstitutional because Hialeah enacted them to suppress religious expression, not to prevent animal cruelty. The Court noted that Hialeah could have used less restrictive alternatives to accomplish its goals.[82] *Lukumi* is also distinguishable from *Stevens* because *Lukumi* involved the free exercise of religion, not freedom of speech.[83]

Notably, the Court *never* held that preventing animal cruelty fails to constitute a compelling government interest.[84] In fact, Justice Blackmun's concurrence in *Lukumi* suggests the opposite conclusion.[85] He emphasized:

> The result in the case before the Court today, and the fact that every Member of the Court concurs in that result, does not necessarily reflect this Court's views of the strength of a State's interest in prohibiting cruelty to animals. This case does not present, and I therefore decline to reach, the question [of] whether the Free Exercise Clause would require a religious exemption from a law that sincerely pursued the goal of protecting animals from cruel treatment.[86]

As the dissenting judges in *Stevens* explained:

> The ordinances . . . [in *Lukumi*] failed not because preventing cruelty to animals was not a sufficiently paramount interest to be deemed compelling; rather, the Court found that the ordinances were so riddled with exceptions exempting all other killings except those practiced by Santeria adherents betrayed that the real rationale behind the prohibitions was an unconstitutional suppression of religion.[87]

The Third Circuit may have misinterpreted *Lukumi* because it had no other precedent to support its assertion that preventing animal cruelty is not a compelling interest.[88] However, just as the Third Circuit misconstrued *Lukumi* to indicate that preventing animal cruelty does not constitute a compelling government interest, without clear guidance to the contrary from the Court, so too, may other courts and legislators misinterpret *Stevens* as requiring them to strike down or narrow the scope of existing animal cruelty legislation and other animal welfare laws, even where the laws differ from Section 48 in language, purpose, or scope.

The widespread adoption and long history of anti-cruelty legislation around the world indicate that preventing animal cruelty constitutes a compelling government interest.[89] Anti-cruelty laws, some of which predate the nation's founding, exist in every state, the District of Columbia, Puerto Rico, the Virgin Islands, and in countries around the world.[90] Congress has also enacted numerous animal welfare laws.[91]

The Massachusetts Colony enacted America's first animal cruelty law over 350 years ago; it prohibited "any Tirrany or Crueltie towards any bruite creature which are usuallie kept for man's use."[92] In 1781, English barrister Jeremy Bentham argued that an animal's capacity for suffering, not its ability to talk or reason, entitles it to legal protection.[93] In 1821, Maine enacted a law, which punished anyone who "cruelly beat any horse or cattle" with fines and up to thirty days in prison.[94] New York followed suit in 1829 when it enacted an animal cruelty law, which stated:

> Every person who shall maliciously kill, maim or wound any horse, ox or other cattle, or any sheep, belonging to another or shall maliciously and cruelly beat or torture any such animals, whether belonging to himself or another, shall upon conviction, be adjudged guilty of a misdemeanor.[95]

Through the years, other states enacted animal cruelty laws. Perhaps in recognition of the significant impact of animal cruelty on public mores, such laws were often incorporated into portions of the legislative code involving public morals and decency.[96]

Animal cruelty statutes even preceded child protection laws.[97] In the 1860s, New York enacted legislation giving North America's oldest animal rights organization—the ASPCA—the power to investigate and prosecute animal cruelty.[98] ASPCA founder Henry Bergh successfully lobbied for enactment of a more comprehensive animal cruelty law in New York, which among other things, applied to any living animal regardless of ownership, expanded the list of unlawful acts to include neglect, torture, starvation, and mutilation, and was the first law to ban animal fighting.[99] Prior to the creation of child protection laws, the ASPCA helped prosecute an infamous child abuse case, but did not, as is widely reported, apply existing animal anti-cruelty laws.[100] Later, Bergh helped to create the Society for the Prevention of Cruelty to Children, underscoring the fact that similar moral arguments underlie the enactment of legislation to protect children and animals—those most vulnerable to wanton acts of cruelty.[101]

Dogfighting is such a tremendous social harm that, despite the existence of general anti-cruelty statutes in every state, separate laws in all fifty states and the District of Columbia specifically prohibit the practice.[102] At the time of the initiation of the *Stevens* case, most states punished dog fighting as a felony.[103] As of 2012, all states now consider this crime a felony and many also ban any and all activities related to dogfighting, such as attending a fight or promoting a match.[104] Furthermore, every state and the District of Columbia ban cockfighting.[105] As of 2006, forty-one states and the District of Columbia also prohibited attending a cockfight, and several states criminalize the possession of cockfighting paraphernalia.[106]

Congress has also vocalized its belief that preventing animal cruelty constitutes a compelling government interest by enacting legislation that does just that.[107] Federal law bans the transport of animals for use in animal fighting,[108] and the Animal Welfare Act prohibits the transportation or export of fighting cocks.[109] Like Section 48, these laws satisfy the public's strong desire that animals be treated humanely.[110] In addition, state and local governments, non-profit organizations, charities, and personal donors annually expend millions of dollars—over and above their tremendous time and effort—to promulgate anti-cruelty legislation, to investigate and prosecute animal cruelty, and to house and rehabilitate animal victims.[111]

The widespread enactment of animal fighting bans and general anti-cruelty statutes suggests that most Americans support the criminalization of animal cruelty. This nationwide consensus strongly indicates that preventing animal cruelty constitutes a compelling government interest. Yet, unlike the *Ferber* Court, which refused to second-guess legislative judgment and afforded deference to research regarding the impact of child pornography, the Third Circuit and the majority appear to have given little or no deference to the indisputable fact that every state outlaws animal cruelty and animal fighting.[112] Instead, as Justice Alito observed, "the Court of Appeals erred in second-guessing the legislative judgment about the importance of preventing cruelty to animals."[113]

Law enforcement officials have long emphasized that existing anti-cruelty legislation is insufficient to prevent and punish animal cruelty.[114] Section 48 was not redundant because existing anti-cruelty laws likely do not cover the creation, sale, or possession of depictions of animal cruelty, and state anti-cruelty laws vary widely in the scope of their coverage.[115] Section 48 aimed "to augment, not supplant, state animal cruelty laws by addressing behavior that may be outside the jurisdiction of the states, as a matter of law, and appears often beyond the reach of their law enforcement officials, as a practical matter."[116] Section 48 filled loopholes in existing anti-cruelty legislation by covering: (i) depictions of animal cruelty rather than the underlying conduct itself, which is sometimes covered under existing law; (ii) all living animals, regardless of ownership or domestic status; and (iii) abusers, regardless of whether they own the animal victim. Section 48 penalized the misconduct more severely, punishing it as a felony whereas many states classify animal abuse as a misdemeanor.[117] The harsher penalty arguably increased the incentive to prosecute and decreased the incentive to commit the crime.[118]

Aside from the non-uniformity and inadequate coverage of most state legislation, many crush and dogfighting videographers cleverly refuse to film (or later edit out) identifying information about participants and the film's setting, making it impossible for prosecutors to establish where the cruelty occurred.[119] Where unable to prove jurisdiction, the case will be dismissed because prosecutors cannot show that the torture was illegal within the laws of the relevant state.[120] Filmmakers also deliberately remove identifying information regarding the depiction's date of creation, making it extremely difficult to prove that the conduct occurred within the applicable statute of limitations.[121] Section 48 solved this problem because the statute of limitations began to toll on the date on which the video was sold, created, or possessed, which was easier to prove and verify.[122] Moreover, filmmakers intentionally record the executioner from the waist down, making it impossible to identify her, and deliberately black out faces in dogfighting videos. For instance, the faces of dog handlers were edited out in *Pick-A-Winna*.[123] As such, there is usually no way to determine when, where, and by whom the animal cruelty occurred; local authorities cannot secure a conviction of those who commit the acts of cruelty portrayed or who make and sell these highly disturbing portrayals.[124] Prior to Section 48's enactment, the sole means by which prosecutors could convict someone for producing such depictions would literally be for undercover law enforcement officers or civilians to discover the scene during filming, arrest the participants, and testify at trial; this situation is extremely unlikely, and perpetrators know it.[125] With no incentive to stop, the cruelty intensified, and the industry grew.

Anecdotal evidence also indicates that prosecuting persons involved in the animal cruelty industry may simultaneously prevent future crimes toward humans (or result in the incarceration of perpetrators of past crimes against humans). In Philadelphia, two men brutally shot Edward Atwood in front of his family. Shortly thereafter, three men attacked and doused six dogs with drain cleaner, bleach, and pancake mix. As a result, five of the dogs had to be euthanized. The men were arrested, and when their photographs were shown on television, Mr. Atwood's wife identified one of them as her husband's murderer. Incredibly, the man had been hired to kill Mr. Atwood because he had complained about a neighbor's improper care of a pet.[126]

Insufficient attention has been paid to the emotional, psychological, and physical harm to humans that animal cruelty causes. In *People v. Garcia*, the Appellate Division of New York struggled to determine whether New York's anti-cruelty statute could be used to prosecute a defendant who deliberately crushed a nine-year-old's pet goldfish before his eyes.[127] The Court's decision appears to have hinged upon the fact that anti-cruelty statutes aim to prevent harm to both the animal and to individuals who have developed emotional ties to the animal as well as potential future harm to humans on the basis of the correlation between cruelty to animals and violence against humans.[128]

Section 48 was uniquely tailored to address each of these concerns. Dog-fighting rings may steal pets for use as bait; not only does the petnapping and brutal slaughter of a beloved companion animal cause severe emotional harm to pet owners, but where the slaughter is recorded and sold for commercial gain, exploitation of the brutal murder exacerbates the harm to pet owners just as the *Ferber* Court noted that circulation of child pornography amplifies harm to the victim. Even excluding petnappings, viewing such depictions can cause harm to the filmmaker and viewer alike.

According to some commentators, the government also has an interest in preventing Americans from accessing materials that encourage a lack of respect for life, erode public morality, and desensitize individuals to violence.[129] As Immanuel Kant observed, "cruelty to animals is contrary to man's duty to himself, because it deadens in him the feeling of sympathy for their sufferings, and thus a natural tendency that is very useful to morality in relation to other human beings is weakened."[130] At least some empirical evidence suggests that Kant was right. Animal cruelty negatively impacts the person inflicting the harm as well as the viewer.[131] Exposure to brutality, whether in person or by viewing a film, desensitizes viewers to suffering; this may provoke violence because viewers lose their ability to empathize with others.[132] In the absence of Section 48 or its replacement—the Crush Act—depictions of animal cruelty would likely have escalated to involve more gruesome killing methods and larger victims, perhaps even infants. After all, early crush videos began with insects and inanimate objects but have evolved to include puppies, kittens, etc.[133] The chilling testimony of a California deputy district attorney reveals that this evolution was already in progress: "We have some stills of a baby doll they're crushing ... [eventually] buyers will get desensitized [and] it'll get to be a baby."[134] Without a law to deter filmmakers, one can only imagine what or who the next victim will be.

Given the widespread availability of the Internet, exposure of children to such depictions is virtually unavoidable.[135] However, by criminalizing depictions of animal cruelty and simultaneously reducing their production, Section 48 would have and the Crush Act will likely reduce the risk that children and other innocent viewers will be harmed and disturbed by exposure to these sadistic depictions.[136]

Psychologists and law enforcement officials have long recognized the strong link between animal cruelty and violent criminal behavior.[137] Thus, Section 48 was (and the Crush Act will hopefully be) an effective crime prevention tool because it could help prevent subsequent crimes against humans and animals committed by depraved viewers of animal cruelty depictions who are so desensitized or aroused by animal torture that they emulate these violent crimes.[138]

An increasing number of research psychologists endorse the existence of a strong causal link between exposure to violence, such as viewing a crush video, and aggressive behavior, particularly in minors.[139] The Meese Commission Report discovered a "strong causal link between exposure to violent pornography and subsequent aggressive behavior," which is particularly relevant since crush videos fulfill violent sexual fetishes.[140] Researchers theorize that the link can be explained in four primary ways: (i) viewers learn violent behavior via imitation and observation; (ii) violent depictions subconsciously "automatize" the viewer's behavior so that the person reacts violently in response to certain stimuli; (iii) recurring exposure to violence desensitizes the viewer, decreasing his or her inhibition to commit violence; and (iv) violent depictions may arouse the viewer, either strengthening his or her reaction to provocation "or causing the viewer to misattribute his state of arousal to the provocation."[141] The Humane Society's First Strike Campaign aims to raise awareness regarding the link between animal cruelty and violent crime.[142] Likewise, the Federal Bureau of Investigation (FBI) has advised that animal cruelty during childhood is a red flag for later violence against humans. [143]

Research also confirms the existence of a strong link between the commission of animal abuse and violence against humans. In one study, seventy-five percent of those charged with violent crimes had histories of animal cruelty.[144] In 1997, the Massachusetts Society for the Prevention of Cruelty to Animals and Northeastern University conducted a study that compared persons prosecuted for intentional animal abuse against individuals of the same gender, age, socioeconomic status, and geographic location who had not abused animals. The study demonstrated that "animal abusers were five times more likely to have been convicted of another violent crime and three times more likely to have been involved in another form of serious criminal behavior."[145] A 1999 study found that "individuals prosecuted for animal abuse were more likely to have an adult arrest in each of four crime categories [person, property, drug, or public order offenses] than the comparison group members."[146] Researchers have found that a history of cruelty to animals during childhood is a strong predictor of subsequent "violent offense recidivism."[147]

Survey evidence also supports the conclusion that animal cruelty is a "predictor crime" for subsequent violence against humans.[148] One FBI study found that more than fifty percent of the thirty-five convicted serial killers questioned admitted to torturing animals during childhood. In a 1988 study of thirty-six sexual murderers (twenty-nine were serial killers), thirty-six percent of the serial killers had committed acts of animal cruelty during childhood and forty-six percent had done so during adolescence.[149] As Dr. Randall Lockwood explained, a "10-year study of at-risk children showed that those who were classified at age 6–12 as cruel to animals were more than twice as likely as others in the study to be subsequently referred to juvenile authorities for a violent offense. Of those reported to be both cruel to animals and firesetters, eighty-three percent had later involvement in violent offenses."[150]

Anecdotal evidence also substantiates the link between animal cruelty and future violent crime against humans. Many serial killers, rapists, and other violent criminals committed acts of animal cruelty during childhood.[151] Serial killer David Berkowitz slaughtered a parrot and a dog before he began murdering humans.[152] Cannibal Jeffrey Dahmer impaled dead dog heads on fence posts.[153] Sixteen-year-old Luke Woodham stabbed his mother to death before embarking on a killing spree at his high school, murdering two classmates and injuring seven others. Six months prior to the killing spree, Woodham confided in his journal that he and an accomplice had beaten, burned, and tortured his dog to death. He described the sound of the dog's crushing bones as "true beauty."[154] Teen shooters in Oregon and Colorado also confessed to torturing animals prior to their multiple victim killings,[155] and a 2000 study revealed that five out of eleven participating school shooters had histories of alleged animal cruelty.[156] Had their conduct been punished at the time, perhaps they could have received treatment or remained behind bars, ultimately preventing the murders that followed.

Sadistic stories ripped from the headlines further illustrate the indisputable link between animal cruelty and violence against humans. In June of 2009, a pet spa owner and alleged animal abuser slit his estranged wife's throat, stabbed her in front of her children, and then committed suicide. He had a history of alleged animal cruelty and was under indictment for the death of Moxie, a beagle, brought to his spa for a bath. A veterinary examination of Moxie uncovered an array of injuries from broken ribs to a lacerated liver, which caused internal hemorrhaging. Moxie's slaying spurred the fourth lawsuit arising from mysterious deaths of pets in the spa's care.[157]

Poignant stories of interpersonal violence illustrate the link between animal and human violence. In January of 1996, a woman returned home to find her two parakeets dead. Her angry ex-husband had broken their necks and then roasted them in her oven. She reported the harassment to the police, and eight months later, she was found shot to death. Authorities charged her ex-husband with her murder. Similarly, in Longview, Washington, a woman's ex-boyfriend was charged with felony animal cruelty and misdemeanor assault after he assaulted her and burned her parakeet to death.[158]

As Frank Ascione and Dr. Randall Lockwood explain, animal abuse "may represent a form of rehearsal for the abuse of humans and, if undetected, embolden the perpetrator to believe he can escape both the authorities and the consequences of his acts."[159] The story of serial killer Arthur Bishop illustrates this theory. Bishop kidnapped, tortured, and slaughtered a child. He was so distressed that, instead of abducting another child, he tortured fifty puppies to death. Rather than satiating his thirst for blood, however, the animal abuse spurred him to abduct, torture, and murder more children.[160]

While animal abusers are often involved in other crimes, the sale of depictions of animal cruelty and/or the commission of animal cruelty may be the easiest to prove and thus, the likeliest to result in incarceration (at least prior to *Stevens*). Getting the offender off the street for animal cruelty may prevent him or her from committing additional and different crimes toward humans, including property and drug offenses, as well as violent crimes.[161]

Famed anthropologist Margaret Mead once remarked, "one of the most dangerous things that can happen to a child is to kill or torture an animal and get away with it."[162] Animal cruelty may be the first serious offense for which a juvenile can be prosecuted, providing an opportunity to intervene at a pivotal stage in development that may prevent the juvenile from committing subsequent crimes against humans.[163] Perhaps not surprisingly, because animal cruelty may be symptomatic of psychological disturbance or conduct disorders that could lead to other crimes,[164] several states mandate psychological assessments of juveniles convicted of animal cruelty.[165]

Animal cruelty is a particularly strong indicator of domestic violence,[166] including elder and child abuse.[167] As Representative Morella noted during legislative debate on Section 48:

My experience in working on domestic violence issues alerted me
to the connection between animal abuse and violent behavior. . . .
Abusers often threaten to harm or inflict pain to the animal to demonstrate control within the home. . . . Raising awareness about the
link between animal cruelty and domestic violence, child abuse and
other forms of violent behavior I think is an important step in trying to prevent such violence.[168]

Research supports the existence of a strong link between animal cruelty and
domestic violence. A Utah study revealed that "71% of pet-owning victims in a
domestic violence shelter reported that their abuser had threatened, harmed, or
killed an animal."[169] Another study indicated that 80% of surveyed pet owners at
twelve domestic violence shelters reported that their abusers had exhibited violence
toward their pets.[170] Comparing 101 women surveyed in shelters to an equal number of women who had not been abused by their partners, battered women were
roughly eleven times likelier to report that their partners had physically abused
a pet. In a 2004 study, 53% of participants indicated that their abusive spouses
physically abused their pets.[171] The study also revealed that:

Of those families where pet abuse had occurred, 48% of the respondents
reported it occurred "often" during the past [twelve] months and another 30% reported that abuse to the family pet had occurred "almost
always" during the past [twelve] months. Victims whose pets had been
abused reported that abuse to the family pets occurred an average of
51% of the time violent outbursts had taken place over the past year.[172]

Pets and service animals may also serve as tools to perpetrate domestic violence. For instance, abusers may force victims and pets to commit bestiality. In
the presence of animal abuse, "the chance of domestic violence lethality generally
increases."[173] As such, prosecuting perpetrators of animal cruelty could perhaps
prevent or reduce incidents of domestic violence.[174]

Fear of pet abuse often deters victims from escaping abusers.[175] In the 2004
study referenced above, "Forty-eight percent of the battered women reported
that they delayed leaving out of fear for the welfare of their pets. Of those situations where the batterer had previously abused a pet, 65% of the battered women
delayed leaving out of concern for their animals."[176] Other research reveals that
"18–48 percent of battered women have delayed leaving an abusive home, or have
returned to their batterer, out of fear for the welfare of their pets or livestock."[177]
A 2000 study indicated that 44% of participants had partners who had abused
or killed companion animals, and 43% stated that concern for their pets' welfare

prevented them from leaving sooner.[178] In a disturbing illustration of such coercive animal abuse, a battered wife returned to her abuser after he mailed photographs to her, which showed him cutting off her dog's ears with gardening shears. He also mailed the ears.[179] Perhaps the most disturbing illustration of coercive animal cruelty comes from Salt Lake City, where a woman alleged that her abusive husband hanged their pet rabbit and began skinning it alive in front of her and their child; as the animal shrieked in agony, he held the baby next to it and remarked, "See how easy it would be?"[180]

As Joshua Friedman and Gary Norman explain, "abusers realize their intended goal by viciously dominating the life of their victim through the threat of harm to a beloved pet or service animal. This course of action instills insecurity and terror in the victims."[181] Congress has also recognized that "women in domestic violence shelters report that their abusers victimize the family pet in order to control their behavior or the children's behavior."[182] Accordingly, animal shelters and battered women's shelters should join forces to care for battered women and their pets.[183] This holistic, interdisciplinary approach is also important because pets "furnish solace, emotional support, and assistance to victims of domestic violence" and "allow for personal exercise and opportunities to search for escape routes."[184]

The strong correlation between animal cruelty and child abuse is also undeniable.[185] A 1983 New Jersey study indicated that out of 53 families where "substantiated child abuse and neglect" had occurred, 60% also possessed abused or neglected pets, and "animal abuse was significantly higher (88 percent) in families where child physical abuse was present than in families where other forms of child maltreatment (e.g., sexual abuse) occurred (34 percent)."[186]

Anecdotal evidence supports the existence of this correlation. In Ohio, for example, police conducted an animal cruelty investigation of a home where neighbors reported seeing dead kittens on the front porch. During the investigation, the police found additional cats in deplorable conditions as well as two young children covered in feces and urine who were locked in a bedroom.[187] After a dog died when its owner taped a toy inside its mouth with packaging tape to prevent it from barking, Michigan Humane Society workers discovered that the same woman had been seen beating her children and had been the subject of prior complaints with Child Protective Services. A man who shot his dog in front of his family because the dog had ruined a window covering was under investigation for child abuse at the time of the shooting.[188]

Abusers often discourage children from reporting abuse by threatening to harm or kill their beloved pets.[189] By way of illustration, according to Susan Crowell, a man charged with lewd conduct and rape of his daughter and half-sister prevented them from reporting the abuse by threatening to kill them and by slaughtering animals in front of them. In another example, a man sexually abused his seven-year-old adopted daughter and her schoolmate during a camping trip, but his victims did not report the abuse in part because he threatened to harm the family pet and subjected it to physical abuse.[190] Abusers may also force child victims to perform sexual acts with pets or force them to wound or murder their favorite pet to compel them to keep the abuse a secret.[191]

Compulsory participation in or witnessing animal abuse is not uncommon and can have extremely negative consequences on a child's development.[192] As Dr. Randall Lockwood explained:

> If children witness a pet being intentionally harmed, it damages any sense of safety and confidence in the ability of adults to protect them from harm. . . . They learn that it is normal to be threatened and hurt by those you love and who claim to love you. . . . Children who are the victims of abuse may seek to re-enact the abuse they have suffered by repeating these behaviors on other victims who are weaker and more vulnerable than themselves . . . [and are] at high risk of establishing life-long patterns of violent behavior. For many children the pain of empathy for animals that have been abused by other family members teaches them that such kindness and sensitivity must be suppressed. Some of these children may still love their pets but kill them in a desperate attempt to have some control over what they see as an inevitable fate for the animal. Others may abuse their own pets to assure themselves and others that their own caring has been stifled and that continuing exposure to the abuse of those they love cannot hurt them anymore. In some cases the child becomes insensitive not only to the feelings of others, but to his or her own feelings. Such children may test the limits of their own desensitization through attempting to cut, burn or mutilate themselves.[193]

A 2004 study revealed that "61% of the women reported that their children had witnessed animal abuse. . . . Children of women in battered women shelters were 'twenty times more likely to have witnessed pet abuse than children from a control group.'"[194] In one case, a woman reportedly shot her batterer when he attempted to force her to hold down a puppy while he had sex with it.[195] A biography of Wayne Dresbach, who murdered his parents at age fifteen, states that when his abusive father was angry about the birth of a new litter of kittens, he piled them into a sack and walked to the creek.

> At the creek [his father] rolled the top of the bag tight, then tossed it into the shallow water. While the kittens screeched, and pawed to get out, and Wayne sobbed for him not to do it, his father took aim and emptied the rifle. . . . Wayne wanted to bury the kittens, but [his father] told him not to bother. Dogs and buzzards would take care of them.[196]

Perhaps it is no surprise that Mr. Dresbach ultimately became a murderer himself.[197]

Exposure to domestic violence during childhood may cause a vast array of other negative consequences, including but not limited to "stuttering, headaches, stomachaches, asthma, bed-wetting, suicidal behavior, clinging behavior, aggressive behavior, passivity, insomnia, phobias, withdrawal, anxiety, or depression."[198] Yet the impact of domestic violence on a child's personality and emotional development is perhaps more disturbing than its physical symptoms. Children exposed to domestic violence are reportedly three times more likely to commit animal cruelty, perhaps due to their desensitization to violence or inability to empathize with victims.[199] A 1992 study indicated that sexually abused children were "significantly more likely" to commit animal cruelty than non-abused counterparts.[200] In a 1983 study of "fifty-three families being treated by New Jersey Family Services because of incidents of child abuse," 88% of the families reported pet abuse; abusive parents were responsible for roughly 66% of the abuse, but children were the animal abusers in the remaining cases.[201] For this reason, taking animal cruelty seriously may not only protect animals but may also unearth and put a stop to child abuse.

Awareness of the link between human and animal cruelty spurred Congress to enact Section 48. Section 48 reflected "a growing awareness . . . that violence perpetrated on animals is unacceptable and often escalates to violence against humans. . . . It is essential that our society recognizes this link and punishes acts of animal cruelty."[202] Accordingly, Congress passed the following resolution, acknowledging the undeniable link between early animal abuse and subsequent brutality against humans:

> The Congress (1) recognizes that individuals who abuse animals are more likely to commit more serious violent crimes against humans; (2) urges social workers, teachers, mental health professionals, and others to be aware of the connection between animal cruelty and human violence and to evaluate carefully and to monitor

closely individuals who have a history of abusing animals because this may indicate a propensity to commit violence against other humans; (3) urges appropriate Federal agencies to encourage and support research to increase the understanding of the connection between cruelty to animals and violence against humans in order to utilize instances of animal abuse to identify and intervene with potentially violent individuals, and urges Federal agencies which are undertaking research on violent crime and its causes to incorporate examination of the link between violence against animals and violence against humans; (4) urges local law enforcement officials to treat cases of animal cruelty seriously both because such cruelty is a [sign] of the potential for domestic and other forms of violence against humans; and (5) commends the fine work of local animal control officials and humane investigators who enforce laws against animal abuse and urges these professionals to work more closely with local law enforcement personnel to identify and prevent potential violence against humans.[203]

For all of the foregoing reasons, the prevention of animal cruelty clearly constitutes a compelling government interest.

Turning to the second *Ferber* factor, the Third Circuit held that the depictions prohibited by Section 48 were not intrinsically related to underlying crimes of animal cruelty.[204] While the majority never addressed the Third Circuit's conclusion, Justice Alito rejected it, noting that the "most important factor" in support of classifying child pornography as unprotected speech was that the speech involved the commission of crimes against children.[205] Likewise, depictions of animal cruelty do more than exacerbate the harm to animals; their creation and sale are often its direct cause.

Because committing a crime is necessary to create depictions of animal cruelty,[206] Section 48 was an effective crime-prevention tool. Section 48's prohibition of the creation, sale, or possession of depictions of animal cruelty likely eliminated or at least reduced the demand for the underlying acts of torture; if the film could not be sold for a profit without risk of criminal prosecution, then what filmmaker would expend the time, money, and effort to create the film, especially when he or she will be unable to earn a profit? This is especially true with regard to made-to-order videos that allow purchasers to specify the victim and method of torture.[207] Without the promise of significant financial gain, the filmmaker is far less likely to commit the other crimes necessary to produce the film, including but not limited to the cruelty itself.[208] By criminalizing one action, Section 48 also effectively prevented the commission of other crimes.

Animals in these depictions experience unimaginable physical and psychological trauma solely for profit.[209] Victims featured in crush videos are slowly ground into a bloody pulp; the length of torture could be prolonged or the killing method made more agonizing to capture "better" footage or to fulfill a customer's specific fantasy. During debate on Section 48's enactment, viewers described one crush video as follows: "the little animal was literally pinned down on the floor as this woman took a high-heeled stiletto shoe, talking vulgar language to it, slowly crushing each of its limbs, listening to its sound on the audio, and working her way to the final death of that animal before . . . the animal was literally crushed into the ground over a period of 10 or 12 minutes."[210] Some films last two hours.[211]

Similarly, a dogfighting video requires a dogfight. Dogfighting is illegal in every state. Additionally, fighting dogs suffer a lifetime of abuse. Puppies are sometimes beaten to condition them to violence.[212] According to one source, as part of training, an owner forced a puppy to fight against a mature fighting dog.[213] Another report indicated that a fighting dog seized after its owner's arrest possessed over a thousand wounds.[214]

The life of a fighting dog is all discipline and no affection. Fighting dogs "are forced to run on a treadmill several hours per day and strengthen their jaws with spring poles. Weights affixed to chains are dangled from their necks to build strength, and owners run them with weights attached; dogs are often *permanently* chained this way." [215] Battered dogs drugged with steroids, weight-gain supplements, and controlled substances (including speed and cocaine) are literally torn apart by opponents.[216] Because of the monetary and reputational harm that ensues from a loss, "the end result, if the losing dog survives the fight, is immediate death, if he is lucky, or torture and mutilation if the owner is embarrassed or irate."[217] Injured winners may also suffer a terrible fate. Owners may fail to take injured dogs to veterinarians for fear that their crimes will be reported, and injured survivors may still die from the substandard veterinary care their owners provide.[218]

Section 48 prohibited materials intrinsically related to animal cruelty because the film's creation is predicated on the commission of multiple crimes in addition to animal cruelty.[219] To film a dogfight, the filmmaker must attend the fight, which is illegal in some states.[220] As Justice Alito observed, "some dogfighting videos are made 'solely for the purpose of selling the video (and not for a live audience),'" which means that the cruelty would never have occurred but for the creation and sale of the film.[221]

By criminalizing depictions of illegal animal cruelty, Section 48 and now the Crush Act promote and preserve public morality and simultaneously prevent, or at least reduce, the commission of related crimes against humans—including gambling, drug and weapons trafficking, murder and other crimes.[222] As Hanna Gibson explained:

> Dogfighting is an insidious underground organized crime and all dog fighters, regardless of their level, embrace many peripheral crimes and gang activities including drug dealing and consumption, gambling, theft, and violence against humans. . . . Many recent dog fighting raids, includ[ing] those in Flint, MI (2003), Buffalo, NY (2004), Port St. Lucie, FL (2004), Jones County, GA (2004), and Oklahoma City, OK (2004), have resulted in the infiltration of major drug distribution networks, and the arrest of the drug kingpins who regularly organized and attended the dog fights. . . . Fighting dogs are clandestine security devices for drug traffickers. Drugs are often stashed in containers to which the dogs are chained in yards or vacant fields. The dogs also provide excellent security inside drug houses and warehouses. Where once the presence of dogs was utilized as an overt warning to potential invaders, it is now increasingly common for criminals to have the dogs debarked (vocal cords severed), to act as silent alarm and attack systems against unsuspecting invaders. The presence of the silent killers poses a significant threat to law enforcement personnel entering these premises. . . . Criminals also use dogfighting to yield large profits through illegal gambling.[223]

As such, criminalizing those who participate in and encourage dogfighting may prevent related crimes against humans, including "drug offenses, gang activity, weapons violations, sexual assault, and domestic violence."[224] Animal cruelty "cases are often easier to prosecute . . . since the effects of the crime on the victim may be easier to document and the intentionality of the offense is more clearly recognized."[225]

Not surprisingly, Attorneys General of numerous states filed amicus briefs in support of Section 48. They argued that Section 48 strengthened law enforcement efforts to deter and enforce state anti-cruelty laws by prohibiting perpetrators (and distributors) from advertising, selling, and profiting from animal cruelty depictions in any market.[226] They further contended that striking Section 48 would severely undermine such efforts by allowing perpetrators to openly profit from their involvement in violent and depraved crimes.[227] Existing anti-cruelty laws have generally required perpetrators to be caught in the act of animal cruelty;

this method is ineffective in light of sophisticated organizations that commercialize animal cruelty. Section 48 and its successor legislation have filled that crucial gap in the law to better guarantee that crime will not pay.[228]

As the drafters of the Crush Act acknowledge, advertising and selling depictions of animal cruelty provide a major economic motive for and are the main incentive for their production.[229] Due to the highly secretive nature of this industry, the most effective way to end the underlying acts of cruelty is to target filmmakers and prevent them from profiting from their instigation of and participation in violent crime.[230] Crush videos enjoy a large audience, and a single video sells for up to $300; annual sales total nearly $1 million.[231]

Animal fighting is also lucrative. As one commentator noted, "dog-fighting is an incredible source of income for gangs and drug traffickers. In fact, the average dog fight could easily net more money than an armed robbery, or a series of isolated drug transactions."[232]

Dogfighting videos perpetuate animal cruelty by promoting illegal dogfighting and increasing the profitability and value of fighting dogs and their issue. A Grand Champion[233] commands substantially higher side bets, purses, entry fees, stud fees, and sale price—up to $10,000—than a Champion.[234] Puppies of Grand Champions may sell for thousands of dollars apiece.[235] Because written certification of a dog's success rate is difficult to verify and easily faked, a film is the best way to memorialize a dog's status and to showcase its fighting style to potential purchasers and breeders.[236] Because a dog's value and profitability hinge on its win rate in "official," refereed fights, dogfighting videos enable owners to profit from their crimes.

Speaking in support of Section 48, one Congressman remarked, "the most effective way of stopping this trade is by getting to the people who are distributing the product and making a profit."[237] He further noted, "the prosecutors from around this country ... appeal to us for this [bill]. ... The producer and distributor of the video, the person making the big bucks, is not violating any current State or Federal laws."[238] The Third Circuit conceded that the drying-up-the-market theory, based on decreasing production, is "potentially apt in the animal cruelty context," but stated that no empirical evidence confirms that theory's validity.[239] According to the HSUS, at least some evidence indicates that Section 48 eliminated the financial incentive driving crush videos (and simultaneously stopped the senseless and illegal acts of animal cruelty depicted therein).[240] According to a member of the Pennsylvania Attorney General's office, taking a popular dogfighting journal out of publication after its owner's arrest reduces profits and thus, diminishes the incentive to participate in the activity.[241] A crush filmmaker recently admitted that publicity about crush videos had forced him out of the business of selling the films via adult magazines.[242] Perhaps in anticipation of a crackdown on crush videos following Section 48's enactment, a crush video website began showing women crushing inanimate objects instead of animals.[243] Likewise, Section 48 had heretofore prevented a Florida company from broadcasting Puerto Rican cockfights on the Internet.[244] Unfortunately, the majority's decision may have undone the progress that Section 48 had achieved; animal cruelty depictions came back online shortly after the Third Circuit's decision.[245] As Strossen observed, the *Ferber* court upheld a ban on child pornography without citing any empirical evidence in support of its drying-up-the-market rationale; "the empirical evidence it did cite actually supported a less restrictive alternative to criminalizing the expression at issue: enforcing obscenity statutes."[246]

The possibility that Section 48 prohibits socially valuable speech is "exceedingly modest, if not, *de minimis*." [247] As Justice Alito observed, "depictions of dogfights that fall within §48's reach have by definition no appreciable social value."[248] According to proponents of Section 48, Congress narrowly tailored the statute such that it covered only depictions that lack redeeming social value and portray criminal acts; as such, Section 48 would have been unlikely to reap negative repercussions on the exercise of free speech.[249] Section 48 exempted "any depiction that has serious religious, political, scientific, educational, journalistic, historical, or artistic value."[250] Significantly, the statute upheld in *Ferber* contained no such exception.[251] Even the obscenity test articulated in *Miller v. California*[252] only exempts works that, taken as a whole, lack serious "literary, artistic, political, or scientific value."[253]

While the majority acknowledged that Congress modeled Section 48's exceptions clause on the Supreme Court's language in *Miller*, well-intentioned reliance on precedent did not save the law. As Chief Justice Roberts explained, "in *Miller* we held that 'serious' value shields depictions of sex from regulation as obscenity. . . . We did not, however, determine that serious value could be used as a general precondition to protecting other types of speech in the first place. . . . Thus, the protection of the First Amendment presumptively extends to many forms of speech that do not qualify for the serious-value exception of §48(b), but nonetheless fall within the broad reach of §48(c)."[254] After noting that the government's interpretation of Section 48's exceptions clause "requires an unrealistically broad reading,"[255] Chief Justice Roberts cautioned that Section 48's requirement of serious value "should be taken seriously."[256] The majority also pointed out that since most hunting videos are designed for entertainment, not instruction, they would potentially violate Section 48.[257]

This argument misses the mark because in order for Section 48 to have applied: (i) the depiction must have included a live animal, not an animated, virtual, stuffed, or dead one; (ii) the animal must have been subjected to intentional and illegal acts of animal cruelty, not legal methods of killing such as fishing, hunting, or lawful euthanasia of a pound animal; and (iii) the depiction must have been created, possessed, or sold and placed in interstate or foreign commerce for commercial gain, not a home video created only for personal enjoyment.[258] As explained during legislative debate on Section 48, Congress never intended the statute to encompass depictions of hunting.

> These exceptions would ensure that an entertainment program on Spain depicting bull fighting or a news documentary on elephant poachers, to state two examples, would not violate the new statute. . . . The bill requires that the conduct depicted be illegal. . . . The sale of depictions of legal activities, such as hunting and fishing, would not be illegal. . . . [The law] will in no way prohibit hunting, fishing, or wildlife videos.[259]

Section 48's record of enforcement spoke for itself. The law had never been used to challenge a hunting channel or program, and neither Stevens nor the Court pointed to any evidence indicating that Section 48 had had a chilling effect on such depictions. Taken together, Section 48's text, legislative history, and record of enforcement seemingly contravened the majority's argument that the law was rightfully invalidated because it could chill depictions of lawful hunting.

Animal violence in films, television, and video games is almost always simulated and conveys a message; thus, it would also have been unaffected by Section 48. Nor would Section 48 apply to *Planet Earth*'s portrayal of a great white shark breaching to capture a seal because the depiction does not show a criminal act of animal cruelty committed by a human against an animal and arguably has redeeming educational, scientific, and perhaps, artistic value.

To the extent a portrayal of animal cruelty is necessary to a film's creation, there is no reason a live animal must be tortured. Animation or computer graphics could simulate the violence.[260] In training videos, dogs could be muzzled, demonstrating attack styles/techniques without injuring themselves or opponents. Bait could also be simulated, fake (for example, a stuffed animal), or dead. This would simultaneously decrease the incidence of abducting pets to be used as bait to train fighting dogs.[261]

As one Congressman explained during legislative debate surrounding Section 48's enactment:

> I do not believe in my entire time in Congress I have ever seen any-
> thing . . . as repulsive as the videotape [crush video]. . . . It was even
> more gruesome as the tape wore on. . . . And I can assure anyone who
> is listening to my comments today that there is nothing redeeming,
> socially or otherwise, about any of the depictions I witnessed in our
> hearing the other day.[262]

He continued, "There is no redeeming value whatsoever. It does not rise to that level at all to be protected as free speech when we are talking about torturing an animal under the purposes here with all the exemptions we have for journalistic and religious and other reasons."[263] Former President Clinton characterized the conduct portrayed in crush videos as "deplorable and indefensible."[264]

Perhaps the strongest criticism lodged against Section 48 is that it was not intended to encompass dogfighting videos. Crush videos spurred Section 48's en-actment, but Congress wisely drafted the statutory language broadly enough to embrace not only existing crush videos but also new and different animal cruelty depictions. Broader language is sometimes necessary to provide a law with suf-ficient flexibility to "evolve" with the times. An extremely narrow "crush video" statute that applies only to films of live animals being stomped to death could not be used to prosecute persons who create dog-burning videos—a new genre in which live dogs are burned on tape to satisfy viewers' depraved sexual interests. Congress would be required to draft and enact an entirely new "dog-burning de-piction" law, which would be costly, inefficient, and wasteful. Had Congress only intended Section 48 to apply to crush videos, it could have included language spe-cific to "crushing"; the fact that it did not indicates that Congress intended Section 48 to cover a broader range of depictions of animal cruelty.

The government argued that prosecutorial discretion would have provided additional safeguards against the application of Section 48 beyond the narrow scope for which it was intended. In rejecting this argument, the majority coun-tered that it "would not uphold an unconstitutional statute merely because the government promised to use it responsibly."[265] The majority even described an Executive Branch announcement clarifying that Section 48 would only apply to "depictions 'of wanton cruelty to animals'" as "an implicit acknowledgement of the potential constitutional problems with a more natural reading [of the statute]."[266]

Banning depictions of animal cruelty comports with First Amendment juris-prudence. Turning to the final *Ferber* factor, it is well settled that certain categories of speech are categorically excluded from First Amendment protection, including fighting words, threats, incitement, child pornography, obscenity,[267] "offers to provide or requests to obtain child pornography,"[268] "offers to engage in illegal transactions,"[269] and "offers to provide or requests to obtain unlawful material, whether as part of a commercial exchange or not."[270] Like the aforementioned categories of unprotected speech, the depictions of animal cruelty that Section 48 was intended to target are devoid of the exposition of ideas, endanger mankind by desensitizing viewers to violence, erode public mores, incite and condone savage acts of violent crime toward defenseless victims, necessitate offers to engage in the crime of animal cruelty, and/or appeal to the prurient interest of depraved individuals aroused by animal brutality.[271]

Furthermore, speech that forms an integral part of a criminal violation is unprotected.[272] Creating a dogfighting video requires the filmmaker to solicit, attend, or promote the fight, which is often illegal.[273] Crush videos are predicated on crimes of animal cruelty and likely require filmmakers to solicit and conspire with others, such as the actress or customer, to plan and record the crime.[274] As the Court announced in *Ferber*, "it rarely has been suggested that the constitutional freedom for speech and press extends its immunity to speech or writing used as an integral part of conduct in violation of a valid criminal statute."[275] Because the depictions of animal cruelty targeted by Section 48 form an integral part of the violation of animal cruelty statutes or the related crimes described above, they do not warrant First Amendment protection.[276]

In determining whether Section 48 satisfies the *Ferber* factors, the Third Circuit erroneously concluded that an analogy to *Ferber* fails primarily because children and animals differ.[277] However, the proper comparison is between depictions of child pornography and depictions of animal cruelty, not between children and animals. *Ferber* stands for the notion that a category of speech does not merit constitutional protection

> where it depicts—and thus necessarily requires—the intentional infliction of physical harm on a class of especially vulnerable victims in violation of law, where the distribution of such depictions spurs their production but laws prohibiting the underlying acts are woefully under-enforced, and where the speech's social value is so *de minimis* as to be outweighed by the important governmental goal of protecting the victims.[278]

Another similarity between depictions of child pornography and depictions of animal cruelty is that their production necessitates harm. *Ferber* prohibits child pornography even where minors have consented to and/or receive compensation for their participation.[279] Animal victims cannot consent to mutilation and torture.[280]

ISAR summarized the Third Circuit's argument as follows:

> Given the seemingly endless varieties of depravity, one could easily imagine underground groups of people who gather and pay to watch live 'performances' of human adults being tortured to death, and narrated videotapes of those events being made and sold. Because the societal value of the 'expression' on those tapes would be zero, no one seriously would doubt the government's power to criminalize the interstate trafficking in such depictions, even though: (a) they would involve adults, not children; (b) the circulation of the videotapes would not cause lingering harm to the dead victims; (c) both the live acts and the later trafficking in depictions of those acts would be money-making activities, so that suppression of the images arguably would not 'dry up the market' for the live performances; and (d) the mere watching of actual murders-by-torture would not necessarily lead viewers to commit that crime. By the Court of Appeals' reasoning, however, a statute criminalizing such depictions would have to be struck down for failure to meet the *Ferber* factors. Indeed, by the Court of Appeals' reasoning, it might well also have reversed Respondent's conviction had the statute reached the sale of depictions of adults engaged in sexual intercourse with animals.[281]

Finally, the Court arguably ignored well-established principles of statutory construction in declaring Section 48 unconstitutional. To successfully claim that Section 48 was unconstitutional on its face would have required Stevens to prove that Section 48 was valid under "no set of circumstances"—an impossibly high burden.[282] For this reason, the Court instead chose to invalidate Section 48 as overbroad on the grounds that "a substantial number of its applications [were] unconstitutional, judged in relation to the statute's plainly legitimate sweep."[283]

The majority found Section 48 to have "alarming breadth."[284] Specifically, the majority found the words *wounded* and *killed* to be especially problematic, explaining, "'Maimed, mutilated, [and] tortured' convey cruelty but 'wounded' or 'killed' do not suggest any such limitation."[285] Under the well-established canon of statutory construction *noscitur a sociis*, courts look to surrounding words to interpret the meaning of an ambiguous term. The majority could easily have applied this principle to conclude that *wounded* and *killed* only encompass acts of unlawful animal cruelty since the accompanying words "intentionally maimed, mutilated, tortured" all involve such cruelty.[286] Professor Harold Lloyd argues that "a better understanding of semiotics . . . including the roles of purpose and framing in statutory interpretation and the various ways living beings might be used as instruments of expression should have led to a more enlightened result" in *Stevens*.[287]

The majority rejected the notion that under *noscitur a sociis*, the terms *wounded* and *killed* may be "given more precise content by the neighboring words with which [they are] associated," and therefore, because they appear under the heading of "depiction of animal cruelty," should be interpreted to require the additional element of cruelty.[288] Instead, the majority concluded that the terms contained "little ambiguity. . . . [and] nothing about that meaning requires cruelty."[289] The majority's arguably erroneous interpretation led it to hypothesize that Section 48 would embrace a video of the "humane slaughter of a stolen cow" and hence, to its conclusion that the statute was unconstitutionally overbroad.[290]

The majority also expressed concern over the impact of Section 48 on hunting depictions. Although Section 48 exempted depictions with "serious religious, political, scientific, educational, journalistic, historical, or artistic value," the majority determined that most hunting videos do not fall into the categories above; yet, the Court could just have easily reached the opposite conclusion.[291] The majority interpreted *serious* to mean "significant and of great import."[292] It observed that "the Government's attempt to narrow the statutory ban, however, requires an unrealistically broad reading of the exceptions clause. As the Government reads the clause . . . anything more than 'scant social value' . . . is excluded. . . . But the text says 'serious' value, and 'serious' should be taken seriously. We decline . . . to regard as 'serious' anything that is not 'scant.' (Or, as the dissent puts it, 'trifling.')."[293] Although Justice Alito correctly observed that *serious* could reasonably be construed as "not trifling,"[294] the majority's interpretation justified its conclusion that Section 48 was unconstitutionally overbroad.[295] According to Professor Lloyd, "proper review of Section 48 must include an intertwined review of the purpose of the statute (. . . the reference level of meaning), the language of the statute (. . . the frame of that reference), and the handling of the reference or parts thereof in ways permitted by the frame (in this context the disposition level of meaning)."[296] Section 48's legislative history makes clear that Section 48 never aimed to embrace depictions of lawful hunting or humane animal slaughter.[297] Nor had such depictions ever resulted in any prosecutions under the statute.

Depictions of lawful hunting could easily be construed as falling under Section 48's broad exemption.[298] It could be considered artistic by TV producers or film students, educational by a hunter hoping to learn new hunting techniques, or journalistic or scientific if the hunting depiction covers, for instance, the quest to capture the elusive Bigfoot. Furthermore, the *value* requirement makes clear that Section 48 does not exempt mere animal cruelty.[299] Therefore, in rejecting Justice Alito's interpretation that *serious* meant "not trifling," the majority opted for a definition that would be likelier to render the statute unconstitutional rather than one that better accords with the statute's underlying purposes.[300] However, doing so contravenes the well-settled principle that where a statute is ambiguous, the court should interpret it in a way as to render it constitutional.[301]

Whether *Stevens* was right or wrong, it is the current law of the land. And, as we will see in the next chapter, Congress reacted swiftly to the decision, quickly enacting a replacement statute tailored to address the Court's concerns. But will the new statute ultimately suffer the same fate as its predecessor?

Notes

1.   U.S. Const. amend. I.
2.   Kerry Adams, Note, Punishing Depictions of Animal Cruelty: Unconstitutional or a Valid Restriction on Speech?, 12 Barry L. Rev. 203, 207 (2009).
3.   Brief Amicus Curiae of the American Society for the Prevention of Cruelty to Animals In Support of Petitioner at 22, *United States v. Stevens*, 130 S.Ct. 1577 (2010) (No. 08-769) [hereinafter ASPCA Brief]; Adams, 220 ("[T]he First Amendment has never been treated as an absolute.").
4.   Elizabeth L. Kinsella, Note, *A Crushing Blow: United States v. Stevens and the Freedom to Profit from Animal Cruelty*, 43 U.C. Davis L. Rev. 347, 356-57 (2009) ("Content-based regulations focus on the communicative impact of speech. In other words, they restrict communication because of the message expressed. The term 'content-based' subsumes two subcategories: restrictions on the subject matter of the speech, and restrictions on the viewpoint of the speaker. For example, a law prohibiting distribution of campaign literature within 100 feet of the entrance to a poll is content-based. The law is content-based because it applies to political campaign literature, a subject matter of speech, but would not apply to a concert handbill. Alternatively, a law barring Republican flyers but allowing Democratic flyers near the same poll is viewpoint-based. The law is viewpoint-based because it restricts only the Republican Party point of view.").
5.   Ibid., 356.
6.   Ibid., 357–58.
7.   315 U.S. 568, 571–72 (1942).
8.   Brief Amicus Curiae of the International Society for Animal Rights In Support of Petitioner at 14, *United States v. Stevens*, 130 S.Ct. 1577 (2010) (No. 08-769) [hereinafter ISAR Brief].
9.   ASPCA Brief, 9 ("Dogfighting videos, such as those for which Stevens was arrested, perpetuate animal cruelty by playing a central role in promoting the dogfighting enterprise.").

10. ISAR Brief, 10 (quoting *Spence v. State of Washington*, 418 U.S. 405, 409 (citing *United States v. O'Brien*, 391 U.S. 367 (1968)).

11. Ibid., 10–11.

12. ASPCA Brief, 22 (citing the *Chaplinsky* Approach).

13. *United States v. Stevens*, 130 S.Ct. 1577, 1585 (2010).

14. Ibid.

15. Ibid., 1586.

16. Ibid., 1585.

17. Nadine Strossen, *A Big Year for the First Amendment: United States v. Stevens: Restricting Two Major Rationales for Content-Based Speech Restrictions*, Cato Sup. Ct. Rev. 67, 88 (2010).

18. *See* Case Comment, "En Banc Third Circuit Strikes Down Federal Statute Prohibiting the Interstate Sale of Depictions of Animal Cruelty," 122 Harv. L. Rev. 1239, 1243 (2009) [hereinafter En Banc] (asserting that, in failing to use the *Chaplinsky* Approach and opting for the *Ferber* Approach instead, the Third Circuit created a precedent inconsistent with the Court's First Amendment jurisprudence).

19. *Stevens*, 130 S. Ct. at 1599–602 (Alito, J., dissenting).

20. ASPCA Brief, at 49-50 (citing *New York v. Ferber*, 458 U.S. 747, 756–64 (1982)).

21. See *Ferber*, 458 U.S. at 756–64.

22. Ibid., 764.

23. *En Banc*, at 1246.

24. *Stevens*, 130 S. Ct. at 1586.

25. Strossen, at 85.

26. Ibid., 85–86.

27. Ibid., 67.

28. Michael Reynolds, Note, *Depictions of the Pig Roast: Restricting Violent Speech Without Burning the House*, 82 S. Cal. L. Rev. 341, 343 (2009) (discussing *Winters v. New York*, 333 U.S. 507, 508 n.1 (1948)).

29. Ibid.

30. Ibid., 349; see also Claire Ponder & Randall Lockwood, *Cruelty to Animals and Family Violence*, Int'l Ass'n of Chiefs of Police, Training Key 526, *2 (2000) [hereinafter Training Key] (noting that one study indicated that among aggressive criminals in prison, "25 percent reported five or more early acts of cruelty to animals, compared to six percent of non-aggressive criminals and none of the sample of non-criminals. Aggressive criminals were also more likely to report fear or dislike of particular animals.").

31. Reynolds, 351–52.

32. Ibid. (citing Douglas A. Gentile & Craig A. Anderson, *Violent Video Games: the Newest Media Violence Hazard, in* Media Violence and Children (Douglas A. Gentile ed., 2003)).

33. *But see* ibid., 353 (stating that violent Internet images are less likely to be seen by unwilling viewers than television or radio broadcasts since one must intentionally search for such images).

34. Ibid., 352 (citing *F.C.C. v. Pacifica Found.*, 438 U.S. 726, 748–49 (1978)); Debra M. Keiser, *Regulating the Internet: A Critique of Reno v. ACLU*, 62 Alb. L. Rev. 769, 776–77,

780, 798 (1998) (discussing the Court's medium-specific First Amendment analysis and arguing that the Internet should be more extensively regulated to protect children from the dangers it poses).

35. Reynolds, 353–54 (discussing *Ferber*, 458 U.S. at 763–64).

36. Snuff videos depict animals being killed or tortured by any method whereas crush videos show animals being crushed to death. As such, crush videos are a subset of snuff videos.

37. ASPCA Brief, 37–42. *But see* Emma Ricaurte, Comment, *Son of Sam and Dog of Sam: Regulating Depictions of Animal Cruelty Through the Use of Criminal Anti-Profit Statutes,* 16 Animal L. 171, 192-94, 199 (2009) (arguing that expanding the obscenity doctrine to include depictions of animal cruelty would be problematic and that covering depictions of animal cruelty with existing Son of Sam laws is preferable).

38. Ibid., 183 (discussing *Miller v. California*, 413 U.S. 15 (1973)).

39. Reynolds, 372 (citing *Miller*, 413 U.S. at 24).

40. *Chaplinsky v. New Hampshire*, 315 U.S. 568, 571-72 (1942); see also *Miller*, 413 U.S. at 18-19 (obscenity constitutes unprotected speech).

41. ASPCA Brief, 38.

42. *See Miller*, 413 U.S. at 24 (stating that obscene materials "appeal to the prurient interest in sex, which portray sexual conduct in a patently offensive way, and which, taken as a whole, do not have serious literary, artistic, political, or scientific value."); *Punishing Depictions of Animal Cruelty and the Federal Prisoner Health Care Co-Payment Act of 1999: Hearing on H.R. 1887 and H.R. 1349 Before the Subcomm. on Crime of the H. Comm. on the Judiciary*, 106th Cong. 1 (1999) [hereinafter *Punishing Depictions*] (statement of Susan Creede, investigator, Ventura County Dist. Attorney Office).

43. *Punishing Depictions*, 127 (statement of William Paul Lebaron, detective, Long Beach Police Department).

44. See *Miller*, 413 U.S. at 24; Brief of Amicus Curiae the Humane Society of the United States in Support of Petitioner at 22–26 (2009), *United States v. Stevens*, 130 S. Ct. 1577 (2010) (No. 08-769) [hereinafter HSUS Brief]. The HSUS argued that rather than exclusively focusing on sex-related speech, America's early obscenity laws banned religious mockery, depictions of violence and crime, materials thought to endanger public morality, and materials deemed "indecent, lewd, lascivious, obscene, libelous, scurrilous, or threatening delineations, epithets, terms, or language, or reflecting injuriously upon the character or conduct of another." As Richard Posner explained, "violent photographs of a person being drawn and quartered could be . . . described as 'obscene,'" and could even be "included within the legal category of obscene . . . even if they have nothing to do with sex." The plain meaning of the term "obscene" further supports the characterization of depictions of animal cruelty as "obscenity." Accordingly, the HSUS argued in its amicus brief: "Modifying the [obscenity] doctrine slightly to also encompass sadistic videos of animal fighting would make the doctrine more coherent and respectful of legislative prerogatives, without genuinely threatening the important values protected by the First Amendment. Under this revised definition material would be obscene if: (a) the average person, applying contemporary community standards would find that the work, taken as a whole, appeals to the depraved or prurient interest; (b) the work

depicts or describes, in a patently offensive way, conduct specifically defined by the applicable law; and (c) the work, taken as a whole, lacks serious literary, artistic, political, or scientific value." HSUS Brief at 22–26; see also Adams, 220–21 (highlighting the way that the obscenity doctrine can and should be used to permit restrictions on "low value violent speech," especially to prevent its access to minors and stating that the Eighth Circuit has allowed limited restrictions on "slasher" films portraying rape, murder, and bestiality); Reynolds, 373–74 (stating that in *Winters v. New York*, 333 U.S. 507 (1948), the Supreme Court "did not foreclose the regulation of violent speech, however, provided that the regulation met the required specificity.").

45. Reynolds, 376–77 ("A recent obscenity prosecution in Pittsburgh involved depictions of women being gang raped and having their throats slit. In another case in 2005, defendants were convicted of selling obscene material for videos purporting to be actual rapes. Federal prosecutors have even secured a guilty plea on an obscenity charge from a woman who wrote stories of young girls being molested, tortured, and killed.).

46. Reynolds, at 374.

47. HSUS Brief, at 30.

48. Ibid., 31.

49. Ibid., 28 (citing *Am. Amusement Mach. Ass'n v. Kendrick*, 244 F.3d 572, 574 [7th Cir. 2001)).

50. *United States v. Stevens*, 533 F.3d 218, 220–21 (3d Cir. 2008).

51. See Randall Lockwood, American Prosecutors Research Institute, *Animal Cruelty Prosecution: Opportunities for Early Response to Crime and Interpersonal Violence* (2006) ("Animal cruelty is increasingly viewed as a serious issue by professionals in law enforcement and mental health—as well as by the general public. Animals are part of the majority of American families, and their victimization is of concern to millions.").

52. Ibid., 9.

53. HSUS Brief, 34, 52–53 (citing *United States v. Davidson*, 283 F.3d 681, 683 (5th Cir. 2002) (involving snuff videos and rape and torture depictions); *United States v. Thomas*, 74 F.3d 701, 705 (6th Cir. 1996) (involving depictions of bestiality and abuse)); see also Reynolds, 382 ("Public reaction to the revelation of Michael Vick's involvement in a dog fighting ring suggests that many people consider animal cruelty to be quite severe."); Lockwood, 1; Ricaurte, 173 n.5 ("Michael Vick is a former quarterback for the Atlanta Falcons who was sentenced to twenty-three months in federal prison in December 2007 for his involvement in the dogfighting operation 'Bad Newz Kennels.' Vick not only financed the operation but also assisted in the execution of underperforming dogs.") (internal citations omitted); Training Key, 2 ("[A]n increasingly concerned public has drawn greater attention to animal abuse . . . ."); Frank R. Ascione & Randall Lockwood, *Cruelty to Animals: Changing Psychological, Social, and Legislative Perspectives, in* The State of Animals: 2001 39, 47 (2001) (discussing a HSUS study, which reported "that 42 percent of respondents believed cruelty to animals to be moderately to extremely serious as a problem . . . . 71 percent supported making animal abuse a felony, and 81 percent felt that the enforcement of cruelty-to-animals laws should be strengthened.").

54. Lockwood, 1.

55. Ibid.

56. See ibid. at 1–2; National Association of Attorneys General AG Bulletin (March 2001) ("Delaware Attorney General Jane Brady hosted a National Conference on Animal Cruelty and Interpersonal Violence . . . to discuss the relationship between animal cruelty and violence against people, and policies that are designed to end the cycle of abuse. According to General Brady . . . 'We've already learned that animal cruelty is both a leading and lagging indicator of violence against human beings. An informed response to incidents of animal cruelty can curb other acts of violence before they happen.' A task force on animal cruelty was created in General Brady's office in November 1999.").

57. The documentary is http://www.ovguide.com/tv_episode/panorama-season-1998-episode-28-the-cruelty-connection-4407115#.

58. Lockwood, 1.

59. HSUS Brief, 27 (citing Kevin W. Saunders, *Media Violence and the Obscenity Exception to the First Amendment*, 3 Wm. & Mary Bill Rts. J. 107, 166 (1994) ["Violence does not, in itself, express a point of view on important issues; its effect is visceral and noncognitive."]).

60. Ibid.

61. P.L. 111-294, H.R. 5566.

62. ASPCA Brief, 23–24 (citing *Brandenburg v. Ohio*, 395 U.S. 444, 447 [1969]).

63. Ibid., 24 (citing Hanna Gibson, *Dog Fighting Detailed Discussion, Animal Legal & Historical Center*, Animal Legal and Historical Center, 2005, *available at* http://www.animallaw.info/articles/ddusdogfighting.htm).

64. P.L. 111-294, H.R. 5566.

65. Section 48 prohibited a person from inciting criminal conduct so that such conduct can be created and sold for commercial gain. A PBS documentary of dogfighting in the United States would be lawful although it memorializes criminal conduct, so long as it possesses serious educational value.

66. *See* N.C. GEN. STAT. § 97-88.2 (2013) (making it a crime for "any person who willfully makes a false statement or representation of a material fact for the purpose of obtaining or denying any [workers' compensation] benefit or payment"); MICH. COMP. LAWS § 750.422 (2013) (making it a crime for "any person who, being lawfully required to depose the truth in any proceeding in a court of justice" to commit perjury); 720 ILL. COMP. STAT. 5/8-1 (2012) (making it a crime for any person to command, encourage, or request another to commit an offense).

67. See *Stevens*, 130 S. Ct. at 1600–02 (Alito, J., dissenting) ("Section 48's ban on trafficking in crush videos also helps to enforce the criminal laws and to ensure that criminals do not profit from their crimes. . . . We have already judged that taking the profit out of crime is a compelling interest. . . . The statutory ban on commerce in dogfighting videos is also supported by compelling governmental interests in effectively enforcing the Nation's criminal laws and preventing criminals from profiting from their illegal activities.") (citing *Simon & Schuster, Inc. v. Members of the N.Y. State Crime Victims Bd.*, 502 U.S. 105, 119 (1991)); Kinsella, 384 ("Admittedly, it remains unclear where exactly courts draw the line between protected depictions and those the government may constitutionally proscribe. Crush videos, however, simply fall on the latter side of the line. There is no First Amendment right to profit from animal cruelty."); Ricaurte, 188 (a Long Island crush

filmmaker used a website and advertising in pornographic magazines to sell "bloodied high heels" used to crush animals during the making of crush videos).

68. ASPCA Brief, 10; Joe Mandak, *Men Charged in Publication of Dogfighting Magazine*, Associated Press, July 26, 2004 ("Some people bet as much as $10,000 on a single [dog] fight, and the purse for a night of fighting could be as much as $50,000 . . . .").

69. Reynolds, 368–70.

70. Ibid., 368 (citing *Ashcroft v. Free Speech Coalition*, 535 U.S. 234, 253 (2002) (discussing virtual child pornography)). This case is distinguishable because virtual child pornography does not necessitate actual harm to living victims. See also Ricaurte, 189–90.

71. *Ferber*, 458 U.S. at 750-51, 756–57.

72. Ibid., 756–63. *But see* Ricaurte, 187 ("Further, the statute is overinclusive because it has the potential to restrict valuable speech. Although the law has an exception for works with 'serious religious, political, scientific, educational, journalistic, historical, or artistic value,' the test is subjective and some fact finders could decide that the work does not have 'serious' value but merely aims to 'shock, titillate, and get ratings.' For example, a video of a bullfight taking place in Spain might well be deemed to have serious value. A harder case would be a depiction of an underground cockfight in Puerto Rico. Like Spain, Puerto Rico has a long history of the sport, and many have argued that it is part of Puerto Rico's culture. However, because the tradition of cockfighting in Puerto Rico might not be as well-known to American juries as bullfighting in Spain, there is a risk it could be deemed to lack serious historical or educational value, whereas the bullfighting in Spain would not. This could lead to dissimilar results in similar cases and could put juries in the position of placing value judgments on the activities of another culture.").

73. ASPCA Brief, 34 (citing *Stevens*, 533 F.3d at 232 (3d Cir. 2008)); see also Kinsella, 373 ("[T]he *Stevens* court failed to assign sufficient weight to the human interest implicit in preventing animal cruelty, and thus made an erroneous distinction between humans and animals.").

74. See Brief for a Group of American Law Professors as Amicus Curiae in Support of Neither Party at 10, *United States v. Stevens*, 130 S. Ct. 1577 (2010) (No. 08-769) [hereinafter Law Professors' Brief]; Reynolds, 384–85 ("Incitement of imminent unlawful activity is a compelling interest, yet there is no requirement that the unlawful activity be directed towards humans. . . . And, more to the point, the reason that most compelling interests involve humans is because the Supreme Court has never had the occasion to consider whether protecting animals is a compelling interest. That the Court has never considered the issue has no bearing on the Court's stance on the issue.") (footnote omitted); Kinsella, 372, 374 ("There is no bright-line test for determining which government interests qualify as compelling. Instead, societal consensus in the form of legislative judgment often informs what constitutes an interest compelling enough to allow infringement on free speech rights. . . . By drawing a First Amendment line between humans and animals, the court neglected societal consensus and erroneously analyzed the compelling interest prong. Certainly, the Supreme Court has not yet recognized a nonhuman interest as sufficiently compelling to justify a content-based restriction. The high court, however, has not had occasion to consider animal cruelty in light of the Free Speech Clause—until now.") (footnotes omitted).

75. *Stevens*, 130 S. Ct. at 1600, 1602 (Alito, J., dissenting).
76. Marion S. Lane and Stephen L. Zawistowski, *Heritage of Care: The American Society for the Prevention of Cruelty to Animals* (Westport, CT: Praeger, 2008), 27–29.
77. Church of the Lukumi Babalu Aye, Inc. v. City of Hialeah, 508 U.S. 520 (1993); see also *Stevens*, 533 F.3d at 227 (concluding that given Lukumi, *inter alia*, the Third Circuit should not create a new category of unprotected speech unless the U.S. Supreme Court instructs it to do so); Kinsella, 362 ("To date, the United States Supreme Court has addressed animal cruelty in the First Amendment context only once.").
78. Kinsella, 372–73 ("The court erroneously suggested there is no compelling government interest in preventing animal cruelty in the First Amendment context. The court erred in its analysis. . . . The court erroneously interpreted *Lukumi* as indicating the Supreme Court's view that" preventing cruelty to animals is not a compelling government interest.); see also Ricaurte, 186 (stating courts cannot rely upon *Lukumi* to support the assertion that preventing cruelty to animals fails to constitute a compelling government interest).
79. Reynolds, 384 ("The Third Circuit found that the Court in *Church of the Lukumi Babalu Aye v. City of Hialeah* at least 'hinted' that prevention of animal cruelty is not compelling enough to overcome fundamental human rights. . . . However, *Lukumi* never confronted such a question. It assumed that protection of animals was a compelling interest, yet found that the ordinance was not narrowly tailored to serve that interest, demonstrating that the true intent of the ordinance was to suppress the practice of Santeria."); Kinsella, 375 ("In *Lukumi*, the Supreme Court held that Church members could freely practice Santeria, including ritual animal sacrifice, under rights guaranteed by the Free Exercise Clause. The Court recognized a compelling government interest in preventing animal cruelty, but ultimately determined the legislature's actual motive was to suppress religion. Thus, the Court did not decide whether a law genuinely seeking to prevent animal cruelty necessitated a religious exemption due to the Free Exercise Clause. The city ordinances at issue in *Lukumi* singled out and directly burdened religion; the ordinances did not implicate the interest in animal protection that the high court recognized as compelling."). *But see* Ricaurte, 194 ("The Supreme Court has never recognized a compelling interest in regard to animals.").
80. 508 U.S. at 540–47.
81. Kinsella, 362–63.
82. Ibid., 363–64.
83. ASPCA Brief, 19.
84. Kinsella, 373 ("The court erroneously interpreted *Lukumi* as indicating the Supreme Court's view that the government interest at issue in §48—preventing animal cruelty—is not compelling.").
85. ASPCA Brief, 20 (citing *Church of the Lukumi Babalu Aye, Inc. v. City of Hialeah*, 508 U.S. 520, 580 (1993) [Blackmun, J., concurring)).
86. *Ibid.*; Kinsella, 373 ("The *Stevens* court ignored Justice Blackmun's concurrence, which makes explicit the high court's belief in the strength of just such a compelling interest.").
87. *Stevens*, 533 F.3d at 240 (Cowen, J., dissenting).
88. Law Professors' Brief, 7–11.

89. ASPCA Brief 4; Kinsella, 374–75 ("When determining whether a government interest is
     compelling, the Supreme Court often looks to societal consensus in the form of nationwide
     legislative prevalence. In *Ferber*, for example, the Court supported its finding of a compel-
     ling interest by citing legislative judgment. Almost all the states and the federal government
     have enacted legislation aimed at combating child pornography. That legislative judgment
     combined with literature detailing the effects on children used as pornography subjects
     'easily passe[d] muster under the First Amendment.' Although noting the comprehensive
     state statutory schemes designed to prevent animal cruelty, the *Stevens* majority failed to
     give this legislative judgment appropriate weight. Indeed, as explained by the dissent, the
     United States has a long-standing aversion to animal cruelty with the first laws proscribing
     such cruelty enacted in 1641. That all fifty states and the federal government have passed
     statutes prohibiting the underlying conduct at issue in §48 demonstrates that preventing
     animal cruelty rises to the level of compelling."); Ricaurte, 177.

90. ASPCA Brief, 5 (citing *Stevens*, 533 F.3d at 224 n.4 (3d Cir. 2008) (listing current state animal
     protection laws); Luis E. Chiesa, *Why Is It a Crime to Stomp on a Goldfish? Harm, Victim-
     hood and the Structure of Anti-Cruelty Offenses*, 78 Miss. L.J. 1, 4 (2008) ("Comprehensive
     anti-cruelty legislation has been adopted in many countries, including the United Kingdom,
     Holland, Australia, and Argentina, to name a few."); Lockwood, 5 ("In England, the first
     comprehensive animal protection law was introduced by Richard 'Humanity Dick' Martin
     and passed June 10, 1822. This 'Act to Prevent the Cruel and Improper Treatment of Cattle'
     also protected horses, sheep, cows and mules, providing for fines of up to 5 pounds and up
     to 3 months in prison for mistreatment of such livestock. The Society for the Prevention of
     Cruelty to Animals (SPCA) was founded in England in 1824 to ensure that this legislation
     would be enforced. It funded its own constables and eventually earned the support of the
     Queen, becoming the Royal SPCA in 1840.").

91. Lockwood, 32 ("Some animal cruelty cases may involve actions that violate . . . federal
     laws including the Humane Slaughter Act, the Endangered Species Act, the Wild Bird
     Conservation Act, the Bald and Golden Eagle Protection Act, the Marine Mammal
     Protection Act and the Wild Horses and Burros Act. Some animal poisoning cases may
     include violations of the Federal Insecticide, Fungicide, and Rodenticide Act. Cases that
     could involve the application of federal charges are likely to also include state animal cru-
     elty violations and may require close coordination of actions with federal prosecutors.").

92. Ibid., 5 ("The earliest printed legal code in America, 'The Body of Liberties' established
     by the Puritans of the Massachusetts Bay Colony in 1641, included among the 100
     'liberties' two provisions protecting animals.").

93. Ibid.

94. Ricaurte, 177; Lockwood, 6 ("The first American law that moved away from these
     limitations was in Maine (1821), prohibiting cruelly beating any horse or cattle—
     regardless of ownership. This was the earliest indication of a law addressing concern
     for the welfare of the animal itself.").

95. Ibid. (citing N.Y. Rev. Stat. tit. 6, §26 [1829]).

96. Lockwood, 6 (New Hampshire's animal cruelty section was included in the same
     section as laws relating to adultery, blasphemy, grave robbing and tomb desecration.

Minnesota's animal cruelty provision was located in the same section as penalties for
attending a dance on the Sabbath.).

97. For a general discussion of the history of legislation criminalizing animal cruelty, *see*
Chiesa, 8–13.

98. ASPCA Brief, 4 (citing ASPCA History Page, http://www.aspca.org/about-us/history.
html (last visited June 10, 2009)); Lockwood, 7; Mark J. Parmenter, *Does Iowa's Anti-
Cruelty to Animals Statute Have Enough Bite?*, 51 Drake L. Rev. 817, 823–824 (2003).

99. Lockwood, 7.

100. Training Key, 1.

101. ASPCA Brief, 4 (citing ASPCA Milestones, *available at* http://www.aspca.org/pressroom/
press-kit/aspca-milestones-2009.pdf (last visited June 12, 2009)).

102. Lockwood, 21.

103. Ibid. ("As of 2006, dogfighting is a felony in all states except Idaho and Wyoming,
where it is a misdemeanor."); Ricaurte, 177 ("Forty-three of the states make certain
acts of animal cruelty a felony.").

104. ASPCA Brief, 6 (citing Gibson (dogfighting is illegal in 50 states and a felony in 48
states, D.C., Puerto Rico, and the Virgin Islands)).

105. Ricaurte, 177 ("Dogfighting and cockfighting are now outlawed in all fifty states, with
Louisiana's 2008 ban making it the final state to ban cockfighting."); Will Connaghan,
"Constitution Shields Questionable Entertainment," *St. Louis Daily Rec.*, July 18, 2007, at 1.

106. Lockwood, 22.

107. ASPCA Brief, 6, n.11 (citing *Stevens*, 533 F.3d at 239–239 (Cowen, J., dissenting) (citing
7 U.S.C. § 2131 (2009) (mandating humane treatment and care of animals to be used
in research or sold); 7 U.S.C. § 1902 (2009) (requiring humane animal slaughter); 7
U.S.C. § 2156 (2009) (making it unlawful to sponsor an animal in a fighting venture))).

108. Lockwood, 21–22.

109. Ibid., 22.

110. ASPCA Brief, 6 (citing H.R. Rep. No. 106-397, at 3 (1999) ("[t]hese legislative enact-
ments evidence society's desire to ensure that animals are treated humanely")).

111. HSUS Brief, 6–7; Lockwood, 26–27 (discussing the tremendous costs incurred when
abused animals require housing, food, veterinary care, etc.); Humane Society of the
United States, *Judge Strikes Major Financial Blow Against Dog Fighting in New York*
(Nov. 22, 2005) (In describing the cost of care to dogs seized from convicted dogfighter
and owner/operator of Sporting Dog Journal James Fricchione, HSUS Program Co-
ordinator Samantha Mullen remarked: "The Shelters that courageously assisted the
law enforcement authorities by taking charge of the dogs seized in this case certainly
deserve to be indemnified . . . . They incurred enormous financial as well as emotional
burdens. In addition, they were targets of burglary attempts because fighting dogs are
notoriously coveted by criminals who know their worth in the underground world of
blood sports."); *People v. Fricchione*, No. 03-00403, 43 A.D.3d 410 (N.Y. App. Div. Feb.
20, 2007) (ordering Fricchione to pay $136,303.13 to Warwick Valley Humane Society).

112. *Stevens*, 130 S. Ct. at 1598–1600 (Alito, J., dissenting).

113. Ibid., 1600.

114. ASPCA Brief, 7 (citing 145 Cong. Rec. H10267, H10267 (daily ed. Oct. 19, 1999) (statement of Rep. McCollum) (discussing difficulties inherent in prosecuting alleged violations of anti-cruelty statutes)).

115. Lockwood, 15–16 (discussing how state anti-cruelty laws contain differing (and sometimes antiquated) definitions of "animal" and "animal cruelty," and noting that several "state laws reserve felony penalties for crimes against companion animals, while others treat only acts against livestock as potential felony offenses."); Ricaurte, 178 (discussing how state laws define "animal" differently); Jennifer S. Rosa, *Recent Developments in New York Law—Chapters 118 and 208 of the Laws of 1999: The New York Legislature Develops a Pseudo Animal Rights Agenda*, 74 St. John's L. Rev. 287, 287–88 (2000).

116. ASPCA Brief, 6–7 (citing H.R. Rep. No. 106-397, at 3 (1999)). As Congressman McCollum explained during legislative debate on the law: "[Section 48] is a necessary *complement* to State animal cruelty laws. Congress alone has the power to regulate interstate commerce, and this bill does just that . . . . It does not create a new Federal crime to punish the harm to the animals itself, rather it leaves that to State law, where it properly lies. What it does do is restrict the conduct that heretofore has gone on unchecked by State law, the sale across State lines of these horrible depictions for commercial gain." 145 Cong. Rec. H10267, H10267 (daily ed. Oct. 19, 1999) (statement of Rep. McCollum) (emphasis added).

117. Beth Ann Madeline, *Cruelty to Animals: Recognizing Violence Against Nonhuman Victims*, 23 U. Haw. L. Rev. 307, 316–17 (2000); Chiesa, 10 (As of 2008, Alabama regarded cruelty in the first degree toward a dog or cat to be a felony; the same abuse to a rabbit, horse, etc., is a misdemeanor).

118. Redundancy would have been an insufficient justification to strike Section 48 since "there is no requirement in Ferber that child pornography laws be limited to depictions that existing child abuse laws would not otherwise reach. . . . [T]here is no requirement [in *Ferber*] that the act depicted even be illegal" as Section 48 required. Reynolds, 385.

119. ASPCA Brief, 7; Ricaurte, 182–83. ("Although acts of animal cruelty were already illegal in all fifty states, proponents of the statute argued that it was necessary to assist states in prosecuting under their anticruelty laws. Prosecuting crush-video production under state animal-cruelty laws is difficult for three reasons. First, there is difficulty in identifying the actor. Women in crush videos are typically shown from the waist down, and the only identifying features are their voices. Second, it is hard for the prosecutor to show that the act took place within the court's jurisdiction and within the statute of limitations. Production of crush videos is by nature a clandestine operation that usually takes place inside the video-maker's home. Therefore, it is difficult to determine the time and place of the act from the video. Third, although the underlying acts of cruelty are illegal under state laws, the production, sale, and distribution of the videos are not. Therefore, prosecution would only be possible under state laws if the person was caught in the act 'through an undercover operation.' Such an undercover operation is unlikely since prosecutors are often reluctant to bring charges of animal cruelty due to limited resources.") (citations omitted).

120. ASPCA Brief, 7.

121. Ibid. (citing *Punishing Depictions* (statement of William Paul LeBaron, Detective, Long Beach Police Dep't)).
122. Ibid. (citing *Punishing Depictions* (statement of Tom Connors, Deputy Dist. Attorney, Ventura Cnty. Dist. Attorney's Office)).
123. Ibid., 8 (citing *Stevens*, 533 F.3d at 245 (Cowen, J., dissenting)).
124. Ibid., 7 (citing 145 Cong. Rec. H10267 (daily ed. Oct. 19, 1999)).
125. Ibid., 8, n.13 (citing *Punishing Depictions* (statement of Tom Connors, Deputy Dist. Attorney, Ventura Cnty. Dist. Attorney's Office); Ricaurte, 183.
126. Training Key, 1.
127. Chiesa, 4, 12 (citing *People v. Garcia*, 812 N.Y.S.2d 66 (N.Y. App. Div. 2006)).
128. See ibid.
129. Kinsella, 379–80 ("Desensitization theory draws support from an increasing body of empirical data. Indeed, over thirty-five years of research suggests a strong link between childhood animal cruelty and adult violent behavior such as domestic abuse and sexual offenses. Considering the potentially extreme consequences of societal indifference to such research, society has a significant interest in preventing animal cruelty. Acting on behalf of society, the government has an equally compelling interest. Section 48 deters human violence by discouraging desensitization of individuals to animal cruelty. By prohibiting the creation, sale, or possession of depictions of animal cruelty, fewer individuals will make and see such depictions. Less exposure theoretically results in fewer persons subject to desensitization. Thus, by concluding the government did not have a compelling interest in preventing animal cruelty, the Stevens court harmed important social policy.")
130. Ascione & Lockwood, 39–40.
131. ASPCA Brief, 17–18 (citing 145 Cong. Rec. H10267, H10271 (statement of Rep. Bachus) ("Psychologists tell us that when we view these activities, they desensitize our young people to a behavior which appears to be a gateway to violent acts of indiscriminate, coldblooded murder."); H.R. Rep. No. 106-397, at 4 (1999) ("If society fails to prevent adults from engaging in this behavior, they may become so desensitized to the suffering of these beings that they lose the ability to empathize with the suffering of humans.")).
132. Ibid., 18, n.37 (citing Reynolds, 349 ("Frequent exposure [to violence] may desensitize the viewer, decreasing the unpleasant reactions to violence which would normally inhibit violent behavior.") (citing Craig A. Anderson et al., *The Influence of Media Violence on Youth*, 4 Psychol. Sci. Pub. Int. 81, 96 (2003))).
133. ASPCA Brief, 18 n.38 (citation omitted); Brief of Florida, Alabama, Arkansas, Arizona, California, Colorado, Connecticut, Hawaii, Illinois, Indiana, Kentucky, Louisiana, Maryland, Michigan, Mississippi, Montana, New Hampshire, New Mexico, North Carolina, Ohio, Rhode Island, South Carolina, Texas, Utah, Virginia, and West Virginia as Amici Curiae Supporting Petitioners at 32, *United States v. Stevens*, 130 S. Ct. 1577 (2010) (No. 08-769) [hereinafter Attorney Generals' Brief].
134. ASPCA Brief, 18 n.38 (citation omitted).
135. For information regarding general Internet regulation, see *generally* Keiser, 785–86 (discussing the Internet's "pervasiveness and its ease of access to children") (citation omitted).

136. See H.R. Rep. No. 106-397, at 4 (1999) (discussing the desensitizing impact exposure to crush videos has on viewers).
137. ASPCA Brief, 11 (citing Randall Lockwood, *Animal Cruelty and Violence Against Humans: Making the Connection*, 5 Animal L. 81, 81 (1999)); Training Key, 1.
138. Chiesa, 31 ("There is ample evidence to suggest that individuals who engage in acts of animal cruelty have a greater probability of committing acts of violence against people as compared to individuals who have no history of committing acts of violence against animals.") (citation omitted); Ascione & Lockwood, 40 ("The escalation hypothesis suggests that the presence of cruelty to animals at one developmental period predicts interpersonal violence at a later developmental period. According to this hypothesis, the five-year-old who abuses animals is on the way to becoming an elementary-school bully, aggressive adolescent, and adult violent offender.").
139. Reynolds, 348; Frank Ascione, *Animal Abuse and Youth Violence*, Office of Juvenile Justice and Delinquency Prevention, Juvenile Justice Bulletin at 3–4, 8 (September 2001) [hereinafter *Youth Violence*] (citing research studies indicating that incarcerated men report committing higher rates of animal cruelty: 36% of male sexual homicide perpetrators reported "childhood animal abuse," 46% reported adolescent animal abuse and 36% adult animal abuse; a 1986 study indicated that 48% of rapists and 30% of child molesters in a study of 64 male convicted sexual offenders reported "animal abuse in childhood or adolescence." A 1988 study of sexual homicide perpetrators indicated that 40% of participants who reported experience sexual abuse in their youth had committed acts of bestiality.).
140. Reynolds, 376.
141. Ibid., 348–49.
142. Chiesa, 31 (citation omitted); *see generally* Parmenter, 830 ("Studies indicate that there is a strong causal connection between animal abuse and violent crime.") (citation omitted).
143. ASPCA Brief, 23 n.25 (citing 145 Cong. Rec. H10267, H10269 (daily ed. Oct. 19, 1999) (statement of Rep. Gallegly) ("Many studies have found that people who commit violent acts on animals will later commit violent acts on people."); ibid. at H10271 (statement of Rep. Bachus) (discussing the case of an 11-year-old boy with a history of animal cruelty who shot ten classmates); Ascione & Lockwood, 48–50 (discussing the connection between animal cruelty and violence toward humans); Randall Lockwood & Ann Church, *Deadly Serious: An FBI Perspective on Animal Cruelty*, Humane Soc'y News 1-4 (Fall 1996) in Cruelty To Animals And Interpersonal Violence: Readings In Research and Application (Randall Lockwood & Frank R. Ascione eds., 1998) (looking at how the FBI recognizes the connection between animal cruelty and future tendencies for violent behavior toward humans);145 Cong. Rec. H10267 (statement of Rep. Morella) (quoting FBI Special agent Allan Brantly who stated "'animal violence does not occur in a vacuum. It is highly predictive in identifying children being abused and cases of spousal abuse. . . . In many cases we have seen examples whereby enjoyment from killing animals is a rehearsal for targeting humans.'").
144. Law Professors' Brief, 23–24; Kinsella, 383 ("Animal cruelty is a form of antisocial behavior closely correlated to human violence.").

145. ASPCA Brief, 12; Chiesa, 32 ("Animal abusers are five times more likely to commit violent crimes ... [and] four times more likely to commit property crimes.") (citation omitted).

146. *Youth Violence*, 5.

147. Ibid., 6.

148. Lockwood, 10 ("Retrospective studies that look backward at the histories of incarcerated serious and violent offenders often reveal a high incidence of animal cruelty offenses in childhood and adolescence. Likewise, prospective studies that follow the offense record of those with a history of animal abuse tend to show a high rate of future offenses against people and property.") (citation omitted); Training Key, 2; Jennifer Robbins, *Recognizing the Relationship Between Domestic Violence and Animal Abuse: Recommendations for Change to the Texas Legislature*, 16 Tex. J. Women & L. 129, 133 (2006) ("Cruelty to animals has been recognized as a warning sign for future interpersonal violence.").

149. Kinsella, 379.

150. Lockwood, 10.

151. Kinsella, 379; Chiesa, 32 ("Some of the most famous serial killers, including Jeffrey Dahmer, the Son of Sam, the Boston Strangler and Ted Bundy had a history of abusing animals."); Joshua L. Friedman & Gary C. Norman, *Protecting the Family Pet: The New Face of Maryland Domestic Violence Protective Orders*, 40 U. Balt. L.R. 81, 86 (2009) ("The common thread is that all of these individuals committed acts of abuse against animals before turning to human targets."); Lockwood, 10; Ricaurte, 181 ("Studies have shown that children who are cruel to animals are more likely to exhibit aggressive or violent behavior towards humans. In fact, some of the most notorious serial killers, including Jeffrey Dahmer and Ted Bundy, tortured and killed animals in their youth before turning to human victims."); Training Key, 2 ("There is compelling anecdotal evidence compiled by the FBI and other law enforcement agencies linking serial killers, serial rapists and sexual homicide perpetrators to acts of animal abuse prior to age 25.").

152. ASPCA Brief, 12 n.22 (citation omitted).

153. Friedman & Norman, 86.

154. Training Key, 3.

155. Madeline, 326.

156. *Youth Violence*, 1.

157. ASPCA Brief, 15–16 (citing J.J. Stambaugh, *Pet Spa Owner Kills Wife, Self in W. Knox*, Knoxville News Sentinel Co., June 3, 2009, *available at* http://www.knoxnews.com/news/2009/jun/03/pet-spaowner-kills-wife-self-in-w-knox).

158. Caroline Forell, "Using a Jury of Her Peers to Teach About the Connection Between Domestic Violence and Animal Abuse," 15 Animal L. 53, 62–63 (2008) (citation omitted).

159. Ascione & Lockwood, 43.

160. Ibid.

161. *See* Lockwood, 10 ("During a 10-year window surrounding an arrest for intentional acts of animal abuse ... [t]he offense rates of animal abusers [for other crimes] were up to five times higher than those seen in non-abusing individuals who were matched on age, gender, race and area of residence. Such studies support the popular notion that perpetrators of animal cruelty are likely to be involved in many and varied offenses. Often

the animal cruelty offenses will be among the easiest to prove and may potentially carry some of the most serious consequences for the offender."); Rosa, 296–97 (suggesting that the primary impetus for New York enacting two new animal cruelty laws was the link between animal cruelty and violence against humans, particularly school shootings).

162. Susan Crowell, "Animal Cruelty as It Relates to Child Abuse: Shedding Light on a 'Hidden' Problem," 20 J. Juv. L. 38, 43 (1999) (internal citation omitted).

163. Lockwood, 13.

164. See ibid. at 10, 13; Training Key 2 ("One survey of psychiatric patients who had reportedly tortured dogs and cats found that all of the subjects had high levels of aggression against people, including one patient who had murdered a boy.") (internal citation omitted). Since the late 1980s, animal cruelty has been listed in the American Psychiatric Association's *Diagnostic and Statistical Manual of Mental Disorders* as a symptom of conduct disorders. Kinsella, 381; *Youth Violence*, 4–5.

165. Ascione & Lockwood, 47–48 ("Since 1998 California has required such assessment in all cruelty-to-animals convictions. Colorado law requires assessment and recommends treatment; New Mexico mandates counseling in cases of animal abuse by juveniles and recommends it for adult offenders. In the last decade, more than a dozen other states have added counseling and treatment as a sentencing option within their cruelty-to-animals codes.").

166. See *generally* Robbins; Naseem Stecker, "Of Interest: Domestic Violence and the Animal Cruelty Connection," 83 Mich. B.J. 36 (2004).

167. See ASPCA Brief, 16 (citing Frank R. Ascione, *Domestic Violence and Cruelty to Animals*, 17 The Latham Letter 1 (1996); Domestic Violence Intervention Project, *Domestic Violence Program*, http://alexandriava.gov/DomesticViolence (last visited June 13, 2009) ("Family abuse crosses all categories, even the family pet. Animal cruelty is often an early warning sign of violent tendencies that may turn into domestic violence."); Barbara Rosen, *Watch for Pet Abuse—It Might Save Your Client's Life, reprinted in* Cruelty To Animals And Interpersonal Violence: Readings In Research And Application 340–47 (Randall Lockwood & Frank R. Ascione eds., 1998) (detailing the link between animal abuse and elder abuse); ASPCA, *The Connection Between Domestic Violence and Animal Cruelty*, *available at* http://www.aspca.org/fight-animal-cruelty/domestic-violence-and-animal-cruelty.html [hereinafter *The Connection*] (looking at the link between domestic violence and animal cruelty and discussing studies that suggest a strong correlation) (last visited June 13, 2009)); see also Crowell; Friedman & Norman, 81 ("There is a demonstrated link between acts and offenses of domestic violence and animal abuse. Domestic abusers often do not think twice about beating or otherwise harming pets that have bonded with the other spouse in order to control, coerce, intimidate, or cause emotional harm to that spouse."); Lockwood, 11 ("Paying attention to the victimization of animals can often lead to the discovery of people who have been harmed by the same perpetrator, or who are at high risk of being harmed. Animal cruelty investigators and humane law enforcement agents are now seen as important sentinels for detecting many forms of abuse, and in some states are key mandated reporters of suspected child and elder abuse."); Training Key, 3 ("Perpetrators [of elder abuse] are the children or grandchildren of the

elderly victim and may abuse the elder's pet as a form of retaliation, out of frustration over their caretaking responsibilities or to extract financial assets from the victim."); Ascione & Lockwood, 46–47; *Youth Violence,* 9 (stating that in a 1998 study of 38 battered women, 71% of those with pets said that their partners had threatened, hurt, or killed at least one of their pets); Randall Lockwood, *Wounded Hearts: Animal Abuse and Child Abuse,* AV Magazine, Winter 2000, at 17 [hereinafter *Wounded Hearts*] ("Veterinarians are mandated reporters of . . . suspected elder abuse in Illinois."); Robbins; Stecker, 36 (quoting prosecutor Gail Benda, who said, "I've seen over the 17 years that I've been a prosecutor that there's a very strong link between other violence and animal cruelty and abuse. To me it's just absolutely proven.").

168. 145 Cong. Rec. H10267 (daily ed. Oct. 19, 1999) (statement of Rep. Morella).

169. ASPCA Brief, 16 (citing Frank R. Ascione, *Domestic Violence and Cruelty to Animals,* 17 The Latham Letter 1 (1996)).

170. Ibid. (internal citation omitted); Training Key, 2.

171. Forell, 56 (internal citation omitted).

172. Ibid.

173. Friedman & Norman, 85 (internal citation omitted).

174. For a general discussion of the severity of the problem of domestic violence in America, see ibid. at 82–83 ("Domestic violence can happen to people of all ages, races, ethnicities, religions, socioeconomic classes, and professions. The statistics, which reflect how disproportionately domestic violence affects women, are overwhelming. 'One in every four women will experience domestic violence in her lifetime.' 'Eighty-five percent of domestic violence victims are women.' 'Over fifty percent of all women will experience physical violence in an intimate relationship,' and twenty-four to thirty percent of those women will experience regular and on-going domestic violence. The majority of domestic violence cases, unfortunately, are also never reported to law enforcement. Additionally, the cost of domestic violence exceeds $5.8 billion each year. To rectify this issue, 'all fifty states now have a version of the civil protection order, which mandates both court and law enforcement participation in instances where persons eligible for relief are in fear of harm.'") (internal citations omitted).

175. ASPCA Brief, 16–17 ("Research has also shown that fear of pet abuse is a major factor in preventing victims from escaping their abusive environments.") (internal citation omitted); Friedman & Norman, 87 ("The bond of a victim with his or her pet or service animal may hinder that victim's ability to seek and acquire help. Victims are unlikely to flee domestic violence for safe harbor, such as a women's shelter, if they must leave pets or service animals in their wake."); Training Key, 2 (citing a 1997 Utah study of victims in domestic violence safehouses, which revealed "72 percent of pet-owning victims reported that their abuser had threatened, harmed, or killed family pets. Researchers also asked victims whether they had delayed leaving their abusive situation out of fear for their pets' safety and found nearly 20 percent had delayed leaving the relationship because of the pet abuse."); Robbins, 129–30 (giving examples of partners who threatened pet abuse to control their partners).

176. Forell, 56 (internal citation omitted).

177. Friedman & Norman, 87 (citing Allie Phillips, *The Few and the Proud: Prosecutors Who Vigorously Pursue Animal Cruelty Cases*, 42 Prosecutor 20, 21 (Jul.-Sept. 2008) ("The actual killing, torturing and beating of pets—or the threat of such actions—is used by abusers as a weapon to ensure submission and silence by women and children."); see also Dianna J. Gentry, *Including Companion Animals in Protective Orders: Curtailing the Reach of Domestic Violence*, 13 Yale J.L. & Feminism 97, 102 (2001) ("It is because of this relationship with animals that abusers readily have the ability to exercise control over domestic violence victims through their pets.").

178. Training Key, 2–3; see also Ascione & Lockwood, 45 (citing a Department of Justice report, in which 9% of female respondents and 6% of male respondents reported that stalkers had murdered or threatened to kill pets).

179. Robbins, 129 (citing Jane Ann Quinlisk, "*Animal Abuse and Family Violence*," in Frank R. Ascione & Phil Arkow eds., *Child Abuse, Domestic Violence, and Animal Abuse* (1999), 168).

180. Crowell, 42 (citing Frank R. Ascione, "Battered Women's Reports of Their Partners' and Their Children's Cruelty to Animals," *J. Emotional Abuse* 1 (1998): 199, 128 (internal citation omitted)).

181. Friedman & Norman, 86 (internal citation omitted).

182. ASPCA Brief, 17 (citing 145 Cong. Rec. H10267); see also Friedman & Norman, 81; Robbins, 129, 134–37.

183. Forell, 61 ("Today many communities have both battered women's and animal shelters. It is not uncommon for women's shelters to work closely with animal shelters to provide care for a battered woman's animal companions, thereby making it easier for battered women with pets to leave their abusers.").

184. Friedman & Norman, 84–85.

185. Training Key, 3; Ascione & Lockwood, 46 (listing studies); see generally Robbins.

186. *Youth Violence*, 8.

187. Training Key, 1.

188. Crowell, 39–40.

189. Ibid., 41; Robbins, 129–30 (Robbins recounts the story of a child whose mother's boyfriend sexually abused her and who abused animals in front of her in an attempt to prevent her from reporting the abuse. He also threatened to abuse her dog, Dusty, if she reported him.); Training Key, 3.

190. Crowell, 41.

191. Training Key, 3.

192. *Wounded Hearts*, 16; Robbins, 135.

193. *Wounded Hearts*, 16.

194. Forell, 56, 57 (citation omitted).

195. Robbins, 130 (citation omitted).

196. Crowell, 42.

197. Ibid.

198. Robbins, 135.

199. Friedman & Norman, 86, 87.

200. *Youth Violence*, 8.

201. Crowell, 40; Training Key, 3 ("Similarly, the 1995 study of domestic violence victims entering shelter in Utah noted that 32 percent of the pet-owning victims reported that one or more of their children had hurt or killed a pet.").

202. ASPCA Brief, 13 (citation omitted).

203. Ibid., 14–15 (citing H.R. Con. Res. 338, 106th Cong. (2000)).

204. *Stevens*, 533 F.3d at 230. In *Ferber,* the Court noted that child pornography was intrinsically related to the sexual abuse of children because it created a permanent record of the abuse, thereby, exacerbating the harm and because closing the distribution network for child pornography was necessary to control its production. *Ferber*, 458 U.S. at 759.

205. *Stevens*, 130 S. Ct. at 1599 (Alito, J., dissenting) ("The videos record the commission of violent criminal acts, and it appears that these crimes are committed for the sole purpose of creating the videos. In addition, as noted above, Congress was presented with compelling evidence that the only way of preventing these crimes was to target the sale of the videos. Under these circumstances, I cannot believe that the First Amendment commands Congress to step aside and allow the underlying crimes to continue.").

206. ASPCA Brief, 23–25 (citations omitted).

207. Ibid., 24.

208. Ibid.

209. Ibid., 25 (citation omitted).

210. 145 Cong. Rec. H10267 (daily ed. Oct. 19, 1999) (statement of Rep. McCollum).

211. *Punishing Depictions*, 126 (statement of William Paul LeBaron, detective, Long Beach Police Department) ("I have watched over 50 videos ranging in length from 10 minutes to 2 hours.").

212. ASPCA Brief, 29.

213. Doug Simpson, "Internet Unleashes US Dogfight Craze," *The Sydney Morning Herald* (January 15, 2004), available at http://www.smh.com.au/articles/2004/01/14/1073877889804.html).

214. Lori Huoy, *Underground Magazine Leads Suspects to Officials*, WPXI (July 26, 2004), *available at* http://www.wpxi.com/news/3579417/detail.html.

215. ASPCA Brief, 29 (citation omitted).

216. Ibid., 30.

217. See Gibson; ASPCA Brief, 30 (citation omitted); Simpson ("The loser may be nursed back to health, if valuable, or it may be shot or abandoned."); *Stevens,* 130 S. Ct. at 1602 (Alito, J., dissenting) ("For these dogs, unlike the animals killed in crush videos, the suffering lasts for years rather than minutes.").

218. ASPCA Brief, 31 (citing Christine Haines, "Pennsylvania, PA: Dogfighting Probe Produces Two Warrants," *Herald-Standard* (July 27, 2004) (noting that in some states, "licensed veterinarians must report suspected dog fighting . . . [so] owners of fighting dogs do their own doctoring"); 720 Ill. Comp. Stat. Ann. 5/48-1 (2013) ("Any veterinarian in this State who is presented with a dog for treatment of injuries or wounds resulting from fighting where there is a reasonable possibility that the dog was engaged in or utilized for a fighting event for the purposes of sport, wagering, or entertainment shall file a report with the Department of Agriculture and cooperate by furnishing the owners' names, dates, and descriptions of the dog or

dogs involved."); Lockwood, 25–26 ("Several states mandate that veterinarians report animal cruelty, including suspected dogfighting activity, to the appropriate authorities. Many other states encourage veterinarians to report suspected animal cruelty by granting immunity to those who make good-faith reports to the appropriate agencies. Such reporting is supported by professional veterinary organizations including the American Veterinary Medical Association (AVMA) and the American Animal Hospital Association (AAHA). The AAHA position statement on reporting, revised in 2003, states: 'Since veterinarians have a responsibility to the welfare of animals and the public and can be the first to detect animal abuse in a family, they should take an active role in detecting, preventing and reporting animal abuse. While some states and provinces do not require veterinarians to report animal abuse, the association supports the adoption of laws requiring, under certain circumstances, veterinarians to report suspected cases of animal abuse. Reporting should only be required when client education has failed, when there is no likelihood that client education will be successful, or in situations in which immediate intervention is indicated and only when the law exempts veterinarians from civil and criminal liability for reporting.'"); *Youth Violence*, 10 (Minnesota and West Virginia require veterinarians to report suspected animal abuse.).

219. *See, e.g.*, Gibson (discussing the crime of dogfighting); Dean Schabner, "Arrest Called Break in Dog Fight Effort," *ABC News* (Apr. 29, 2003) (detailing a NY arrest made in connection with animal cruelty and dogfighting); "Leashing a Blood Sport," *Wash. Times*, Jan. 13, 2004, *available at* http://www.washingtontimes.com/news/2004/jan/12/20040112-115320-5139r/print ("Dogfighting is illegal in all states and a felony in 47, but the activity is on the rise.").

220. ASPCA Brief 5 (citation omitted); 720 Ill. Comp. Stat. Ann. 5/48-1 (2013) (making it illegal to knowingly attend a dogfight); Tex. Penal Code § 42.10 (2011) (same).

221. *Stevens*, 130 S. Ct at 1601 (Alito, J., dissenting).

222. Ibid., 1601 ("[T]hose who stage dogfights profit not just from the sale of the videos themselves, but from the gambling revenue they taken in from the fights; the videos 'encourage [such] gambling activity because they allow those reluctant to attend actual fights for fear of prosecution to still bet on the outcome.'") (citing Brief of the Center on the Administration of Criminal Law as Amicus Curiae in Support of Petitioner 12 ("Selling videos of dogfights effectively abets the underlying crimes by providing a market for dogfighting while allowing actual dogfights to remain underground."); Kinsella, 370–72 (discussing whether the Secondary Effects Doctrine applied to Section 48); Ricaurte, 188 ("In the case of dogfighting, the main revenue generator is the gambling and sale of illegal drugs, activities which are associated with dogfighting.").

223. Gibson; see also *Stevens*, 130 S. Ct. at 1601 (Alito, J., dissenting) ("dogfight videos are very often produced as part of a 'low-profile, clandestine industry' and 'the need to market the resulting products requires a visible apparatus of distribution'") (citing *Ferber*, 458 U.S. at 760); Lockwood, 20.

224. Lockwood, 20.

225. Ibid.

226. Attorneys' General Brief, 1; *Stevens*, 130 S. Ct. at 1600–01 (Alito, J. dissenting) ("Section 48's ban on trafficking in crush videos also helps to enforce the criminal laws and to ensure that criminals do not profit from their crimes.").

227. Attorney Generals' Brief, 2.

228. Ibid., 4–6. It is no defense to argue that the underlying acts of animal cruelty would still occur regardless of Section 48 because the same can be said of child pornography and many other criminal laws. The mere fact that a law cannot prevent every act it criminalizes is insufficient to warrant invalidating it. See HSUS Brief, 20 (explaining that the Third Circuit erroneously labeled Section 48 "underinclusive," but Congress was merely respecting potential limits on congressional powers).

229. ASPCA Brief, 33, n.61.

230. *Punishing Depictions*, 130 (statement of William Paul Lebaron, detective, Long Beach Police Department); *Stevens*, 130 S. Ct. at 1598–1600 (Alito, J., dissenting); Reynolds, 386 ("Halting distribution is necessary to halt production of animal cruelty videos because of the difficulty in prosecuting the actual offenders.").

231. ASPCA Brief, 9 (citing *Punishing Depictions*) (stating that a video typically sells for $40 to $45; made-to-order videos sell for up to $300 apiece; one video distributor had pending orders totaling $3,349 at the time of arrest; crush video distributors derive "a lucrative income from the sales and making of these videos"); ibid., 62 ("Devotees buy nearly $1 million worth of the tapes every year."); 145 Cong. Rec. H10267, H10273 (statement of Rep. Lantos) (stating that videos sell for up to $100 and "over three thousand titles [are] now for sale"); see also 145 Cong. Rec. H10267, H10267 (statement of Rep. McCollum) ("Entire industries have sprung up appealing to these unusual sexual fetishes.").

232. Gibson.

233. ASPCA Brief, 9, n.15. A Grand Champion has won five fights, while a Champion has won three.

234. See ibid., 9 (citing Haines) ("[P]itting champions or grand champions against one another can drive up the stakes in a dogfight to as much as $10,000."); ibid., 9–10 (asserting that championship status increases stud fees and the cost of puppies); Simpson (noting that wagers at organized fights range from $100 to $50,000); Huoy (purse runs up to $50,000).

235. Julie Bank & Stephen Zawistowski, "History of Dog Fighting," *ASPCA Animal Watch* (1997), available at http://www.aspca.org/fight-animal-cruelty/dogfighting/history-of-dogfighting.html ("The owner of a grand champion . . . can sell the dog's pups for as much as $20,000 apiece.").

236. ASPCA Brief, 10.

237. Ibid., 8, n.13 (citation omitted).

238. Ibid., 8 (citing 145 Cong. Rec. H10267, H10270 (statement of Rep. Gallegly)).

239. *Stevens*, 533 F.3d at 230.

240. ASPCA Brief (citing David S. Jackson, "Congress Stamps Out Animal-Snuff Videos," *Time*, Sept. 6, 1999; HSUS Brief, 3–5 (citing Elton W. Gallegly, "Beyond Cruelty," *U.S. Fed. News*, Dec. 16, 2007, internal citations omitted)).

241. Haines.

242. ASPCA Brief, 10 n.18 (citation omitted).

243. Ibid. (citing Jackson, "Congress Stamps Out Animal-Snuff Videos").

244. Reynolds, 386.

245. ASPCA Brief, 10–11 (citing *Crush-Fetish Net Clip Store*, http://xxxfetishmedia.com/shop68/shop.php?&dept=313&type=VIDEO&page=1 (last visited June 10, 2009) (crush videos); *Crush Cuties*, http://www.crushcuties.com (last visited June 10, 2009) (same).

246. Strossen, 96.

247. *Ferber*, 458 U.S. at 762.

248. *Stevens*, 130 S. Ct. at 1602 (Alito, J., dissenting) ("As noted, §48(b) exempts depictions having any appreciable social value, and thus the mere inclusion of a depiction of a live fight in a larger work that aims at communicating an idea or a message with a modicum of social value would not run afoul of the statute."). Some critics of Section 48 agree that crush videos lack any redeeming social value. See Adams, 219; Reynolds, 386 ("[T]he depictions prohibited by §48 lack any serious value.").

249. *Ferber*, 458 U.S. at 762.

250. ASPCA Brief, 26 (citing 18 U.S.C. §48(b) (2009)).

251. Ibid. (citing *Ferber*, 458 U.S. at 750–51 (discussing N. Y. Penal Law § 263.15)).

252. *Miller*, 413 U.S. at 15.

253. ASPCA Brief, 26 (citing *Miller*, 413 U.S. at 15).

254. *Stevens*, 130 S. Ct. at 1591.

255. Ibid., 1590.

256. Ibid.

257. Ibid.

258. Brief for the United States at 15, *United States v. Stevens*, 130 S. Ct. 1577 (2010) (No. 08-769) [hereinafter Gov't Brief].

259. 145 Cong. Rec. H10267 (statement of Rep. McCollum); *but see* Adams, 207 (Rep. Ron Paul of Texas stated that while the law was not intended to punish hunting or fishing depictions, "legislation often 'gets carried away and is misinterpreted.'").

260. ASPCA Brief, 26 (citing *Ashcroft*, 535 U.S. at 239–40).

261. Ibid., 24, n.42 (citing Mary Ann Mott, "U.S. Dogfighting Rings Stealing Pets for Bait," *Nat'l Geographic News* (2004), available at http://news.nationalgeographic.com/news/2004/02/0218_040218_dogfighting.html (family pets are often kidnapped and killed as bait to train fighting dogs)).

262. Ibid., 28 (citing 145 Cong. Rec. H10267 (statement of Rep. McCollum)).

263. 145 Cong. Rec. H10267, H10272 (statement of Rep. McCollum).

264. President's Statement on Signing Legislation to Establish Federal Criminal Penalties for Commerce in Depiction of Animal Cruelty, 34 Weekly Comp. Pres. Doc. 2557 (Dec. 9, 1999) (Section 48 will "assist in reducing or eliminating . . . deplorable and indefensible practices.").

265. *Stevens*, 130 S. Ct. at 1591.

266. Ibid.

267. ASPCA Brief, 23.

268. Ibid. (citing *United States v. Williams*, 553 U.S. 285, 299 (2008)).

269. *Williams*, 553 U.S. at 297.

270. Ibid., 298.

271. The Third Circuit conceded that the aforementioned categories could be supplemented, which was appropriate in this case because the depictions that Section 48 prohibited lack redeeming social value, instigate violent crime, and erode public mores. *See Stevens*, 533 F.3d at 224.

272. ASPCA Brief, 24 (citing *Ferber*, 458 U.S. at 761–62 (citing *Giboney v. Empire Storage & Ice Co.*, 336 U.S. 490, 498 (1949))); see *Stevens*, 130 S. Ct. at 1598–99 (Alito, J., dissenting) ("The First Amendment protects freedom of speech, but it most certainly does not protect violent criminal conduct, even if engaged in for expressive purposes. Crush videos present a highly unusual free speech issue because they are so closely linked with violent criminal conduct. The videos record the commission of violent criminal acts, and it appears that these crimes are committed for the sole purpose of creating the videos.").

273. ASPCA Brief, 5 n.10 (citing Huoy (noting that in Pennsylvania it is a criminal offense to aid in or promote illegal dogfighting); see also 720 Ill. Comp. Stat. 5/48-1 (2013) (making it illegal to knowingly attend a dogfight); Tex. Penal Code Ann. § 42.10 (2011) (same)).

274. Ibid., 24 n.40 ("Creating a crush video requires the filmmaker to solicit and conspire with another to commit a crime of animal cruelty and aid or abet that crime.") (citing Gibson).

275. Ibid., 24–25 (quoting *Ferber*, 458 U.S. at 761–62).

276. Ibid., 24 (citing *Brandenburg*, 395 U.S. at 447; *Ferber*, 458 U.S. at 761–62).

277. Ibid., 34 (citing *Stevens*, 533 F.3d at 232); *see* Reynolds, 385–86 ("The Third Circuit correctly notes that the depiction of the animal cruelty does not cause any psychological harm on the animal in the same way that a depiction of sexual abuse might cause harm to a child. . . . Whether or not the child is truly affected by the existence of a depiction of abuse, the primary rationale behind Ferber is the desire to prevent the underlying abuse in the first place. The constitutionality of §48 should not turn on this factor."); Robbins, 131–32 (Some may argue that to many American pet owners, pets are like children. In fact, a recent study found that 99% of dog and cat owners thought of their pets as family members, not mere property.).

278. *Stevens*, 533 F.3d at 243.

279. *See* Reynolds, 380 ("The age of consent in some states is as low as sixteen, and some states allow minors to engage in consensual sex with other minors. These acts are not illegal, but to film them and distribute the film across state lines would be. Furthermore, the age of consent in some foreign countries can be as low as thirteen. Despite the fact that a sexual act with a thirteen-year-old may be legal in that country, possessing any depiction of the act in the United States would subject the possessor to criminal liability.").

280. Ibid., 381.

281. ISAR Brief, 26 n.23.

282. Stevens, 130 S. Ct. at 1587 (quoting *United States v. Salerno*, 481 U.S. 702, 740 (1987)).

283. Ibid. (quoting *Wash. State Grange v. Wash. State Republican Party*, 552 U.S. 442, 449 n.6 (2008)).

284. Ibid., 1588.

285. Ibid.

286. See *Black's Law Dictionary* (9th ed. 2009) available at Westlaw BLACKS; see also *S.D. Warren Co. v. Maine Bd. of Evtl. Prot.*, 547 U.S. 370, 378 (2006) ("The canon, *noscitur*

a sociis, reminds us that 'a word is known by the company it keeps', and is invoked when a string of statutory terms raises the implication that the 'words grouped in a list should be given related meaning.'") (citations omitted).

287. Harold Anthony Lloyd, *Crushing Animals and Crashing Funerals: The Semiotics of Free Expression*, 12 First Amend. L. Rev. 236 (2013).

288. *Stevens*, 130 S. Ct at 1588 (citation omitted).

289. Ibid.

290. Ibid., 1588–89.

291. 18 U.S.C. §48(b) (2006).

292. *Stevens*, 130 S. Ct at 1590. The Court obtained this language from the District Court's jury instructions which the government defended as "a commonly accepting meaning of the 'word 'serious.'"

293. Ibid.

294. Ibid., 1595 (Alito, J., dissenting).

295. As Lloyd explains, ironically, in his subsequent decision upholding the Affordable Care Act, Chief Justice Roberts, who authored *Stevens*, acknowledged that the statute's "penalty" meant "tax": The text of a statute can sometimes have more than one possible meaning. To take a familiar example, a law that reads "no vehicles in the park" might, or might not, ban bicycles in the park. And it is well established that if a statute has two possible meanings, one of which violates the Constitution, courts should adopt the meaning that does not do so . . . . The question is not whether that is the most natural interpretation . . . , but only whether it is a "fairly possible" one. . . . As we have explained, "every reasonable construction must be resorted to, in order to save a statute from unconstitutionality." *Nat'l Fed'n of Indep. Bus. v. Sebelius*, 132 S.Ct. 2566, 1293-94 (2012). See Lloyd, 266–67.

296. Lloyd, 269.

297. See *Stevens*, 130 S.Ct. at 1588 (majority opinion).

298. Lloyd, 269–70.

299. Ibid., 271.

300. Ibid., 272–73.

301. Ibid.

CHAPTER 10

The Aftermath of
United States v. Stevens[1]

While *Stevens* will have significant consequences on the battle to end animal cruelty, it neither signals the end of animal welfare legislation nor stands for the notion that preventing animal cruelty is not a compelling interest. As Chief Justice Roberts remarked, "we therefore need not and do not decide whether a statute limited to crush videos or other depictions of extreme animal cruelty would be constitutional."[2]

Congress took the hint, and on April 21, 2010, a day after the Supreme Court issued its decision in *Stevens*, Representative Elton Gallegly and 50 co-sponsors introduced H.R. 5092—a bill to amend Section 48 that prohibited persons from "knowingly sell[ing] or offer[ing] to sell an animal crush video in interstate or foreign commerce for commercial gain."[3] It was hastily constructed without significant input or review from animal protection and animal law experts, but in response to the majority's concerns, it limited the restrictions specifically to animal crush videos and added an exemption that stated "nothing . . . shall be construed to prohibit the selling or offering to sell a video that depicts hunting."[4] This had been a major sticking point for many groups that had filed amicus briefs in *Stevens* and was the focus of many of the "fanciful hypotheticals" proposed during oral argument to demonstrate how Section 48 could be used to suppress the distribution of outdoor life style hunting videos in areas, such as the District of Columbia, where hunting is illegal.

After receiving comments on the original bill, Rep. Gallegly and 262 co-sponsors ultimately introduced H.R. 5566 on June 22, 2010.[5] That same month, the House Judiciary Committee approved H.R. 5566 by a unanimous vote of 23–0.[6]

The subsequent progress of H.R. 5566 was even more rapid than that of Section 48. There continued to be a sense of urgency in passing new legislation since animal protection groups had documented a return of crush videos to the market, discovering more than 100 videos for sale on one Internet site alone.[7]

217

The House of Representatives passed H.R. 5566 by a vote of 416 to 3 on July 21, 2010—less than a month after its introduction.[8] The Senate passed it on September 28, 2010, amending it to embrace the international distribution of materials. The Senate also added exemptions for "good-faith distribution to a law enforcement agency; or a third party for the sole purpose of analysis to determine if referral to a law enforcement agency is appropriate."[9] The House accepted these changes on November 15, 2010, and the Senate approved them four days later. On December 9, 2010, President Barack Obama signed Public Law 111-294, the Animal Crush Video Prohibition Act of 2010 (Crush Act), into law.[10]

The Crush Act contains key differences from the statute deemed unconstitutional in *U.S. v. Stevens*. Table 1 summarizes several of its key provisions.

Table 1. Key Provisions of the Crush Act

Provision	The Crush Act
Mens Rea	Knowingly create, sell, market, etc.; intentionally crush, burn, etc.
Prohibited Conduct	Creation where one intends or has reason to know that the video will be distributed in, or using a means or facility of, interstate or foreign commerce or the video is distributed in, or using a means or facility of, interstate or foreign commerce; sell, market, advertise, exchange, or distribute

Table 1 (continued).

Interstate or Foreign Commerce	Creation where one intends or has reason to know that the video will be distributed in, or using a means or facility of, interstate or foreign commerce or the video is distributed in, or using a means or facility of, interstate or foreign commerce; sell, market, advertise, exchange, or distribute in, or using a means or facility of, interstate or foreign commerce
Penalty	Fine or a maximum of 7 years in prison or both
Exceptions	Exempts works that are not obscene; see additional exceptions below
Depictions	Any photograph, motion-picture film, video or digital recording, or electronic image
Living Animal	Living non-human mammal, bird, reptile, or amphibian
Prohibited Cruelty	Crushed, burned, drowned, suffocated, or otherwise subjected to serious bodily injury (as defined in section 1365, etc.)
Obscenity	Depiction must be obscene
Conduct Criminal under State or Federal Law	N/A
Preemption	Law does not preempt state or local law

Table 1 (continued).

Extraterritorial Application	Applies extraterritorially under certain circumstances
Good Faith Distribution Exception	Permits good faith distribution to law enforcement or a third party for the sole purpose of analysis to determine if a referral to a law enforcement agency is appropriate
Veterinary Exception	Depiction of customary and normal veterinary practices
Animal Husbandry Exception	Depiction of customary and normal agricultural husbandry practices
Animal Slaughter Exception	Depiction of the slaughter of animals for food
Hunting Exception	Depiction of hunting, trapping, or fishing

Justifications for the law included that:

1. preventing extreme animal cruelty is a compelling government interest;
2. every state and the District of Columbia criminalize intentional acts of extreme animal cruelty;
3. the clandestine nature of certain acts of animal cruelty allows the perpetrators of such crimes to remain anonymous, thus frustrating the ability of Federal and State authorities to enforce the criminal statutes prohibiting such behavior;
4. these criminal acts constitute an integral part of the production of and market for so-called crush videos and other depictions of animal cruelty;
5. the creation and sale of crush videos provide an economic incentive for, and are intrinsically related to, the underlying acts of the criminal conduct;
6. the United States has a long history of prohibiting the interstate sale of obscene and illegal materials; and
7. animal crush videos appeal to the prurient interest and are obscene.[11]

These justifications have been expanded to reflect the views and opinions of the federal government and various amici that endorsed upholding Section 48. They now emphasize, among other things, the "long history of prohibiting the interstate sale, marketing, advertising, exchange, and distribution of obscene material and speech that is integral to criminal conduct" and state that "there are certain extreme acts of animal cruelty that appeal to a specific sexual fetish. These acts of extreme animal cruelty are videotaped, and the resulting video tapes are commonly referred to as 'animal crush videos.'"[12] The latter finding narrows the Crush Act's scope and application because it could be read to exclude from coverage videotapes not made to satiate a sexual fetish, perhaps providing the accused with a defense, that is, that the film was not made to appeal to the prurient interest in sex. The findings also make clear that in the judgment of Congress, at least some crush videos constitute obscenity, and the Crush Act only applies to obscene speech. As such, one might argue that under a literal reading of the statute, a snuff film of a living puppy being gagged, burned alive, and decapitated would not be covered so long as it was made for entertainment, but not to appeal to the prurient interest in sex. Depictions of unlawful animal fighting are also excluded. These statutory changes may address the concerns raised by the majority in *Stevens*, but they may also reduce the law's scope and effectiveness. Furthermore, the mere fact that a film is not intended to sexually arouse a viewer does not change the harmful effects flowing from the depiction or prevent the underlying act of animal cruelty its creation necessitates.

The findings also raise questions regarding whether the prevention of criminal animal cruelty, as opposed to *extreme* animal cruelty, constitutes a compelling government interest. The Crush Act asserts that "the Federal Government and States have a compelling interest in preventing intentional acts of extreme animal cruelty."[13] This could be read to imply that, in Congress's view, preventing animal cruelty, not extreme animal cruelty as defined by the Crush Act, does not constitute a compelling government interest.

The Crush Act defines "animal crush video" as:

> any photograph, motion-picture film, video or digital recording, or electronic image that—(1) depicts actual conduct in which 1 or more living non-human mammals, birds, reptiles, or amphibians, is intentionally crushed, burned, drowned, suffocated, impaled or otherwise subjected to serious bodily injury (as defined in section 1365 and including conduct that, if committed against a person and in the special maritime and territorial jurisdiction of the United States, would violate section 2241 or 2242); and (2) is obscene.[14]

While Section 48 applied to living animals, including fish, crustaceans, insects, worms, etc., the Crush Act is limited to "living non-human mammals, birds, reptiles or amphibians."[15] Ironically, the specificity of the new law regarding the animals protected creates a large loophole for producing and distributing crush videos that feature acts involving non-designated animals, including insects, fish, earthworms, cephalopods and others. Insect and worm crush videos soon surfaced on YouTube and other widely accessed sites because filmmakers had no concern over legal action. Such species are not protected under the new law and would not be covered under most state anti-cruelty laws. The Crush Act further limits the scope of animal protection because it only applies to visual depictions, whereas Section 48 also applied to auditory recordings.

Section 48 embraced depictions of maiming, mutilation, torture, wounding, and killing that would constitute criminal animal cruelty under federal, state, or local law. However, the Crush Act applies to crushing, burning, suffocation, drowning, impaling, or otherwise subjecting to serious bodily injury as defined in Section 1365. Removal of the words "wounding" and "killing" directly addresses the overbreadth concerns raised in *Stevens*, but inclusion of the term "serious bodily injury" may not encompass all of the harms that the law should ideally address, including interspecies sexual assault.

As explained above, Section 48 applied to depictions of animal cruelty generally, but the Crush Act's application is limited to obscene depictions, that is, those that appeal to the prurient interest in sex, are patently offensive, and lack serious literary, artistic, political, or scientific value. Addition of the phrase "is obscene" aimed to bring the Crush Act in line with existing constitutionally upheld obscenity laws and to return the law to the original spirit of its legislative intent. However, this addition could limit the application of the law to videos that are specifically sexual in nature. Other videos that display animal crushing in a non-sexual context without the dominatrix setting or sadomasochistic overtones of earlier crush videos could conceivably be outside the law's scope. As such, the law could be read to exclude (and thus permit) the sale of a depiction of a living dog being intentionally burned so long as the depiction was not created to satiate a sexual fetish. Evidence suggests that crush videos are created to appeal to specific sexual fetishes, but the legislative history of Section 48 nowhere mentions sexual fetishes linked to burning, drowning, or other acts of extreme animal cruelty. Although the absence of such evidence does not preclude the possibility of its existence, this definition could heighten the burden of proof to secure a conviction since, in addition to proving each element of prong one, that is, the victim was alive, the perpetrator acted intentionally, and the animal was subjected to "serious bodily injury" as defined by Section 1365, the prosecutor must also prove that the depiction is obscene.

In narrowing Section 48, Congress also removed its broad exceptions clause, which excluded works having serious religious, political, scientific, educational, journalistic, historical, or artistic value. By comparison, the Crush Act exempts non-obscene works having literary, artistic, political, or scientific value and adds exceptions for good faith distribution to law enforcement as well as visual depictions of customary and normal veterinary practices, agricultural husbandry practices, animal slaughter for food, and hunting, fishing, and trapping.[16] At first glance, these exceptions appear to address the concerns of the majority, but a more thorough analysis suggests that the Crush Act remains susceptible to overbreadth challenges because it no longer expressly exempts works having educational, religious, journalistic, or historical value. It also fails to exempt, among other things, visual depictions used for animal research and forms of lawful gaming *other* than hunting, trapping, and fishing. In sum, congressional attempts to narrow the law gave it less bite but did not necessarily guarantee that it will survive future overbreadth challenges.

As of January 2013, the Crush Act had been used only once. In August 2012, Brent Justice and Ashley Nicole Richards were arrested in Houston, Texas, on charges of animal cruelty documented on camera and promoted for sale.[17] The couple "allegedly tortured a puppy, kittens, a rabbit, mice, a pigeon, fish, lobsters, crabs, and other animals using high heeled shoes, a meat cleaver, knives, screwdrivers, pliers, and other devices," and "as many as 27 videos were seized."[18] Another source stated that puppies, kittens, chickens, and mice were tortured to death in the films. It observed that a pit bull puppy was slashed and then beheaded with a meat cleaver, and an actress stabbed a kitten's eye with her stiletto heel. Richards and Justice claim to have created the films for paying customers.[19] Justice and Richards were indicted on five counts of violating the Crush Act, but the district court granted their motions to dismiss.[20] The district court concluded that the depictions were neither obscene nor speech integral to criminal conduct.[21] According to the district court, "the acts depicted in animal crush videos are disturbing and horrid," yet are still considered protected speech.[22] Because the district court determined that the depictions were protected speech, it applied strict scrutiny but concluded that the statute was not sufficiently narrowly tailored.[23] It determined that preventing animal cruelty is a compelling interest, but that the Crush Act did not serve the dry-up-the-market rationale.[24] Thus, although the district court acknowledged the interest in preventing animal cruelty to be "compelling," it held that that the Crush Act was not sufficiently narrowly tailored to survive strict scrutiny.[25] It remains to be seen whether their case will lead to invalidation of the new Crush Act.

Notes

1. Portions of this chapter are excerpted from Abigail Lauren Perdue, *When Bad Things Happen to Good Laws: The Rise, Fall, and Future of Section 48*, 18 VA. J. Soc. Pol'y & L. 469 (2011), and have been reprinted herein with the permission of the Journal and Author.

2. *United States v. Stevens*, 130 S. Ct. 1577, 1592 (2010) (emphasis added).

3. H.R. 5092, 111th Cong. (2d Sess. 2010).

4. Ibid.

5. H.R. 5566, 111th Cong., (2d. Sess. 2010) ("H.R. 5566").

6. "The HSUS Applauds Signing of Animal Crush Video Prohibition Act," *The Humane Society of the United States*, December 9, 2010, accessed March 7, 2013, http://www.humanesociety.org/news/press_releases/2010/12/crush_bill_signed_120910.html.

7. "Crush Videos Make a Comeback," *The Humane Society of the United States*, September 15, 2009, accessed March 7, 2013, http://www.humanesociety.org/news/news/2009/09/crush_video_091509.html.

8. "The HSUS Applauds Signing of Animal Crush Video Prohibition Act."

9. H.R. 5566 Bill Tracking, 111th Cong. (2d Sess. 2010).

10. Ibid.

11. P.L. 111-294, H.R. 5566.

12. Ibid.

13. Ibid.

14. Ibid.

15. Ibid.

16. Ibid.

17. Tal Kopan, "Feds Bring First Case Under New 'Animal Crush' Video Law," *Politico*, November 29, 2012, accessed January 13, 2013, http://www.politico.com/blogs/under-the-radar/2012/11/feds-bring-first-case-under-new-animal-crush-video-150700.html.

18. "Brent Justice, Ashley Nicole Richards 'Crush Video' Bust: Pair Charged With Animal Cruelty," *Huffington Post*, August 21, 2012, accessed March 7, 2013, http://www.huffingtonpost.com/2012/08/21/brent-justice-ashley-nicole-richards-crush-video-animal-cruelty_n_1819198.html.

19. "Texas Judge Says Animal Snuff Films Are Constitutional," *Life With Dogs*, April 24, 2013, accessed April 20, 2013, http://www.lifewithdogs.tv/2013/04/texas-judge-says-animal-snuff-films-are-constitutional/.

20. *U.S. v. Richards*, 940 F. Supp.2d 548, 550 (S.D. Tex. 2013).

21. Ibid., 553–55.

22. Ibid., 559.

23. Ibid.

24. Ibid.
25. Ibid., 560.

Afterword:
Implications for the Future

In the wake of *Stevens*, the Supreme Court is unlikely to categorically exclude depictions of animal cruelty, even crush videos, from First Amendment protection primarily because such speech has not historically been prohibited.[1] As such, some feared that *Stevens* would provoke a domino effect of unintended negative consequences: (i) enabling the brutal and unchecked slaughter of countless animals via unlawful animal fighting; (ii) facilitating the commission of animal cruelty; (iii) clogging already back-logged courts and law enforcement agencies with animal cruelty-related prosecutions; (iv) increasing the likelihood of children's exposure to gruesome depictions of animal cruelty and animal fighting; (v) enhancing the risk of petnappings to procure bait or victims for use in dogfighting and crush videos, respectively; (vi) desensitizing Americans to violence against humans and animals; and (vii) facilitating the continued erosion of already imperiled public mores.

Some also feared that *Stevens* would have the indirect effect of endangering existing animal cruelty legislation nationwide or preventing enactment of new laws even where the laws differ from Section 48 in purpose or effect, because as with *Lukumi*, courts may misinterpret *Stevens* to indicate that preventing animal cruelty does not constitute a compelling government interest.

Moreover, there was some concern that the majority's declaration that use of the words *wounded* or *killed* made Section 48 overbroad could also imperil animal welfare legislation nationwide by prompting challenges to state anti-cruelty laws with similar language. For example, New York prohibits the unjustifiable "killing" of an animal, with certain exceptions.[2] It remains unclear whether *Stevens* will make laws like New York's susceptible to challenges or whether state legislatures will preempt such challenges by amending their laws to comport with the decision. Such amendments may narrow the laws' coverage, perhaps reducing their effectiveness.

On the other hand, *Stevens* has heightened public awareness of animal cruelty issues and specifically, the crush video industry. Through extensive media coverage of the legislative and legal battles, the public was made aware of a bizarre form of animal cruelty and the inadequacies of existing law to address it and related practices. This attention has fueled efforts to recriminalize animal sexual assault and look more closely at such crimes as indicators and predictors of interpersonal violence against humans. There has been a strong effort to extend the same kind of action against crush videos around the world. The website stopcrush.org tracks these activities worldwide and has reported significant legal and legislative efforts against crush videos in the United Kingdom, Canada, Italy, Greece, China, the Philippines, and South Africa.

Stevens also impacted humane law enforcement. The passage of stronger state laws protecting animals, including provisions for prosecuting some abuses as a felony in forty-nine states, has come at a time of declining law enforcement and animal care and control resources. While the public increasingly demands a response to incidents of animal abuse, the response is often considered inadequate. There is often a disconnect between the cases that produce public outrage and those that police and prosecutors feel are important enough to devote time and money to investigate and pursue. It is not unusual for law enforcement officials to receive hundreds or thousands of communications regarding a high-profile animal cruelty case while an assault, murder, or abduction may seem to go largely unnoticed by the public.[3] In addition, prosecutors may be reluctant to pursue charges if there is concern that a law is flawed or if the investigation or documentation was inadequate.

One solution has been the greater involvement of community-oriented policing and the establishment of local level task forces to deal specifically with animal cruelty cases through the coordinated actions of police, prosecutors, animal care and control, animal protection groups, veterinary forensic specialists, and social services. This approach has been used to address general animal cruelty, dogfighting, and animal hoarding.[4]

Fortunately, the failure to use Section 48 successfully in *Stevens* has not had a noticeable chilling effect on prosecuting actual dogfighting. In fact, law enforcement agencies have shown great interest in materials specifically providing guidance for investigating and prosecuting dogfighting.[5] They have recognized that such cases will require the traditional forms of evidence (paraphernalia, injured dogs, undercover video) and newer applications of veterinary forensics.[6]

Another concern was whether the Supreme Court in *Stevens* would hold that preventing animal cruelty is not a compelling government interest. The government, many amici, and several legal scholars all considered such a ruling to be erroneous.[7] As explained earlier in this volume, the Third Circuit's conclusion that the state did not have a compelling interest in preventing animal cruelty in the context of the First Amendment arguably resulted from a misreading of *Lukumi v. City of Hialeah*. Unlike *Stevens*, the case involved freedom of religion, not freedom of speech. The district court upheld the ordinances, and the Eleventh Circuit affirmed. However, the Supreme Court reversed, stating that the ordinances aimed to suppress Santeria and thus target religious conduct. The Supreme Court did not resolve whether preventing animal cruelty was a compelling government interest; rather, it indicated that the state had less restrictive means of achieving its goals.[8]

Although some read *Lukumi* as making all animal sacrifice legally untouchable, subsequent events reveal otherwise. In June of 1993, Roberto Zamora, a Miami Santeria practitioner, held a press conference where he performed a Santeria ritual that involved sacrificing three goats and one sheep by slitting their throats.[9] Videotaped records of the conference showed that one goat continued to bleat after the first knife cut, although the cut appeared to enter the animal's trachea. A second goat was clearly conscious after being stabbed in the neck and struggled while Zamora made more cuts in a haphazard sawing fashion. The sheep required seven cuts to the throat before dying.

Animal cruelty charges were filed against Zamora in July of 1995. Dr. Michael W. Fox and Dr. Melanie Adcock of the Humane Society of the United States and livestock handling and slaughter expert, Dr. Temple Grandin, provided detailed veterinary testimony, concluding that the slaughter had been cruel and unnecessarily painful. Zamora was charged with four counts of animal cruelty. He moved to dismiss the charges on the grounds of religious freedom, but his motion was denied. In July of 1996, he pled no contest to the charges and received two years' probation and 400 hours of community service.[10] He appealed his conviction to the circuit court, which affirmed in October of 1997.[11] This demonstrates that animal cruelty committed in the name of religious freedom may still be successfully prosecuted.

To the relief of animal advocates, the *Stevens* Court chose not to rule on the compelling state interest issue.[12] As Cassuto notes, "the *Stevens* holding left the Court and the law with respect to animal cruelty in much the same limbo in which it had found them. . . . [and] could have been a lot worse."[13]

Stevens also has implications with regard to the use of graphic imagery in animal advocacy. The use of graphic imagery to educate the public about animal cruelty and animal welfare issues has been a significant part of animal advocacy for over fifty years. *Stevens* and the potential for restriction of depictions of animal cruelty raised concerns that animal activists should exercise caution in trying to save Section 48 from invalidation since many of the images used to raise awareness of abuse could theoretically be subjected to the same restraint that was attempted with the videos at issue in *Stevens*. However, these concerns may have been unfounded as most, if not all, such images would likely have fallen within one of Section 48's exceptions.

However, the question is important because the assumption has always been that graphic depictions *are* needed to effect change in attitudes and behavior. This has been a widespread strategy not only of animal rights and animal welfare advocates but also of efforts aimed at abortion, smoking, drunk driving, and other issues.

In the case of anti-smoking efforts, the Centers for Disease Control (CDC) embraced the graphic approach. In 2012, the CDC reported that its ad campaign showing diseased smokers had been such a success that it planned to repeat it.[14] The assumption of the ads' effectiveness is based on the fact that the ads generated 192,000 extra calls—more than double the usual volume—to its national toll-free quit line and 417,000 new visitors to its website offering cessation tips, which was triple the site's traffic before the ads.[15]

There has been little research on the effectiveness of such "shock advocacy" in animal issues or specifically linking changes in behavior to specific kinds of media messages. Scudder and Mills looked at various forms of messaging around the factory farming of pigs using investigative videos from People for the Ehical Treatment of Animals (PETA).[16] They found that watching negative media depicting the conditions pigs faced in intensive farming led viewers to have a significantly more positive image of the organization.[17] The negative nature of the advocacy message did not appear to be held against PETA.[18]

Another concern is that the media presentation of information on illegal or undesirable behavior can create a "copycat" or "outlaw" response. Widespread attention to crush and related videos may actually stimulate rather than suppress interest in and the market for such material, as seen in the proliferation of "legal" crush videos involving invertebrates on the Internet noted earlier. Likewise, widespread media attention to the evils of dogfighting may, despite improved reporting and response, contribute to the escalation of the problem by those inspired to emulate the offenders who receive media attention.

The effectiveness of media campaigns designed to bring attention to animal welfare and other issues, particularly those making use of graphic video depictions of animal cruelty, has created a large backlash against such campaigns by corporations and other entities that feel threatened by the dissemination of such media, whether accurate or distorted. The backlash against such efforts often relies on tactics of suppression and intimidation of such coverage that clearly raise many of the same First Amendment issues that were hotly debated in *Stevens*. Effective actions exposing animal cruelty or environmental risks now almost invariably galvanize special interest groups and create a response that is potentially damaging to past and future legislative efforts in the form of unfavorable laws or added exemptions, weakened regulations or costly litigation aimed at suppressing criticism. This backlash has taken several forms. It includes the use of "food disparagement" laws and litigation, laws restricting investigations of factory farms and the proliferation of state "right to hunt" legislation.

The First Amendment's protection of legitimate exposure of social issues is well-established. In the 1964 case, *New York Times v. Sullivan*, the Supreme Court held that the First Amendment protects individuals who make defamatory statements related to matters of public concern, so long as such statements are not made with actual malice or in reckless disregard of the truth.[19] The Supreme Court affirmed the notion that "debate on public issues should be uninhibited, robust, and wide-open."[20]

The sentiment of that decision seems to have eroded in recent years with the proliferation of so-called "food disparagement laws" or "veggie-libel laws" pushed by meat, dairy and agricultural interests. Such efforts emerged after a 1989 *60 Minutes* exposé on the hazards associated with the pesticide Alar resulted in millions of dollars in lost sales for apple growers and the removal of the chemical from the market. Washington state apple growers filed a $250 million lawsuit against CBS, which was ultimately dismissed.[21]

In 1992, the American Feed Industry Association drafted model legislation for food disparagement laws that 13 states have adopted. Such laws set a much lower standard for action against critics of industries, requiring only negligence, rather than malice, in making false or disparaging statements and setting a much lower standard for who might claim injury by such statements to include virtually anyone in the industry being criticized.[22]

The most prominent test of the legality of such laws came in 1996 when Oprah Winfrey aired an episode entitled "Dangerous Foods" featuring former cattleman Howard Lyman, an HSUS staffer well known for his conversion to vegetarianism and his criticism of the meat industry. The show focused on recent concerns about "Mad Cow Disease" and its potential link to livestock rearing practices, particularly including remains of dead cows in feed for other cattle.[23] Following the show, beef sales and prices dropped dramatically.[24] Oprah offered industry groups an opportunity to respond, but Texas cattleman Paul F. Engler and Cactus Feeders,

Inc. (Texas Beef Group) sued Winfrey and Lyman for $10.3 million in damages under Texas' False Disparagement of Perishable Food Products Act.[25] The court dismissed the lawsuit but did not address the law's constitutionality.[26]

The Civil Liberties Defense Center (CLDC) confirms that, to date, no one has been found liable under any food disparagement lawsuit, but the chilling prospect of facing expensive legal action without the financial resources of Oprah Winfrey continues to have a stifling effect on criticism of agricultural practices.[27] The CLDC maintains that food disparagement laws undermine basic First Amendment rights and threaten a reversion to the pre-*Sullivan* days when fears of liability constrained public debate.

The proliferation of so-called "Ag-Gag" laws has followed a path similar to that of food disparagement laws. For more than a century, reformers and animal welfare investigators have revealed severe animal abuse and raised additional concern about industrial farms, such as the potential contamination of eggs and meat.[28] This process began with Upton Sinclair's *The Jungle* and has seen increasing impact through the decades.[29] Increasingly, these investigations have made extensive use of photographic and video documentation of abuses—depictions of animal suffering and death that echo the concerns raised in *Stevens*. They have led to product recalls, decisions by retailers to drop suppliers, legal prosecutions of employees, and hard questions posed to the animal agribusiness industry.[30] Video footage was a major component of a 2007 HSUS investigation at a slaughterhouse in Chino, California, that revealed the abuse of downer cows and spurred criminal prosecutions and the largest meat recall in U.S. history.[31]

The response of the agricultural industry to the perceived threat of documenting animal cruelty in commercial operations stimulated a reaction similar to that raised as a result of the proliferation of undercover laboratory animal investigations and exposés by animal rights groups in the 1980s and 1990s. At least twenty-eight states have passed "animal enterprise interference statutes" since 1988.[32] Some penalize common acts of undercover investigators, such as entering an animal facility to commit unauthorized acts or committing fraud on a job application, but do not appear to have been enforced against undercover investigations.[33] Several of the animal enterprise interference statutes contain language that presaged a new round of laws launched in 2011.

Beginning in 2011, several states sought to pass bills seeking to criminalize the recording, possession, or distribution of still images (photos), live images (video) and/or audio at or upon a farm, industrial agricultural operation or "animal facility."[34] Bills in some states seek to bar potential investigators from gain-ing employment on farms. The first two such laws were passed in Iowa and Utah in March of 2012.[35] Iowa's law establishes the crime of "agricultural production facility fraud."[36] Utah outlaws "agricultural operation interference," making it a crime to record farm animals and farm animal workers without permission of the farm owner.[37] Kansas, North Dakota, and Montana prohibit "unauthorized filming at animal facilities."[38]

Finally, many states and the federal government have enacted "hunter harassment" laws.[39] Most of the proscribed behaviors involve actual interference with legal hunting ranging from direct confrontation to the spreading of human hair, urine, and feces with the intent of scaring away wildlife.[40] However, the simple act of documenting someone's hunting activity could result in threats of arrest and can act to suppress criticism, dissent, and documentation of possible illegal or unethical actions.

"Right to hunt" laws further affirm the legitimacy of sport hunting. According to the National Conference of State Legislators, seventeen states guarantee the right to hunt and fish.[41] Vermont's law dates back to 1777, but as late as November of 2012, voters in four more states—Idaho, Kentucky, Nebraska, and Wyoming—overwhelmingly passed legislatively referred ballot measures to add a constitutional right to hunt and fish. Seven other states—Hawaii, Michigan, Missouri, New Jersey, New Mexico, New York, and Pennsylvania—considered legislation to amend the constitution to add the right to hunt and fish in 2012 but were unsuccessful.

Conclusion

The competing concerns regarding the prevention of animal cruelty and the preservation of free speech will likely clash again as they did in *U.S. v. Stevens*. Although the outcome of such a collision remains unclear, the certainty of its recurrence does not. Depictions of animal cruelty have been and will remain part of the media landscape whether they are used to advocate for animal protection or to satisfy the base motives of those who would exploit animals for utilitarian, prurient, or pathological purposes. *Stevens* highlighted the fine line between a documentary that shows how livestock are raised and one that shows their abuse. As long as such distinctions remain blurred, the best recourse for policymakers and law enforcement is to continue to focus on the actors and actions that place animals at risk. Animal advocates must use the media to alert the public and law enforcement to persistent forms of animal cruelty and utilize existing animal protection laws to seek justice for the voiceless victims of animal cruelty.

Notes

1. See Nadine Strossen, "United States v. Stevens: Restricting Two Major Rationales for Content-Based Speech Restrictions," Cato S. Ct. Rev., 2009–2010 (2010): 101–2.

2. Jennifer S. Rosa, "Chapter 118 and 208 of the Laws of 1999: The New York Legislature Develops a Pseudo Animal Rights Agenda," 74 St. John's L. Rev. 287, 287–88 (2000).

3. Randall Lockwood, *Animal Cruelty Prosecution, Opportunities for Early Response to Crime and Interpersonal Violence* (Virginia: American Prosecutors Research Institute, 2006), 12.

4. Phil Arkow and Randall Lockwood, *Animal Abuse and Human Violence: Toolkit For Starting A Link Coalition In Your Community* (National Link Coalition, 2012), 4.

5. See *generally* Arkow and Lockwood, *Animal Abuse and Human Violence.*

6. Randal Lockwood, *Veterinary Forensic Evidence in Animal Cruelty Cases* (North American Veterinary Conference, 2013).

7. Joseph J. Anclien, "Crush Videos and Case for Criminalizing Criminal Depictions," 40 U. Mem. L. Rev. 1 (2009); Elizabeth Kinsella, "A Crushing Blow: United States v. Stevens and the Freedom to Profit from Animal Cruelty," 43 U.C. Davis L. Rev. 347, 382 (2010); David N. Cassuto, "United States v. Stevens: Win, Loss, or Draw for Animals?," *Journal of Animal Ethics* 2, no. 1 (2012).

8. Elizabeth Kinsella, "A Crushing Blow," 362.

9. Raju Chebium, "Santeria Priest Pleads No Contest to Animal Cruelty Charge," *Associated Press*, July 20, 1996.

10. Ibid.

11. Leslie Sinclair, Melinda Merck, and Randall Lockwood, *Forensic Investigation of Animal Cruelty* (Washington D.C.: Humane Society Press, 2006), 188.

12. David N. Cassuto, "United States v. Stevens: Win, Loss, or Draw for Animals," *Journal of Animal Ethics* 2, no. 1 (2012): 13.

13. Ibid., 17, 18.

14. Wendy Koch, "CDC Says Graphic Anti-Smoking Ads Work, More On Way," *USA Today,* August 6, 2012.

15. Ibid.

16. Joseph N. Scudder and Carol Bishop Mills, "The credibility of shock advocacy: Animal rights attack messages," *Public Relations Review* 35 (2009): 162.

17. Ibid., 163.

18. Ibid., 164.

19. *New York Times Co. v. Sullivan*, 376 U.S. 254, 270 (1995).

20. Ibid., 272.

21. "Veggie Libel Laws: Attempts at Silencing Animal Rights Advocates," *Civil Liberties Defense Center* (2012).

22. Ibid.

23. Howard Lyman and Glen Merzer, *Mad Cowboy: Plain Truth from the Cattle Rancher Who Won't Eat Meat* (New York: Scribner, 1998), 14.

24. Ibid., 15.

25. "Veggie Libel Laws"; Howard Lyman, Glen Merzer, and Joanna Samorow-Merzer, *No More Bull! The Mad Cowboy Targets America's Worst Enemy: Our Diet* (New York: Scribner, 2005), 9.

26. Lyman, *No More Bull*, 10.

27. "Veggie Libel Laws."

28. Lewis Bollard, "Ag-Gag: The Unconstitutionality of Laws Restricting Undercover Investigations on Farms," *Environmental Law Report* 42, no. 10 (2012): 6–7.

29. Gail Eisnitz, *Slaughterhouse: The Shocking Story of Greed, Neglect, and Inhumane Treatment Inside the U.S. Meat Industry* (New York: Prometheus Books, 1997), 6; Ruth Harrison, *Animal Machines: The New Factory Farming Industry* (London: Vincent Stuart Ltd., 1964); Jim Mason and Peter Singer, *Animal Factories* (New York, Crown Publishers, 1970).

30. Randall Lockwood, Interview with Randall Lockwood, Winston-Salem, NC, May 17, 2013.

31. Bollard, *Ag-Gag*, 8.

32. Ibid., 9.

33. Ibid.

34. Ibid., 11.

35. Bollard, *Ag-Gag*, 3.

36. Ibid., 14.

37. Ibid., 15.

38. Ibid., 9.

39. Jeffery Banke, "Hunter Harassment," *Examiner.com*, http://www.examiner.com/article/hunter-harassment.

40. Ibid.

41. *See* Douglas Shinkle, "State Constitutional Right to Hunt and Fish," *National Conference of State Legislatures*, http://www.ncsl.org/issues-research/env-res/state-constitutional-right-to-hunt-and-fish.aspx).

Bibliography

Arkow, Phil, and Randall Lockwood. *Animal Abuse and Human Violence: Toolkit for Starting a Link Coalition in Your Community.* Stratford, NJ: National Link Coalition, 2012.

Burt, Jonathan. *Animals in Film.* London: Reaktion Books, 2002.

Eisnitz, Gail A. *Slaughterhouse: The Shocking Story of Greed, Neglect, and Inhumane Treatment Inside the U.S. Meat Industry.* New York: Prometheus Books, 1997.

Essig, Mark. *Edison and the Electric Chair.* New York: Walker & Company, 2003.

Evans, Edward Payson. *The Criminal Prosecution and Capital Punishment of Animals.* London: Faber and Faber, 1906.

Garner, Bryan A. (Ed.). *Black's Law Dictionary.* 9th ed. Eagan, MN: West, 2009.

Greenwald, Marilyn. *Cleveland Amory: Media Curmudgeon and Animal Rights Crusader.* Lebanon, NH: University Press of New England, 2009.

Harrison, Ruth. *Animal Machines: The New Factory Farming Industry.* London: Vincent Stuart, 1964.

Kadri, Sadakat. *The Trial: A History, from Socrates to O. J. Simpson.* New York: Random House, 2005.

Kalof, Linda. *Looking at Animals in Human History.* London: Reaktion Books, 2007.

Lockwood, Randall. *Animal Cruelty Prosecution: Opportunities for Early Response to Crime and Interpersonal Violence.* Alexandria, VA: American Prosecutors Research Institute, 2006.

Lockwood, Randall. *Dogfighting: A Guide for Community Action.* Washington, D.C.: U.S. Department of Justice, 2012.

Lyman, Howard F., Glen Merzer, and Joanna Samorow-Merzer. *No More Bull! The Mad Cowboy Targets America's Worst Enemy: Our Diet.* New York: Scribner, 2005.

Mason, Jim, and Peter Singer. *Animal Factories.* New York: Crown Publishers, 1970.

Merzer, Glen, and Howard F. Lyman. *Mad Cowboy: Plain Truth from the Cattle Rancher Who Won't Eat Meat.* New York: Scribner, 1998.

O'Brien, David M. *Animal Sacrifice and Religious Freedom:* Church of the Lukumi Babalu Aye v. City of Hialeah. Lawrence: University of Kansas Press, 2004.

O'Brien, David M. *Storm Center: The Supreme Court in American Politics.* New York: W.W. Norton & Company, 2011.

Oran, Daniel. *Oran's Dictionary of the Law.* 4th ed. New York: Delmar Cengage Learning, 2007.

Regan, Tom. *Animal Rights, Human Wrongs: An Introduction to Moral Philosophy.* Lanham, MD: Rowan and Littlefield, 2003.

Sinclair, Leslie, Melinda Merck, and Randall Lockwood. *Forensic Investigation of Animal Cruelty: A Guide for Veterinary and Law Enforcement Professionals.* Washington, D.C.: Humane Society Press, 2006.

Walker, L. E. *The Battered Woman Syndrome.* 3rd ed. New York: Springer, 2009.

Index

www.ingramcontent.com/pod-product-compliance
Lightning Source LLC
Chambersburg PA
CBHW061007280326
41935CB00009B/863

* 9 7 8 1 5 5 7 5 3 6 3 3 4 *